The Lyric Poem and Aestheticism

Edinburgh Critical Studies in Victorian Culture
Series Editor: Julian Wolfreys
Volumes available in the series:

Visit the Edinburgh Critical Studies in Victorian Culture web page at edinburghuniversitypress.com/series/ecve

Also Available:
Victoriographies – A Journal of Nineteenth-Century Writing, 1790–1914, edited by Julian Wolfreys
ISSN: 2044-2416
www.eupjournals.com/vic

The Lyric Poem and Aestheticism

Forms of Modernity

Marion Thain

EDINBURGH
University Press

Edinburgh University Press is one of the leading university presses in the UK. We publish academic books and journals in our selected subject areas across the humanities and social sciences, combining cutting-edge scholarship with high editorial and production values to produce academic works of lasting importance. For more information visit our website: edinburghuniversitypress.com

Edinburgh University Press Ltd
The Tun – Holyrood Road, 12(2f) Jackson's Entry, Edinburgh EH8 8PJ

Typeset in 11/13 Adobe Sabon by
IDSUK (DataConnection) Ltd, and
printed and bound in Great Britain by
CPI Group (UK) Ltd, Croydon CR0 4YY

A CIP record for this book is available from the British Library

ISBN 978 1 4744 1566 8 (hardback)
ISBN 978 1 4744 1567 5 (webready PDF)
ISBN 978 1 4744 1568 2 (epub)

Contents

Contents

Series Editor's Preface

'Victorian' is a term, at once indicative of a strongly determined concept and an often notoriously vague notion, emptied of all meaningful content by the many journalistic misconceptions that persist about the inhabitants and cultures of the British Isles and Victoria's Empire in the nineteenth century. As such, it has become a by-word for the assumption of various, often contradictory habits of thought, belief, behaviour and perceptions. Victorian studies and studies in nineteenth-century literature and culture have, from their institutional inception, questioned narrowness of presumption, pushed at the limits of the nominal definition, and have sought to question the very grounds on which the unreflective perception of the so-called Victorian has been built; and so they continue to do. Victorian and nineteenth-century studies of literature and culture maintain a breadth and diversity of interest, of focus and inquiry, in an interrogative and intellectually open-minded and challenging manner, which are equal to the exploration and inquisitiveness of its subjects. Many of the questions asked by scholars and researchers of the innumerable productions of nineteenth-century society actively put into suspension the clichés and stereotypes of 'Victorianism', whether the approach has been sustained by historical, scientific, philosophical, empirical, ideological or theoretical concerns; indeed, it would be incorrect to assume that each of these approaches to the idea of the Victorian has been, or has remained, in the main exclusive, sealed off from the interests and engagements of other approaches. A vital interdisciplinarity has been pursued and embraced, for the most part, even as there has been contest and debate among Victorianists, pursued with as much fervour as the affirmative exploration between different disciplines and differing epistemologies put to work in the service of reading the nineteenth century.

Edinburgh Critical Studies in Victorian Culture aims to take up both the debates and the inventive approaches and departures from convention that studies in the nineteenth century have witnessed for the last half century at least. Aiming to maintain a 'Victorian' (in the most positive sense of that motif) spirit of inquiry, the series' purpose is to continue and augment the cross-fertilisation of interdisciplinary approaches, and to offer, in addition, a number of timely and untimely revisions of Victorian literature, culture, history and identity. At the same time, the series will ask questions concerning what has been missed or improperly received, misread, or not read at all, in order to present a multifaceted and heterogeneous kaleidoscope of representations. Drawing on the most provocative, thoughtful and original research, the series will seek to prod at the notion of the 'Victorian', and in so doing, principally through theoretically and epistemologically sophisticated close readings of the historicity of literature and culture in the nineteenth century, to offer the reader provocative insights into a world that is at once overly familiar, and irreducibly different, other and strange. Working from original sources, primary documents and recent interdisciplinary theoretical models, Edinburgh Critical Studies in Victorian Culture seeks not simply to push at the boundaries of research in the nineteenth century, but also to inaugurate the persistent erasure and provisional, strategic redrawing of those borders.

Julian Wolfreys

Acknowledgements

Poems by Arthur Symons are reproduced by kind permission of Brian Read, the copyright holder. The frontispiece image is *Mars and Venus*, or *Parnassus* by Andrea Mantegna, and is reproduced courtesy of RMN-Grand Palais and Art Resource NY (© RMN-Grand Palais / Art Resource, NY) on behalf of the Louvre Museum, Paris.

Chapter 4 contains some material first published in 'Decadent Forms: Parnassus in the Age of Mechanical Reproduction', in Jason Hall and Alex Murray (eds), *Decadent Poetics* (2013), and is reproduced with kind permission of Palgrave Macmillan. Chapter 7 contains some material first published in 'Thomas Hardy's Poetics of Touch', *Victorian Poetry* (2013), and it is reproduced by kind permission of the journal's editor, John Lamb. Chapter 9 was first published as 'Desire Lines: Swinburne and Lyric Crisis', in Catherine Maxwell and Stefano Evangelista (eds), *Algernon Charles Swinburne: Unofficial Laureate* (2013), and is reproduced by kind permission of Manchester University Press.

This project was supported by a book grant from the Center for the Humanities at New York University, and I thank the committee for this contribution to the completion of this project. Many thanks also go to the series editor, the staff and the anonymous readers at EUP, for their prompt professionalism and their keen insights; and to all those who have commented so helpfully on earlier versions of these chapters.

Andrea Mantegna, *Mars and Venus*, or *Parnassus* © RMN-Grand Palais / Art Resource, NY

Introduction

'A fundamental and fascinating crisis in literature is now at hand.'
This is how Stéphane Mallarmé's Oxford lecture, 'Crisis in Poetry',
began in 1894.[1] Walter Benjamin too writes of a sense of 'the
approaching crisis of lyric poetry' in the final third of the nineteenth
century.[2] T. E. Hulme's 1908 'A Lecture on Modern Poetry' identi-
fies in the late nineteenth century an end to the age of the Romantic
lyric, and a remaking of poetry.[3] It is easy simply to equate this 'lyric
crisis' with the 'remaking' of poetry in early twentieth-century liter-
ary modernism: a process that abandoned traditional verse forms,
but also embraced modernity in its use of vernacular language
(a process of modernisation owing much to Wordsworth, of course),
its imagistic techniques, and its urban subject matters. But the poetry
published in the later decades of the nineteenth century – the period
identified by all three writers as the temporal location for the crisis
they describe – did not, for the most part, look 'modernist' (particu-
larly in terms of its form), so how was it engaging with the pressures
these writers describe? Indeed, was it engaged at all? The causes and
effects of the lyric crisis identified by turn-of-the-century commenta-
tors are various, but all see a problem in the purpose or relevance of
the lyric genre in relation to the new contexts that resulted from a
process of rapid industrialisation across the previous hundred or so
years. It is the awareness of, and response to, this problem within
what can broadly be characterised as 'aestheticist' poetry of the last
third of the nineteenth century that is my object of study.

Scholarly histories of the modern formation of the lyric genre
have often ignored or dismissed the last few decades of the nine-
teenth century, seeing this as a period of nostalgic indulgence in a
conception of poetry already irrelevant to the modern world. A Pre-
Raphaelite interest in the myths of the past and the paintings of the
Renaissance; Swinburne's giving voice to Sappho and Catullus; the

Parnassian revival of medieval French forms; the Decadent 'gem-like' forms: these have all appeared to seek a retreat from the urbanised, industrialised and commodified world in which poets found themselves. Scholars have long identified a link between the more socially responsive dramatic-hybrid poetic forms of the mid-nineteenth century and the epic and dramatic 'innovations' of modernism in the early twentieth, but aestheticist poetry is awarded little place in these narratives of the modernisation of lyric form and genre. For example, in a brilliant and still much-cited essay from 1985, Herbert Tucker writes of aestheticist lyric as something of an aberration within a trajectory of poetic modernisation: 'When the lyrical bubble burst within its bell jar, poetry became modern once again in its return to the historically responsive and dialogic mode' of Tennyson and Browning.[4] The story of poetic modernity is, implicitly at least, often one of a move away from the lyric genre. Similarly, scholars such as Carol Christ wrote at length about 'The Victorians' concern with what they feel are the dangers of Romantic subjectivity', which 'cuts the artist off from both the real world and a communal tradition'.[5] Christ identifies Victorian poets (her focal examples are early and mid-Victorian works by Tennyson, Browning and Arnold) and modernist poets (Yeats, Pound and Eliot) as united in their concern to reject Romantic interiority in favour of 'a more objective basis for poetic discourse'.[6] For Christ too it is the introduction of narrative or dramatic elements in mid-Victorian poetry that brings a new 'objectivity' to poetry, and the hybrid forms that result (most notably the dramatic monologue) crucially modify lyric to better fit it for modern use. Christ's main concern in her book is to complicate and correct large-scale narratives of poetry that – in key part as a result of the 'anti-Victorianism' of the modernists – are based around a rift between Victorian and modernist literature.[7] Yet her narrative of poetic continuity between Victorian and modernist poetics, like the narrative of discontinuity that she rejects, effaces the particular interest and experiment in the lyric in the last few decades of the nineteenth century.

These critical narratives have remained influential. The importance of hybrid-lyric forms to the modernisation of poetry in the mid-nineteenth century has remained a vibrant topic of scholarship[8] (this is particularly true of the dramatic monologue),[9] and much twenty-first-century scholarship stresses innovations in hybrid forms as the fate of lyric poetry in the age of the novel.[10] Scott Brewster's book on the history of lyric, for example, moves from Romantic and mid-Victorian poetry to T. S. Eliot and high modernism, and attributes to the experiments of high modernism the desire to confront lyric's poor fit with modernity: 'the provocative challenge to the staleness of everyday language, to mass culture and to bourgeois attitudes in the modernist lyric suggests confrontation with, rather than evasion of, this inhospitable climate'.[11] The association of late nineteenth-century poetry with a nostalgic and introspective model of lyric also endures in scholarship on lyric. In her important entry in the 2012 *New Princeton Encyclopaedia of Poetry and Poetics*, Virginia Jackson writes that 'at the end of the 19th c., the tendency to work variations on lyric in relation to social complexity moved toward an idea of lyric as a refuge from mod[ern] life'.[12] Yet it is precisely the relationship between the lyric genre and modernity in this period that I take as my focus. My interest, then, is in forms of lyric that in larger narratives of the development of the genre are still commonly either elided, or defined in opposition to modernity as a nostalgic last gasp of Romanticism interjected between the modernising hybrid forms of the mid-century and the continuation of that more 'objective' turn in the poetry of literary modernism.

To be sure, recent decades have seen a flourishing field of scholarship exploring how late nineteenth-century poetry was engaged with the tropes, languages and experiences of modernity (such as the urban world, modern transport systems, or the economics of the commodity revolution).[13] This work has been valuable in many ways, not least in showing how such poetry connects with the values of the twentieth century, and it is within this trajectory that my book is situated. However, the narrative of aestheticist poetry's irrelevance to the modernisation of poetry is persistent because, however much the concerns of modernity were reflected in the content, and even the aesthetics, of this work, the more fundamental problem of *genre* remains for *lyric* poetry after the mid-century attacks by Robert Browning and others: the very underlying conventions of the genre risk appearing to be in tension with the experience of modernity. It is this problem that I take as my focus, exploring not so much lyric poetry's thematic engagement with the tropes of modernity but its response to the threat of the redundancy of its own generic conventions. I ask how lyric poetry responds not to a changing subject matter but to the idea that the underpinning ideals of its very genre are somehow out of step with modernity. So, the aim of my study is to open up avenues of investigation into aestheticist lyric poetry's own discourse on the relationship between the lyric genre and modernity. In the following series of chapters I suggest, crucially, that we might find not so much a nostalgia or a retreat from modernity, but an *engagement* with the risk of irrelevance of a nineteenth-century conceptualisation of lyric poetry to the modern world. It is this idea that drives the book throughout.

The idea of the Romantic poetic inheritance was often, for commentators in the final third of the nineteenth century, as much a touchstone for a particular set of ideas as an accurate engagement with the work of their forebears, but it was a crucial and recurrent one. As I will explore in the fuller context for this study offered in Chapter 1, it was in key part lyric's association with transcendence that was at the heart of this perceived poor fit with late nineteenth-century modernity. For many Romantic theorists, lyric poetry was a special mode of communication, perhaps even a special mode of thinking. Hegel writes of poetry demanding: 'a new domain, a new ground on which we can only tread after forsaking the prose of the theory and practice of our ordinary life and way of thinking'.[14] For Hegel, poetry represents something of an aspiration to take up a position outside of space, time and individual subjectivity: an escape, however paradoxical and unsustainable, from our everyday world and our own human condition. Models such as this one seemed increasingly untenable as the century progressed; and the genre was particularly challenged by the new ways of thinking that, particularly in the last third of the century, resulted from a culture radically changed by processes of urbanisation, industrialisation and commodification.

Rather than seeking a retreat into the transcendent ideals of lyric, however, I suggest that aestheticist lyric poetry registered these pressures and responded to them – and, crucially, what was found within a Romantic lyric heritage was an ideal experimental arena for the interplay of the different forces that structured experience. The lyric could be used to explore the pull between the personal and the universal; a communicative transaction and a profound solipsism; the individual voice and the chorus; the time-bound and the timeless; strict conventional form and freer verse; personal sentiment and public expression. It is perhaps in this capacity, I will suggest, that the lyric became a genre in some ways particularly responsive to conceptual shifts, and able to formulate the new philosophies of modernity through its very forms. Within this study I argue for a diverse set of responses within aestheticist poetry, but my three-part structure organises the discussion around three key axes of the 'problem' of lyric transcendence: time, space and subjectivity. These headings offer a shorthand for a set of issues explained and contextualised more fully in my next chapter, but which all stem from a recognition of the challenges of writing within a genre characterised by a Romantic aspiration to an eternal moment, profound introspection, and a desire for the lyric subject to represent a 'universal' voice. This book argues that reflection on the possibilities for poetry in the modern world can be seen as central to the practice of the lyric genre at this time, and through close engagement with the poems themselves it seeks fresh ways of thinking about the relationship between lyric and modernity. In particular, my study explores this relationship through a close consideration of poetic form. The revival of strict forms in aestheticist poetry is at the heart of the problem of genre that interests me: it is a distinctive and characteristic feature of poetry of the period, and one which looks like a retreat into the formal certainties of lyric from the uncertainties of a rapidly changing world. It is the formal presence of late Victorian poetry – and particularly the investment in 'quaint', highly patterned, strict forms characteristic of aestheticist lyric – that determines my methodological focus.

Thinking about how the new era of industrialised modernity was reflected in poetry of the final third of the century might more readily bring to mind aspects of poetic content, such as the use of the city and industrial technology as poetic subject matter, or the intensification of a turn to vernacular speech in opposition to 'high' and antiquated poetic diction – those things, in short, that Arthur Symons identifies in 'Modernity in Verse' (1897) as marking the modernity of W. E. Henley's poetry.[15] Yet the equally, if not more, characteristic vogue for strict verse forms and frequently 'old-fashioned' poetic tropes (retrospective even at the time of use) is much less redeemable in relation to the values of 'modernism' and still poses a real problem for today's commentators. In 'Modernity in Verse', Symons recognises the need for poetry to respond to modernity, but suggests this can be done from within regular metrical forms.[16] The essay begins, after all, by praising Henley's Parnassian verse which appeared in Gleeson White's 1887 collection *Ballades et Rondeaus*.[17] Take, for example, his liking for forms such as the rondeau (I will quote just the first stanza of 'In Rotten Row' here to give a flavour):

> In Rotten Row a cigarette
> I sat and smoked, with no regret
>   For all the tumult that had been.
>   The distances were still and green,
> And streaked with shadows cool and wet.[18]

How, today, do we square the use of these antiquated forms with what Symons praises as 'a certain freshness, a daring straightforwardness' in Henley's content?[19] How do these *forms* respond to modernity?

While the middle of the century is better known for its experiments with dramatic, narrative and hybrid forms, from the 1860s (with Swinburne's *Poems and Ballads* in 1866) until the early twentieth century we see something of a shift in focus. While 'dramatic monologues' and other types made popular in the mid-century continued to be written and new vogues for hybrid forms such as the prose poem emerged, it is perhaps all the more striking to see a new concentration of experimentation with intricate and compressed fixed lyric forms. This might include and be characterised by, among others, Swinburne's interest in Sappho's Aeolic lyrics, Dante Gabriel Rossetti's developing commitment to the sonnet, and the Parnassian fashion for medieval French forms. Confronting the 'problem' of these forms seems to me central to understanding the period, and it would be a mistake, I think, to turn away from these unfashionable structures in favour of poetry less representative but more easily assimilated to today's canon.[20] Driving my study from a particular emphasis on the structural or formal parameters of lyric, then, enables me to take on a distinctive and unresolved challenge in thinking about the relation between poetry and modernity. In her recent work *On Form*, Angela Leighton suggests that we might think of form 'as a way of knowing, not as an object of knowledge'.[21] It is by seeing lyric form as not only a site of epistemological struggle but as a way of feeling – as a sentient poetic skin – that I trace something of poetry's response to modernity before modernism.

The forms I consider can be assimilated neither to the search for more dramatic, narrative or 'objective' poetic forms that characterised the innovations of the mid-century, nor to the free-verse experiments of the early twentieth century. My study is not a search for the much-explored 'innovations' of modernist poetry *prefigured* in poetry of the later nineteenth century, and for this reason, the poetry I explore will frequently not appear very 'modern' – in fact, it is particularly this poetry in which I am interested and which determines my choice of focal poems (and explains the absence of poets of the period better known as 'modernisers', such as John Davidson). I analyse a set of responses to modernity that precede the better-known reactions of high modernism and that, however much the two are related, manifest a distinctive set of strategies.[22] Jonathan Freedman has given us the useful and liberating method of reading aestheticism not as a 'proto-modernism', but as an aesthetic closer to postmodernism in its playful performativity.[23] No wonder, then, that it often fares badly under readings searching for the 'authenticity' of high modernism. Following this lead, I prefer to think of the literature I study here as 'post-Victorian', in a sense that implies a similar relationship to the Victorian that postmodernism has to modernism. Viewing the later decades of the century in this way provides a productive way of approaching the quirkiness found there, and of recognising something of the type of self-conscious reflection on the status of the lyric genre in relation to modernity that it harbours.

The book begins, in Chapter 1, by providing a fuller context for my study – a necessary prelude to any use of the terms 'lyric' and 'modernity' in aestheticist poetry. Following on from this chapter are the three major sections of the book – each designed, as noted above, to organise my readings around a key axis of aestheticist poetry's response to the problem of lyric's association with transcendent aspirations. Each of the three sections begins with a brief chapter setting up my exploration of the genre in relation to one particular historically relevant conceptual axis. These initial chapters open up broader aesthetic and literary trajectories as well as providing a conceptual context. In each part of the book, this first, short chapter is followed by two 'case study' chapters, in which those ideas are explored in relation to particular poems and poets. In the first part ('Time') I explore rhythm and metrical patterning in relation to what Hegel theorised as lyric's dialectic between the earthly and the eternal, arguing that we can see in lyric of the later decades of the nineteenth century a confrontation with and absorption of post-Enlightenment modes of temporal experience. The most Romantic *and* most modern of poetry, D. G. Rossetti's sonnets reflect this shift in microcosm. This leads me to recognise the significance for the rhythms of Parnassian poetry of the reiteration and repetition of the commodity – and ultimately leads to a theorisation of Parnassianism's affective rhythmical historicism. Part II ('Space') aims to highlight lyric's awareness of its own spatial embodiment, attending both to its investment in its own formal presence and its negotiation of a deep-rooted notion of lyric address (the poem as a transaction across space between 'I' and 'you', or as an invocation of a lyric other). This part engages with two of the key issues of aestheticism's poetic modernity: the phenomenological possibilities for its intricate forms; and the threat of solipsism that is particularly pressing for the lyric genre. The work of Arthur Symons (and other Decadent poets) is central to this part, as are Alice Meynell's and Thomas Hardy's sophisticated meditations on lyric address in relation to a phenomenology of the printed page. Part III ('Subjectivity') explores issues related to the construction of the lyric subject itself, and some of the ways in which poetry tackled the problems posed by lyric introspection at a time when its validity as a method of reaching shared universal truths was deeply suspect and when the very idea of a reified, unified subjectivity was untenable. This section highlights the significance of A. C. Swinburne's and Ezra Pound's search for historical models, and argues that they both seek from them a poetic subject newly relevant for the modern age: a subject that enables a voice both personal and communal.

*   *   *

In the rest of this introduction, I will explain further the structure of the book, outline some of the factors that have determined my choices within it, and then contextualise my methodology. As can be seen from the outline above, the overall structure is determined by my conceptual axes rather than governed by chronology (which within the few decades of my relatively short focal period is not the main consideration). However, each Part does, internally, recognise the significance of chronology within my period of study through the ordering of the two case studies. In addition, the choice of writers for the first and final case study chapters – starting with Dante Gabriel Rossetti's rewriting and publication of poems from the 1840s and ending with the early publications of Ezra Pound – also recognises something of the chronological arc of aestheticism. My case studies explore poems that represent the canonical, the once-popular and the rediscovered – and that range historically from the 1860s to the early years of the twentieth century. Choosing to engage with a relatively small number of poems in detail, rather than offering a broad survey of poetry, allows for the close engagement necessary to explore the textual and conceptual issues and strategies that are my focus. This approach is appropriate because my study aims not to present an all-encompassing theory of aestheticist lyric but rather to highlight areas of lyric's response to modernity that have been not well recognised and that might provide new impetus for our exploration of the genre.

My choice of poems and poets in relation to the remit of a broad 'aestheticism' might be usefully elaborated, however. Recent scholarly usage sees literary 'aestheticism' reaching from the 1860s into the early years of the twentieth century, with 'Decadence' as a distinctive subset within a broader 'art for art's sake' impetus, and early modernism as in some ways a natural extension of it.[24] Such terminology enables a body of literature (well described neither as Victorian or modernist) to become an object of study in its own right, and it is in this spirit I use the term. Within this remit I include Thomas Hardy, who of all my subjects is perhaps least obviously an aesthete as such but whose work is an important marker of the trajectory I follow. There is good historical precedent for this inclusion in the form of an essay published in the *Edinburgh Review* in 1918, in which Edmund Gosse identifies and outlines the trajectory of lyric history that interests me. Identifying its origins in the 1860s, Gosse sees Swinburne leading the poetic 'revolution' with *Poems and Ballads*.[25] It was Swinburne's success in poetic revolution that paved the way, Gosse concludes, for Hardy's turn to lyric: 'although he [Swinburne] approached the art from an opposite direction he prepared the way for an ultimate appreciation of Mr. Hardy'.[26] Despite their differences, Gosse sees both Swinburne and Hardy as part of a 'revolution against the optimism and superficial sweetness of [their] age'.[27] Although Hardy did not begin publishing volumes of poetry until the late 1890s, Gosse pinpoints '1865 to 1867' as the starting point of Hardy's poetic vocation, and attributes Hardy's late-career turn to poetry to doubts about 'whether his poems would have been received in the mid-Victorian age with favour, or even have been comprehended'.[28] Dante Gabriel Rossetti might be introduced as a third major marker of this 'revolution' as he returns to lyrics often written as long ago as the 1840s, revising them considerably and publishing them in 1870. Rossetti's recovery of his poems from Elizabeth Siddal's grave in the 1860s is perhaps not just a personal story of resurrection, but one also symbolic of this new trajectory in lyric. Each of these three authors is a major poetic presence in the period I explore and it is for this reason they each provide focal subject matter for one of my six case studies.

While Rossetti, Hardy and Swinburne might form particularly visible markers of the shift in poetry I study, there are writers less well recognised but equally important to tracing its trajectory. The other case study in each part of the book explores its theme in relation to either Parnassian poetry, the Decadents or early modernist writing, to represent other significant impetuses within the longer aestheticist trajectory traced here and to connect it with the more fully explored poetics of the twentieth century. Necessarily selective in terms of the writers examined within each of these three categories, choices have been taken to keep the focus on poetic responses to the problem of what many at the end of the century saw as a Romantic formulation of lyric's aspiration to transcendence. This means that specifically religious poets are not included because of the different significance that transcendence holds in their work. As a result my book has a focus very different from – but complementary to – works such as Elizabeth Gray's *Christian and Lyric Tradition in Victorian Women's Poetry* (2009), in which the women poets who are important to the trajectory I explore (for example, Michael Field and Alice Meynell) appear only in passing. Significantly, Christina Rossetti is not a subject for my study: as Emma Mason has persuasively argued, Tractarianism brought to Rossetti's work a very specific transcendent aesthetic, one that puts it outside my remit.[29] For similar reasons, I do not include the work of Gerard Manley Hopkins; the fact that Hopkins's poems were not published until after the start of the First World War also places his work rather outside the remit of my study as his voice was not integral to the period. Issues of national identity also determine my choices: my discussion of W. B. Yeats in Chapter 3, for example, shows why there might be significantly different issues of lyric formation in play for Irish writers in this period (indeed, the particular significance of lyric within a Celtic tradition is a thread to which I will return). In choosing to figure both the more familiar Decadent poets but also the less well-known (although highly characteristic) poets of the Parnassian movement, I aim to represent the importance of the *fin-de-siècle* cult of the 'minor poet' as well as representing a once-popular vogue. My final chapter takes Ezra Pound as its focus in order to connect the trajectory I examine with a major modernist inheritor whose work comes, in a significant way, out of an engagement with aestheticist lyric. My coverage does not aim to be comprehensive, but rather to offer case studies of some key trajectories.

I end in the early twentieth century, with Pound's turn to free verse, even though modernist poetry (with its French precedents and aesthetic principles) is in important ways a natural extension of the phase of lyric I study. This is not the end-point of the story, but it is the start of a better-known part of that story. Indeed, it would be wrong to see free verse as the ultimate incarnation of modernity in lyric. Eliot and Pound were already reacting against it as early as 1917,[30] and in an interesting piece from *The Saturday Review* of June 1922, Louis Golding writes of the perceived 'failure of free verse': 'Certainly no notable poet who has emerged during and since the War is continuing the experiment of free verse. Here and there an isolated practitioner who has been successful might be quoted, but his is not in the current of the time.'[31] Free verse did not turn out to be the temporary 'fad' that this predicts, but neither did free verse proper come to be the only vehicle of lyric in the twentieth century. D. H. Lawrence's legacy represents something of the position free verse went on to hold as one of lyric's forms, along with the sonnet and other strict forms. By the time modernism was at its height, however – and in part due to the massive cultural shifts occasioned by two world wars – the prerogatives of art had changed. Peter Howarth writes of the shift between 'early modernism based on impressionism and the personal, and the later modernism based on order and impersonality'; in terms of a high poetic tradition at least, I suggest this meant a turn away from the lyric genre that was thriving in a more popular context.[32]

It is worth clarifying at this point that I am using the term 'cultural *modernity*' to designate those contexts that resulted towards the end of the nineteenth century from a process of industrialisation, and that formed the basis of the urbanised society in which we still live.[33] The term 'modernity' enables me to talk of this cultural context before the advent of literary '*modernism*' – a term at least implicitly premised on the notion of a 'radical break' with the nineteenth century. I use the term '*modern*', on the other hand, to denote a period from, roughly, the later eighteenth century onwards, distinguished by a process of industrialisation and by the key philosophical shifts that partnered it. The 'modernity' I take as my cultural context is what Matthew Arnold saw as a moral chaos, debased by the dominant values of science, which gives free rein to selfish and unenlightened behaviour; a society comprising 'a materialized upper class, a vulgarized middle class, and a brutalized lower class'.[34] It is the same period in which Adorno finds the growth of capitalism changing the way we experience the world, and which Stephen Kern shows to hold a distinct set of experiences of time and space that resulted from the new technologies of industrialised modernity.[35] This context will be elaborated further – in relation to ideas of lyric specifically – in my next chapter; my focus thereafter, however, will be on the development of a literary genre within an aesthetic context that supervenes on that culture.

The poetic strategies I trace within this context are not necessarily unique to this particular period (it is certainly not the only time in history that, for example, a communal lyric subject or lyric chorus has been imagined), but these motifs have a particular meaning and importance in relation to a nexus of concerns about lyric expressed at this time. At the heart of the distinctiveness of the poetry I study lie two things in addition to the interest in compressed, fixed verse forms, both of which are in some sense responses to a period of economic history marked by the 'second' industrial revolution (the revolution of the commodity): a culture of aestheticism; and the culmination of what Matthew Rowlinson has described as the 'totalization' of lyric in print – an idea I will introduce in the following chapter. Across all three parts of the book, then, there are recurring themes (such as an engagement with the past, a drive towards collecting and summation, and a symbiotic relationship between economic and aesthetic impulses) that bind the book together. More specifically, for my purposes, this period was one that saw an intensification of interest in the potentialities of 'lyric' poetry and of the structures of lyric form. I will pursue all of this in Chapter 1, but for now it is worth noting that an interest in the history of lyric as a genre rooted in Classical, medieval and Elizabethan sources is central to this period, which produced much new scholarship on Sappho, the troubadours and the Elizabethan songbooks. Works that 'defined' or sought to claim, retrospectively, a lyric tradition will be explored throughout my study.

*   *   *

Methodologically this study is a long way from the 'genre theory' of the 1970s, which was primarily interested in genre as an ahistorical framework for interpretative practices. Drawing on a tradition of genre theory from E. D. Hirsch and Croce, William Elford Rogers' *The Three Genres and the Interpretation of Lyric*, states its aims as follows,

> Precisely because my genres are meant to be *interpretive* categories, they give us conceptual knowledge *not* about works, but about *interpretations*. And since interpretation is merely the making-explicit of understanding, we might say that this genre-theory gives us conceptual knowledge not of the works themselves, but of our own understanding of the works.[36]

In contrast, I suggest that we can see poems and poetic discourse as offering as much of a 'theory' of lyric as that which appeared in new paradigms of interpretative literary criticism in the early twentieth century. In this study I am interested in 'lyric' as a historically created and inflected category that is as much a category of production as interpretation. Attending to the way the genre of 'lyric' poetry was understood as a literary category within the period is important, and review essays will be cited to this end. This understanding forms a context for production when poets are also, as is usually the case here, part of that community of readers.

Here my study differs from, although I hope might be complementary to, Virginia Jackson's work on Emily Dickinson, where her interest is primarily in lyric as a theory of interpretation (although crucially, unlike the old 'genre theory', her interest is in historicising that theorisation). While Dickinson's work was not written for print publication, the writers I look at were published authors who wrote with full awareness of how their work might circulate in print, and how it would be received in relation to the genre categories of the day: it is explicitly a conceptualisation of lyric as a print genre that I explore. While Jackson is concerned with the posthumous publication and categorisation of Dickinson's manuscript writings as 'lyrics', the poems I analyse were frequently framed and presented in that way by their authors. In this sense, the works I explore here might be seen as contributing to the definition of lyric poetry that was consolidated by the New Critics, rather than as unwitting subjects of its interpretation. Poets actively writing for print publication often did not have full control over the publication of their material, but there is no doubt that their poetry itself engages with what a context of mass print publication might mean for lyric as a genre. The writer's choice of genre, as T. S. Eliot points out, connects them with their readership through shared paradigms: 'there is already something given which I can recognise and which exists for others as well as myself'.[37] However, my interest is not in individual instances of authorial intention *per se* but in the operation of poems themselves in relation to contemporaneous conceptualisations of lyric poetry in print. My interest is in the aesthetic potential of the genre, and particularly in the potential of the highly patterned and compressed fixed forms characteristic of aestheticist poetry to register something of the relationship between lyric and modernity. Read as historical documents, but historical documents of an aesthetic nature, poems offer us rhetorical strategies and textual operations; they are documents, in other words, that are centrally concerned with offering us ways to read them. It is this evidence that can be used to explore poetry's formal response to modernity: genre might be seen in this sense as the most historically and culturally reflexive incarnation of text's specific rhetorical operations.

Many other approaches to lyric are possible and valuable, and in the current critical field the resurgence of interest in the idea of genre has prompted a pleasing variety of responses. For example, in the 2008 issue of *PMLA* in which Virginia Jackson outlines her interest in the history of lyric theory, Jonathan Culler calls for that kind of historical study to be 'joined to a revival of the idea of the lyric as a poetic activity that has persisted since the days of Sappho, despite lyric's different social functions and manifestations'.[38] This is something Culler has undertaken at length in his *Theory of the Lyric*, a trans-historical study of poetics in which he explores the utility of 'lyric' to identify retrospectively a particular, and persistent, type of poetry and to analyse its operations. Susan Stewart and Mutlu Konuk Blasing's recent theories of lyric (of poetry and the senses, on the one hand, and twentieth-century lyric subjectivity, on the other) both offer rich work that situates lyric not so much historically as conceptually. Helen Vendler's *Poems – Poets – Poetry* offers a theorisation of lyric based on a formal affinity with music and what I call in Chapter 1 its transcendent ambition – the idea that lyric seeks independence from time and space.[39] The relationship between music and language is an area that has also flourished in recent years with scholarship ranging from Lisa Goldfarb's study of the significance of Valéry's musical ideas in Wallace Stevens's poetic theory and practice to Simon Jarvis's philosophical theorisation of prosody.[40] Each of these methodologies takes the discipline in interestingly different directions, and develops the study of poetry in multiple forms and modes.

My approach to lyric takes its cue from another recent trend within the discipline: the insistence that we return to the text itself. I respond particularly to those claims made by the 'new formalism'. While recognising the excellent work done through interdisciplinary initiatives, Marjorie Perloff has written about the allure of '*other-disciplinarity*', where the 'merely' literary is so suspect.[41] She also writes in her MLA presidential address about the tendency for literary studies to analyse content without much awareness of literary form.[42] The casualties have sometimes been the specifics of the text itself as a formal aesthetic object and the larger *literary* trajectories or frames of reference in which those texts might be located. E. Warwick Slinn expressed similar views in *Victorian Poetry as Cultural Critique*. Here Slinn worries about methods of reading that, in a backlash against New Criticism, privilege 'context' and risk 'the privileging of the cultural value of these other discourses, as if cultural meaning were always located in discourses from institutions outside literature – medicine, law, politics, public media'. Slinn is particularly keen to address the importance of recognising 'the potential, particularly in poetry, for formalist features to problematize literal-figurative choices. This problematizing is often a source of verbal brilliance or aesthetic delight and the very mainstay, therefore, of conventional formalist analysis.'[43] This is an important foundation stone for my study because I explore poetry that can be broadly characterised both by a self-proclaimed lack of interest in overt critique of modernity in its content, and, I argue, by an engagement with those very cultural conditions through its form. This is a poetry that, I suggest, explores an inhabitation of modernity even while its content may seem deliberately to invoke a nostalgic counter-reaction. Detailed close reading of specific texts will be used to open up avenues for investigating the connection between particular poetic characteristics and a broader narrative of the lyric genre.

As well as responding to current concerns within the discipline, my methodology is, in an important way, dictated by the subject matter. In his investigation of the influence of German lyric theorists on British Romanticism, David Duff acknowledges that there is no equivalent body of Romantic genre theory in English. Yet his book argues that much of what we see in German theory can be found in the practice of English literature, where it finds 'more indirect expression'.[44] The primary site of formulation in British literature was in the poetry itself:

> The 'internalization' of genre which Harold Bloom defines as a hallmark of Romanticism was thus, in part, a *theoretical* self-consciousness about genre. To write poetry in this period was also, of necessity, to write *about* poetry: its form, its purpose, its value, its destiny.[45]

This continues to be true over the course of the nineteenth century, and I argue throughout that the poets I study explore concerns about the potential incompatibility of lyric with modernity in ways that are intelligent, interesting, subtle and witty; and, moreover, that this exploration took place through the form of lyric itself. Indeed, reading form is a method particularly crucial for approaching a body of poetry that is so invested in formal patterns, and if we are to appreciate aestheticist poetry it must be with such an awareness. As well as studying poetry's own discourse on genre, I am interested in the potential for reading in the other direction: how reflection on the formation of the concept of lyric might motivate fresh thinking about the operations of particular poems and particularly poetic features or vogues. When taken collectively, these case studies do not build a comprehensive narrative, but rather establish of a set of lines of enquiry for how aestheticist poetry might be inflected by, and responsive to, the poetic context explored in more detail in my next chapter. As Friedrich Schlegel put it, the study of genre can be nothing short of 'a classification which at the same time would be a history and theory of literature'.[46] Or to put it in terms that will resonate more strongly for my study: 'genre' is another word for the historically contingent incarnation of literary form – what I termed earlier the sentient skin of poetry.

Notes

1. Mallarmé, 'Crisis in Poetry', p. 34.
2. Benjamin, *Charles Baudelaire*, p. 25.
3. Hulme, 'A Lecture on Modern Poetry', passim.
4. Tucker, 'Dramatic Monologue and the Overhearing of Lyric', p. 239.
5. Christ, *Victorian and Modern Poetics*, pp. 6, 8.
6. Ibid., p. 3.
7. Ibid., p. 12.
8. This is usefully reviewed by Monique R. Morgan in her 2007 piece on 'Lyric Narrative Hybrids in Victorian Poetry', and indeed her own 2009 book, *Narrative Means, Lyric Ends*, is an important recent example.
9. See, for example, Glennis Byron's *Dramatic Monologue*; discussion of the form in James Phelan's *Living to Tell About It*; and Melissa Valiska Gregory's 'Robert Browning and the Lure of the Violent Lyric Voice'.
10. See, for example, Ivan Kreilkamp's *Voice and the Victorian Storyteller*, p. 156.
11. Brewster, *Lyric*, pp. 92, 100.
12. Jackson, 'Lyric', p. 832.
13. This is thanks to the work of a group of scholars too large to name, but which would include, for example, Joseph Bristow, Regenia Gagnier, Linda Hughes, Ruth Livesey, Tricia Lootens, Yopie Prins, Margaret Stetz and Ana Parejo Vadillo. Ruth Robbins's chapter 'Rhymers and Reasoners: Poetry in Transition' gives a useful overview of these issues (*Pater to Forster, 1873–1924*, Chapter 2).
14. Hegel, *Aesthetics*, pp. 1011–12.
15. Symons, 'Modernity in Verse', passim.
16. Ibid., p. 58.
17. Ibid., p. 44.
18. White, *Ballades and Rondeaus*, p. 170.
19. Symons, 'Modernity in Verse', p. 56. Symons finishes this essay with the statement: 'A new subject, an individual treatment, a form which retains all that is helpful in tradition, while admitting all that is valuable in experiment; that, I think, is modernity becoming classical' (p. 59).

20. For example, a retrospective canon might favour the sprung rhythm of Gerard Manley Hopkins as representative of lyric musicality, but such a focus would be to privilege a voice that was more marginal both to the period and to the 'art for art's sake' impetus I take as my particular focus.
21. Leighton, *On Form*, p. 27.
22. See Bristow, *The Fin-de-Siècle Poem*, p. 39: poets of the 1880s and 1890s were 'devising fresh poetic models that could engage with the modern before further shifts in poetics became identifiably modernist'.
23. Freedman, *Professions of Taste*, pp. 1–78.
24. The change in the use of the term 'aestheticism' to designate not just the early 'art for art's sake' movement in the 1860s and 1870s but an aesthetic trajectory that continued across the next few decades is identified and discussed by Nicholas Shrimpton in his essay 'The Old Aestheticism and the New' (passim).
25. Gosse, 'Mr Hardy's Lyrical Poems', pp. 273–4.
26. Ibid., p. 274.
27. Ibid., p. 274.
28. Ibid., p. 273.
29. Mason 'Christina Rossetti and the Doctrine of Reserve', p. 200: 'Poetry, then, represents God's truths indirectly like a parable, allowing only those armed with faith and knowledge to recognise what Keble elsewhere called "parabolical lessons of conduct" within its 'symbolical language in which God speaks to us of a world out of sight'.
30. Beasley, *Modernist Poetry*, p. 56.
31. Golding, 'Mr Hardy and the New Poetry', pp. 649–50: 'It is possible that this new tendency . . . is a profound reaction from the chaos of the War'.
32. Howarth, *British Poetry in the Age of Modernism*, p. 34.
33. My book therefore takes a very different focus from Paul de Man's essay on 'Lyric and Modernity' which is interested not in a particular period of history but in 'the problematical possibility of all literature's existing in the present, of being considered, or read, from a point of view that claims to share with it its own sense of a temporal present' (p. 166).
34. Arnold, 'The Study of Poetry', p. 161.
35. Adorno, *Aesthetic Theory*, passim; Kern, *Culture of Time and Space*, passim.
36. Rogers, *The Three Genres*, p. 56.
37. Eliot, *The Three Voices of Poetry*, p. 22.
38. Culler, 'Why Lyric?', p. 202.
39. Vendler, *Poems – Poets – Poetry*, passim.
40. Goldfarb, *The Figure Concealed*, passim; Jarvis, 'Musical Thinking', passim.
41. Perloff, 'Presidential Address 2006', p. 655.

42. Ibid., p. 658.
43. Slinn, *Victorian Poetry as Cultural Critique*, p. 13.
44. Duff, *Romanticism and the Uses of Genre*, p. 9.
45. Ibid., p. 10.
46. Schlegel, *Dialogue on Poetry*, p. 76.

Chapter 1

Lyric, Aestheticism and the Later Nineteenth Century

This chapter prefaces the subsequent three major parts of the book with an expansion of the contexts for lyric very briefly gestured towards in the introduction. Hegel wrote that 'To define the poetic as such or to give a description of what is poetic horrifies nearly all who have written about poetry'.[1] In 1970 René Wellek called for critics to 'abandon attempts to define the general nature of the lyric or the lyrical'.[2] My study is not primarily concerned with defining the *extension* of the term 'lyric', even as it is used historically within the few decades I cover. What I offer is rather an investigation of what were considered core features of the genre (inherited by the Victorians from formative Romantic theorisations) as they run up against the radically changed circumstances of the later part of the century. It is primarily to outlining these circumstances, as well as a critical context, that I devote this initial chapter; yet I will dwell here a little on issues of definition to set up the main matter. How do we identify aestheticist 'lyric' poetry in the later nineteenth century? Intrinsic to the term is a connection with music and song that is often taken as a key feature of the genre throughout the ages. One might, then, invoke as the quintessential lyrical utterance of the period the songs of Ernest Dowson and A. Mary F. Robinson, the ballads of D. G. Rossetti, or the early work of W. B. Yeats. Less obvious, but with perhaps a greater claim, are Dollie Radford's poems, of which D. H. Lawrence said: 'They make me think of the small birds in the twilight, whistling brief little tunes, but so clear, they seem like little lights in the twilight, such clear, vivid sounds.'[3] The terms in which he praises this 'fine, exquisite verse' register a particularly aesthetic quality in both poem and commentary. Emily Harrington has recently argued for a self-consciousness to Radford's work, suggesting that she questions the value of song even as her poetry is constructed around it;[4] whether a critique or a celebration, poems such as the simply titled 'song' (from Radford's first collection in 1891) perform its tropes explicitly:

> In the first light of the morning,
>   When the thrush sang loud and clear,
> And the black-bird hailed day's dawning,
>   How I wished my love could hear.
>
> When the sun shone on the sand there,
>   And the roses bloomed above,
> And the blue waves kissed the land there,
>   How I longed to see my love.
>
> Now the birds good-night are calling,
>   And the moonbeams come and go,
> And my tears are falling, falling,
>   Because I want him so.[5]

The trochaic tetrameter invokes a sung rather than spoken rhythm and connects her to both folk song and nursery rhyme. In content, however, the motifs of birdsong, lost love, tears and nature combine in a set of familiar tropes that link her with a heritage of lyric poetry, and Radford's metrical ease carries a melodic line that is suspended in time like the timeless call of the blackbird she evokes.

Such poems may enact an apparently timeless lyrical quality in the late nineteenth century, yet it is not sung forms *per se*, or the relationship between music and text, that is the focus of my study.[6] While music and song have a long history of association with the lyric genre, it would be a mistake to impose on the late nineteenth century a *definition* of lyrics poetry that rests on its perceived relation to music. The strict-form poetry I explore shows an awareness of the tension between lyric's aural heritage and a context of mass print circulation that had become, over the course of the nineteenth century, not just the medium but ever-more essential to the character of the published lyric poem. Of course, print was not a new medium for poetry in the late nineteenth century, but there did seem to be a growing sense that a printed lyric poem was no longer inherently a textually recorded aural form – and that changed its nature fundamentally. Lyric poetry was seen by some late nineteenth-century commentators to have completed its long transformation from something constitutively encountered on the airwaves to something constitutively encountered on paper. Indeed, this is central to the anxiety about the relevance of lyric to the modern world that I suggest is motivating many of the poetic responses I trace in this study. In a little-known essay that provides me with a substantial theorisation of the lyric genre in the late nineteenth century, J. A. Symonds claims it is a mark of the better poetry of the age that it exploits its textual medium so that it can exist complete without added music: 'the best lyrics of the Victorian age are not made to be sung'. Symonds claims that the *lyric* poem has become a textual genre, which, while it may be set to music, exists on its own terms, finding its melody within itself rather than in an accompanying strain. For Symonds, this goes along with an idealisation of the Elizabethan age as a time when lyric poetry was still inherently connected to a sense of song and a vocal encounter with an audience (although, of course, even then it was written down and circulated as text in manuscript and print form).[7] The point here is not whether such Victorian narratives of lyric history are accurate, but what they say about the concerns of the period in which they are written. Symonds's essay sets the agenda for the issues I explore throughout this book, and I will return throughout to his analysis.

This essay by Symonds expresses what the scholar Matthew Rowlinson much later termed the 'totalization in print' of the lyric genre around the 1860s. While poetry had been printed for many centuries, it was only at this point that 'print become[s] for lyric the hegemonic medium': 'As the nineteenth century progressed, lyric came with increasing self-consciousness to reflect on its own mediated character.'[8] One might consider that a poet such as Thomas Hardy, for example, a musician and a highly musically minded man, brought that experience to his poetry, but he also wrote with a keen sense of the dissemination of literature in print and how lyric worked within its visual encoding.[9] As I will explore in the final chapter, key modernist theorists in the early twentieth century sought to return the concept of 'lyric' to a central affiliation of words with music. In so doing, they felt they were returning to a more 'authentic' and precise taxonomy, but to impose that definition on the nineteenth century is to side-step some of the dilemmas that are most crucial to an understanding of poetry of the period. One of the questions that motivates this book is how we might find ways of discussing the character of a broad genre that, while it includes song forms, is no longer defined simply, at this time, in relation to musical accompaniment, oral performance or aurality.

The term 'lyric' had come, by the 1860s, to encompass a raft of different forms and impetuses. 'Song' is still at the core of the genre – sometimes as a ghostly or imagined aural echo – but it is not a genre limited to traditional sung forms. Virginia Jackson has recently argued that much of our understanding of the 'lyric' genre is fundamentally anachronistic, suggesting that early twentieth-century New Critical formulations of the lyric genre mark a crucial point in its formation.[10] Central to this process is 'the lyricization of poetry itself – the historical transformation of many varied poetic genres into the single abstraction of the post-Romantic lyric'.[11] Jackson and Prins argue in their anthology of twentieth-century lyric theory that this 'lyricization of poetry is a product of twentieth-century critical thought'.[12] Yet, interestingly, J. A. Symonds's 1889 essay might be seen to set out a theory of poetry's 'lyricisation' as a nineteenth-century phenomenon in advance of the more systematic movement that Jackson and Prins identify. Symonds's piece provides crucial evidence of late nineteenth-century lyric theory in the days prior to the birth of literary criticism as an academic discourse, and it reflects at length on the concept of the 'Victorian lyric'. Here Symonds writes:

> But what a complex thing is this Victorian lyric! It includes Wordsworth's sonnets and Rossetti's ballads, Coleridge's 'Ancient Mariner' and Keats' odes, Clough's 'Easter Day' and Tennyson's 'Maud,' Swinburne's 'Songs before Sunrise' and Browning's 'Dramatic Personae,' Thomson's 'City of Dreadful Night' and Mary Robinson's 'Handful of Honeysuckles,' Andrew Lang's Ballades and Sharp's 'Weird of Michael Scot,' Dobson's dealings with the eighteenth century and Noel's 'Child's Garland,' Barnes's Dorsetshire Poems and Buchanan's London Lyrics, the songs from Empedocles on Etna and Ebenezer Jones's 'Pagan's Drinking Chaunt,' Shelley's Ode to the West Wind and Mrs Browning's 'Pan is Dead,' Newman's hymns and Gosse's Chaunt Royal. The Kaleidoscope presented by this lyric is so inexhaustible [. . .][13]

This list is notable for its eclecticism, which demonstrates Symonds's claim for the absorption of many different poetic forms into an abstracted 'lyric'. Yet it is also revealing in that it implicitly positions song as something analogous to a dead metaphor within lyric: the sonnet, for example, may be etymologically a 'little song', but by the late nineteenth century it is one of the pre-eminent *textual* forms. The same might be said of Gosse's Chant Royals, which while invoking the 'chant', existed as part of the compendious textual collation of medieval French forms for which the technologies of print were key. A. Mary F. Robinson's *Handful of Honeysuckle* contains a variety of forms and types of what she calls 'lyrics', but again, while including some songs, the book was purposefully planned as a textual performance.[14] According to this list, then, lyric already signifies a range of types of poetry, in which aural song exists sometimes only as a fossil at its core.

Indeed, Thomas Bayne, writing in 1880, also provides a clear statement that 'lyric' poetry is no longer a category unified by a concern with music and song when he writes that, 'As modern dramatic poetry is largely composed without reference to the stage, so a wide latitude is now assumed in the application of the title lyric poetry. [. . .] the twanging of the actual lyre is not in the thoughts of many modern lyricists.'[15] Writing again in 1882, on D. G. Rossetti's poetry, Bayne declares that 'the lyric poet has many outlets for the application of his special powers'.[16] Even earlier, in 1870, Swinburne, also writing about Rossetti, identifies distinctive modes of 'narrative', 'lyric' and 'dramatic' poetry that act as categories over and above an identification with individual forms such as 'ballad' or 'sonnet'.[17] More specifically for the aestheticist lyric, one might say that the musical impetus was often transmuted into an interest in highly patterned, compressed, fixed forms which relied on visual patterning and eye-rhyme as much as any aural effect. This distinctive revival of a plethora of fixed-form verse structures capitalises on a textual as well as an aural presence.

The above evidence shows why a variety of poetic forms are considered in this study to be of the 'lyric' genre, and why 'song' does not define my remit (although song forms are included within it). Indeed, the problems for 'lyric' poetry I go on to outline later in this chapter are precisely attendant on that 'lyricisation' of poetry. Certainly much of what is central to the 'modern' understanding of the lyric as a genre (the short, non-narrative poem focused on subjective experience)[18] was in evidence as early as Hegel's early nineteenth-century theorisation, and certainly in reviews of poetry in my period of study. Take, for example, a review of 'Mr Swinburne's Lyrics' (*Poems and Ballads*) from 1890, which opens its examination by dwelling for several pages on what 'lyrical poetry' is, and drawing out its key features. The anonymous writer identifies 'lyric' poems as having three major qualities: 'beauty of versification' or 'perfect form', which reflects its musical origins; 'reflective or subjective' thought as content; and, above all, 'concentration': 'Few, indeed, are the *long* lyrical poems which have met with any general acceptance.'[19]

The dominant current critical narrative sees the Romantic period as a time when literary genre began to be conceptualised in its modern form. This is not to underestimate the variety and divergence of uses of the term 'lyric' in that period, but to see the emergence of an overall trajectory. Scott Brewster begins his study of lyric with the claim that our current understanding of the lyric as a textual poetic genre was 'developed in the later eighteenth century, which defined lyric in terms of heightened emotion and authentic sentiment, and presented it as a (usually brief) moment of intensified awareness'.[20] Brewster gives plenty of evidence for believing that 'From the early nineteenth century onwards, lyric came to be identified as the very essence of poetry, the most intense, passionate and authentic poetic mode' and an umbrella for many varied poetic forms.[21] M. H. Abrams has been particularly influential in the formation of this narrative, arguing, in *The Mirror and the Lamp*, that only towards the end of the eighteenth century is lyric conceptualised as the dominant poetic genre.[22] John Stuart Mill, for example, identifies 'lyric poetry' as 'the earliest kind', but also 'more eminently and peculiarly poetry than any other'.[23] Frederick Garber gives a useful summary of the sources preceding Mill's claim that help contextualise it. Writing of William Jones's 1772 'Essay on the Arts called Imitative' he points out:

> Some sixty years before Mill, Jones came to the same conclusion Mill would arrive at in his own essays on poetry: the characteristics of lyric – brevity, intensity, passion – are those of poetry as such. And if made by Sir William Jones in a relatively obscure essay, that point was made more famously in chapter 14 of Coleridge's *Biographia Literaria* [. . .][24]

In a recent study, David Duff has explored the Romantic period as that which not only established the 'modern' definition of lyric as a genre encompassing many forms (albeit through many competing schemas), but which also marked a hyper-consciousness around genre that ensured it was an expressive category, hugely influential for poetic production.[25] I would suggest that the appropriate critical formulation is one that has been in currency from at least the 1960s: 'from the late eighteenth century the lyric impulse became diffused over an ever-widening area, till today one could almost say there is no lyric poetry since every poem has a lyrical quality'.[26] Twentieth-century theorisations of lyric mark an important point in this process, but not an original point of formation. Already in the later nineteenth century a definition similar to the one we know now was in circulation.

While New Criticism was guilty of a 'retro-projection' of its own definition of lyric on to literary history, this too is already much in evidence in the later decades of the nineteenth century. 'Lyric' had, arguably, become a genre that not only subsumed many and varied other poetic forms, but also one that subsumed its own lyric history. Rowlinson has suggested that in the final third of the century, 'British lyric poetry displays a new sense of confronting the prior history of lyric as a totality, a sense which [. . .] results from confronting it in print'.[27] At this point, the print lyric 'was able to incorporate the totality of its own antecedents, becoming the medium for a coherent summing up of its own history'.[28] In this period, Rowlinson claims, the aural and the manuscript incarnation were combined with and mediated through print as the primary mode of transmission that incorporated and replaced all others. This tendency for lyric of the period to 'at once [preserve] and [supersede] its multiple pre-decessors'[29] might be seen most clearly in works such as Edward FitzGerald's *The Rubáiyát of Omar Khayyám*. This example shows, crucially, that an argument for print 'totalisation' is not an argument for print providing textual stability in the later decades of the nine-teenth century. First published in 1859, FitzGerald's *Rubáiyát* went through five different editions up to 1889, each edition presenting a rather different text: expanded, revised and changed in various, sometimes quite radical ways. Christopher Decker has documented the impossibility of identifying one 'definitive' text for this work, and it is a good example of the potential instability of the printed poetic text at this time.[30] In their overview of scholarship on precisely this issue, Josephine Guy and Ian Small conclude that such textual his-tory 'can have surprisingly little to tell us about the nature of those poetic works which survive today, and this is because . . . such an approach has relatively little to say about value'.[31] Yet this print his-tory does, I suggest, have something fascinating to say in relation to our understanding of the concept of lyric in the period, and about the values that emerge in the reception of this poem as a key 'lyric' text of the period. The text is a selection of verses taken from manu-script sources in the Bodleian and in Calcutta, 'mashed' and 'tes-sellated' together, as FitzGerald himself described his method. This involved not only rearranging the order of the quatrains but 'creating completely new ones by conflating lines and images from more than one of the originals'.[32] Add to this FitzGerald's linguistic misunder-standings of his sources and his attempt to Hellenise and Orientalise them,[33] and one sees how the text is an important example of how a rich aural and manuscript history of lyric was combined with, and in a sense superseded by, a print rendition that largely fabricated its own generic origins.

FitzGerald's text is, along with Palgrave's *Golden Treasury* (1861), an important landmark of the start of a renewed interest in the lyric genre and of the currency it held throughout my period of study. We see this desire to explore, preserve and supersede lyric history continued in the zest for publication of complete editions of works considered formative in the history of lyric, such as Henry Thornton Wharton's edition of *Sappho* (1885). Such editorial work was accompanied in the nineteenth century by a flurry of philological and historical study. The rediscovery of Sappho across the nineteenth century has been charted in detail by scholars including Yopie Prins and Margaret Reynolds, although the huge amount of interesting philological and historical work that brought the troubadour poets back to poetic consciousness between 1860 and 1900, before the better-recognised work of Pound, has been far less acknowledged. Robert Browning had already marked his strong interest in the troubadours, but his highly sceptical engagement with lyric history contrasts strongly with the much more welcoming reception such poets received in the later part of the century, as I will explore later. An interest in the history of lyric is, of course, not new to my period of study (as Coleridge and Wordsworth's rethinking of the eighteenth-century lyric, for example, attests), but the shift from the mid-century lyric-scepticism of Browning to the later desire to translate and celebrate complete bodies of medieval French work is striking.

If the period of lyric history I study can be characterised by an interest in the past that is in equal parts voracious and subsuming, then the implications of this might usefully be explored by turning back to John Addington Symonds's essay, in which he explicitly declares 'Victorian poetry' to be 'in large measure the criticism of all existing literature'. Here again, Symonds provides clear evidence for the idea of a process of lyric 'totalisation'. Symonds goes on to consider very interestingly the effects this had on poetry of the period. In his comparison of Elizabethan and Victorian lyric, he mourns the loss of the 'spontaneous and joyful utterance' of the Elizabethan lyric and finds such unmediated effusion replaced in his own age by a lyric whose freshness is compromised by its awareness of the genre as a summation of its own history: 'The result is a polychromatic abundance of what may be called cultured poetry, which does not reach the heart of the people, and does not express its spirit.'[34] Here Elizabethan poetry is associated with the immediacy of song unhampered by the cultures of knowledge that he sees as the curse of the nineteenth century print lyric. Symonds projects on to Elizabethan poetry an alternative defined in opposition to a 'modern' literature caught up within a network of cultural processes: 'each man in that age wrote what he thought best, wrote out of himself, and sang spontaneously. He had no fear of academies, of censorship, of critical coteries, of ecclesiastical censure, before his eyes.'[35] In spite of his talk of 'Victorian poetry', there are indications that Symonds is writing particularly of a trajectory that had come to a head in recent years rather than earlier in the century. When he comments how, in comparison with Elizabethan poetry, 'We have exchanged the hedgerow flowers for heavy-headed double roses, and instead of honey we are not infrequently reminded – pardon the expression – of jam', he is perhaps thinking, in 1889, of Swinburne and Rossetti and of what Tennyson called the 'poisonous honey' of aestheticism.[36]

This investment in a myth of spontaneous and expressive song as a contrast and precursor to what Symonds finds in his own age can easily look like a flight from the conditions of modernity: from the isolated, alienated nature of both the modern subject and the lyric in print culture. Yet in this study I argue that such gestures are at least as much an engagement with modernity as an eschewal of it. It is in such a desire to look back to a pre-mass-print, and often pre-textual, moment of lyric as song – however mythical that moment may be – that we find an attempt to reflect on the current status and purpose of the genre, and an attempt to remake its forms in ways that better responded to the conditions of modernity. Much as Herbert Tucker saw the aestheticist lyric as a moment of 'nostalgia for lyric', and a yearning for an escape from modernity, he acknowledges that it does not seek a return to any type of lyric that can be found within Romanticism.[37] The aestheticist poets 'wanted to read in their French and English antecedents an expurgated lyric that never was on page or lip. It was, rather, a generic back-formation, a textual constituent they isolated from the dramatic monologue and related nineteenth-century forms.'[38] Aestheticism offers a form of lyric that represents a 'severely purist poetics' and a 'surprisingly revisionist history of poetry' in its rejection of the 'exteriority' and 'rhetoric' of mid-century hybrid forms.[39]

In fact, the drive towards compendious expansion and summation within the conceptual scope of the totalised print lyric sat, within aestheticist poetry, alongside a desire for a compression, distillation and 'reduction' in lyric form. The focal poetry of my book might be thought of as representing a fairly expansive understanding of the many manifestations of this drive towards a 'purist' lyric. This might be seen to encompass the Dollie Radford song quoted earlier, and Olive Custance's 'A Sleep Song'.[40] It might include Hardy's domestically gnomic 'glimpses', such as 'At Tea',[41] and Wilde's liturgically gnomic 'Helas!'[42] It brings with it a tendency towards the metapoetical, as in D. G. Rossetti's 'The Sonnet' and Alfred Douglas's 'Sonnet on the Sonnet' ('some deliberate cage/ Wherein to keep wild thoughts like birds in thrall').[43] It certainly includes, among many others, Swinburne's highly wrought roundels and Arthur Symons's brief theatre-hall impressions.[44] A particularly central example of the kind of lyric purism to which I think Tucker refers might be found in Selwyn Image's compress of images, seen here in 'Suavis et Decora':

> Like a willow, like a reed,
>   Is my Love's grace:
>   And her face,
>
> Like a soft, pale-petalled, rose:
>   And my Love's breast,
>   Like the rest
>
> Of a snow-drift, calm and white:
>   And to kiss there!
>   Ah! What compare,
>
> Can I find in rhyme for that;
>   Where is Love's own
>   Jewelled throne?[45]

Regular rhyme schemes and strict verse forms characterise these examples. The sheer variety of types of tightly crafted formal presence in this brief selection gives something of an introduction to the significance of form in the poetry I will be exploring.

Like Image's rose petals and snowflakes, the 'purist' lyric seeks a finely wrought beauty in microcosm. Aiming to represent a slice of experience, colour or emotion in all its complexity and multiplicity, it often employs symbol, impression, refrain or image to achieve its compression. Image's work also gives an indication of the importance of pre-Romantic sources within this search for a 'purer' lyric, as the striking design of *Poems and Carols* itself harks back to decorated medieval manuscripts. To be sure, Wilde's *Poems* are frequently invested in a Romantic heritage, yet here, as much as with Image's imagism, we would do well to be suspicious of labelling this a 'nostalgic' gesture. The critic Cosmo Monkhouse describes in 1887 a '*modern* movement towards greater perfection in lyric form' (my emphasis), which owes its origins to the work of Swinburne and Rossetti, even when expressed through the medieval French forms he reviews in that essay.[46] I will argue that the aestheticist search for a form of lyric that is as pure as possible is more of a deliberate *reductio ad absurdam* of the lyric impetus that was theorised in the late eighteenth century, drawing on many pre-Romantic models in order to imagine a form of art as separate as possible from modernity, society and the world of commerce. After all, while the Romantics may have formulated 'lyric' in terms recognisable under our current definition, it should not be overlooked that it frequently functioned at that time more as a poetic *mode* – which could be identified as a register, sometimes dominant, sometimes not, within many different types of poems – than as a genre.[47] What we see by the final decades of the nineteenth century is an idea of lyric as an isolatable poetic genre.[48]

This search for a purer, more perfect and more self-sufficient form of lyric is in many ways emblematic of the 'art for art's sake' impulse. Yet in practice British aestheticism always ultimately uses this position as one from which to reflect on the nature of society, modernity, commerce and all the things it is apparently designed to exclude. Indeed it 'comes to problematize the very art it would seem to erect as the locus of value; moreover, it problematizes that art by the same gesture with which it valorizes it'.[49] As Angela Leighton has written, in a chapter devoted to exploring the significance of what might be summarised as the crack in the Golden Bowl: 'For all its beautiful indifference, its cool isolation, this art object bears the pressure of what it shuts out, or in: the pressure of context, content, reference, memory.'[50] The aestheticist conceptualisation of lyric is no exception, and in this book I argue that the turn to an 'essence' of lyric ultimately represents as much a confrontation of the genre's relationship with modernity as an escape from it. Moreover, the exploration of pre-Romantic sources, in particular, is indicative of a desire not just to register the problems of that relationship but to re-imagine the possibilities for lyric in the modern world.

*   *   *

If the above gives an introduction to how we might usefully conceptualise aestheticist lyric poetry through the twin impetuses of conceptual expansion and formal reduction, more needs to be said here to position it culturally – particularly to explain what I mean by the pressures of 'cultural modernity' to which I suggest it was responding and which I will invoke throughout this study. When Symonds writes, as quoted above, of the 'fear' of a network of cultural surveillance, he goes on to elaborate more generally on the place of poetry in the modern age:

> We are oppressed with social problems which admit of no solution, due to the vast increase of our population, to the industrial changes which have turned England from an agricultural to a manufacturing country, to the unequal distribution of wealth, to the development of huge, hideous towns, the seething multitudes of vicious and miserable paupers which they harbour. We watch the gathering of revolutionary storm-clouds, hear the grumbling of thunder in the distance, and can only sit meanwhile in darkness – so gigantic and unmanageable are the forces now in labour for some mighty birth of time.[51]

This cannot help but deny poetry the freedom of spontaneous song he feels characterises the Elizabethan lyric:

> Victorian poets cannot be spontaneous in the same sense as our ancestors were. Like Iago, they are nothing if not critical. Science has imposed on them her burden of analysis, and though science reveals horizons far beyond the dreams of Bacon, it fills the soul with something well-nigh akin to hopelessness. Man shrinks before the Universe. We have lived through so much; we have seen so many futile philosophies rise like mushrooms and perish; we have tried so many political experiments [. . .] that a world-fatigue has penetrated deep into our soul.[52]

Lyric of the period, he asserts, is characterised by the anxiety resulting from what recent scholars call the 'crisis of abundance' – the overwhelming feeling of a world whose understanding was outside any individual's grasp: that great proliferation of historical knowledge, scientific discovery, the size of individual communities and the commodity.[53] Yet, within this most un-singing of worlds, there is, somewhat ironically, a particular emphasis on the lyric genre within poetry: 'No literature and no age has been more fertile of lyric poetry than English literature in the age of Victoria.'[54] Even when we discover that Symonds is loose enough in his designation of 'Victorian poetry' to include much of the Romantic poets' work, this might still come as a surprise when our established critical narrative characterises nineteenth-century literature through the growing importance of the novel and of narrative and dramatic poetic forms. The novel, writes Symonds, has taken over the role that dramatic and epic poetry used to fill, and poetry is left to focus on what he calls the 'lyric' and the 'idyll'.[55] With the loss of a rationale for epic and dramatic forms, he argues, poets of his time 'have had to sing from their inner selves, subjectively, introspectively'.[56]

It is the fate and function of the lyric Symonds describes above that interests me. My period of study is characterised by a combination of the marginalisation of poetry within the marketplace and the dominance of lyric within poetry – undoubtedly in part a consequence of the established position held by the novel, which ultimately encouraged poetry to find its distinctive qualities in non-narrative features. This leads to the problematic that lies at the heart of my study: the simultaneous recognition of the poor fit of some of the central qualities of the lyric genre with the realities of modernity *and* the move towards its instatement as the dominant modern poetic. While the general readership for poetry declined, Palgrave's *Golden Treasury*, a book aimed at the newly populous middle-class reading public, was thriving and sales were strong. First published in 1861, the anthology provides a marker of the beginning of the crucial period in lyric history I study here, and a clear marker in the formation of 'lyric' as understood today.[57] The book has long been recognised as indicating an important moment in 'the codification of Romantic theory, with its gradual privileging of the lyric above the other literary modes'.[58] One can argue that the anthology format privileged lyric (in practical terms it is possible to represent a range of shorter poems where space would not permit a diversity of long poems), but also that the turn to lyric might be part and parcel of the marginalisation of poetry, as the lyric was associated through Romantic theorisations with the lone poetic voice, a seer separated from society: a form of high art that is both valuable and a little disconnected from society.[59]

Yet the decline in the readership for poetry generally across the second half of the nineteenth century stands in stark contrast to its popularity in the first half.[60] Ezra Pound asserts that 'The main expression of nineteenth-century consciousness is in prose', and connects this shift away from the importance of poetry to the rapidly increased pace of modern life and the attention required to read poetry: 'The art of popular success lies simply in never putting more on any one page than the most ordinary reader can lick off it in his normally rapid, half-attentive skim-over.'[61] Hardy turned from prose to poetry because, scholars have argued, it was both 'respected and ignored': in being above the marketplace, poetry had also become in danger of seeming rather irrelevant.[62] Evidence can be found in articles such as Calvin Thomas's 'Have We Still Need of Poetry' (1898), Gosse's 'Is Verse in Danger?' (1890–91), and even W. B. Yeats's 1902 piece 'What is Popular Poetry', in which he saw the large reading public that arose across the nineteenth century as being incapable of understanding poetry. Walter Benjamin also notes retrospectively that by the late nineteenth century 'the climate for lyric poetry has become increasingly inhospitable'. He dates the change back 'roughly to the middle of the last [nineteenth] century', and writes:

> If conditions for a positive reception of lyric poetry have become less favourable, it is reasonable to assume that only in rare instances is lyric poetry in rapport with the experience of its readers. This may be due to a change in the structure of their experience.[63]

This change in the nature of experience is for Benjamin, as for Symonds, related to the process of industrialisation that character-ised nineteenth-century modernity. Earlier in the same book he con-nects the nineteenth-century sense of 'the approaching crisis of lyric poetry' with 'the increasing rift between the city and the country'; for Benjamin, the very nature of industrialised modernity 'render[s] the possibility of lyric poetry questionable'.[64] Why? At root because the lyric quest for transcendence is incompatible with – or at least in tension with – the values of modernity: 'the lyric poet with a halo is antiquated'.[65]

Indeed, all the declarations of 'lyric crisis' with which I began this book are, no matter how different their poetic affiliations, also premised on very broadly similar statements. Mallarmé's Oxford lecture, 'Crisis in Poetry', is fundamentally about the failure of language in the modern world to enable transcendence, and his hopes that free verse might help poetry rediscover the 'suggestiveness of things'.[66] T. E. Hulme is equally clear about his sense of both the centrality of the quest for transcen-dence to a nineteenth-century conception of lyric and its irrelevance to modernity. He begins the lecture with the statement:

> I will give you an example of the position exactly opposite to the one I take up. A reviewer writing in the *Saturday Review* last week spoke of poetry as the means by which the soul soared into higher regions, and as a means of expression by which it became merged into a higher kind of reality. Well that is the kind of statement that I utterly detest.[67]

Contrary to Mallarmé, Hulme rejects this characterisation of lyric altogether, and rather than seeing it as an essential part of the genre brought into crisis, he declares it a fiction no longer subscribed to: 'Now the whole trend of the modern spirit is away from that; phi-losophers no longer believe in absolute truth'; 'In all the arts, we seek for the maximum of individual and personal expression, rather than for the attainment of any absolute beauty.'[68] The Symbolism of Mallarmé is different in many ways from Hulme's imagism,[69] but for my purposes the significance here is that Benjamin, Mallarmé and Hulme – three very different writers, from different parts of Europe – all recognise very clearly through their description of the 'crisis' that it is the conceptualisation of lyric as a genre with transcendent aspirations that is at the root of its incompatibility with the values of industrialised modernity. (This is not a new concern, of course, but it is one that, I will argue, takes on different and more acute forms as the century progresses.) This is what Theodor Adorno identifies as the genre that 'hopes to attain universality through unrestrained individuation'; this is the genre that eschews the 'bustle and commotion' of modern society in order to find something that transcends the material world.[70]

Yet, crucially, the reference Benjamin makes to the lyric poet with the halo is to Baudelaire, and to a piece written almost half a century before the remaking of poetry in high modernism. It is worth dwelling a little here on a writer of such fundamental significance for British aestheticism. Baudelaire famously attempted a reconciliation when in 1863 (in *Le Peintre de la vie moderne*) he theorised art as the finding of the transcendent ('the eternal and the immovable') in modernity ('the transient, the fleeting, the contingent').[71] The desire to forsake neither leads him to the idea of '*Correspondance*', denoting points of connection between modernity and eternity.[72] It is these moments that enable the artist to 'distil the eternal from the transitory'.[73] Yet while Baudelaire's 1857 *Les Fleurs du mal* is celebrated as a poetic demonstration of this theory, his oeuvre as a whole represents a more complex meditation. Scholars have drawn attention to the need to read Baudelaire's work as ironic and deliberately inconsistent – noting that *Correspondance* ultimately fails, in Baudelaire's eyes, to awake the eternal in the fleeting: *Correspondances* are 'ineluctably personal because the collective experience that might have made them public no longer exists'.[74] Indeed, in Benjamin's discussion, noted above, it is Baudelaire's prose poem, 'Perte d'auréole' ('The Loss of a Halo') that he references. Published posthumously in *Petits poèmes en prose* (also known under a later title as *Le Spleen de Paris*) in 1869, the piece depicts an angel on earth who loses his halo while dodging the mud and the horse-and-cart-traffic in the process of crossing a busy Parisian street.[75] Enjoying his new-found disguise as a 'ordinary mortal', the angel decides not try to reclaim his divinity, musing

> I think with joy that some poor poet will pick it up, and will impudently deck himself out. To make someone happy, what joy! and especially a happy one that makes me laugh! Think of X. . ., or of Z. . . Oh! That would be comical![76]

The incongruity and incompatibility of the angel in the compellingly materialist rough-and-tumble of the modern street speaks concisely of the failure of the attempt to find the eternal in the flux of modern life – and the poet who might attempt this is a figure of fun.[77] Credited with inaugurating the modern genre of prose poetry, Baudelaire's later works appear to turn away from lyric to hybrid forms. In his prose poems, reference to the lyre is almost always ironic, and recent scholarship has explored the critique within this later work of the 'rarefied terms of Romantic lyricism'.[78]

Ultimately, then, Baudelaire's bold assertion of reconciliation between modernity and lyric's transcendent quest is as much an acknowledgement of the problems as a solution, and it gives a context for the English aestheticist lyric's struggle with those issues that forms my central problematic. Whether the conceptualisation of lyric that emerges from the Romantic period is a revolutionary or an evolutionary one,[79] lyric 'transcendence' was frequently seen by commentators at the end of the century as a key component of the conceptualisation of lyric inherited from that formative period.[80] Shelley's 'Defence' is, of course, a central statement, which resonated across the nineteenth century and which set some of the key terms of the debate for poetry thereafter, but Wordsworth's claims for lyric universalisation (the subject as a 'man speaking for men') also attested to transcendent ambition.[81] Just as crucial, however, is the influence of a much more substantial body of lyric theory from early nineteenth-century Germany: the work of Hegel influenced 'mainstream British criticism' in the late nineteenth century in key part through Walter Pater.[82] Indeed, it is at the end of the century that we begin to see a retrospective awareness of the larger formative currents of 'Romanticism'.[83] Hegel's lengthy discussion of 'lyric' poetry – distinct from 'epic' and 'dramatic' – claims its particularity to be in a focus on the 'inner life': it is concerned with subjective feelings, and the expression, or articulation, of what was formerly only felt.[84] Yet it is crucial too that something transcendent is reached through this introspection:

> in order that this expression may not remain a merely casual expression of an individual's own immediate feelings and ideas, it becomes the language of the *poetic* inner life, and therefore however intimately the insights and feelings which the poet describes as his own belong to him as a single individual, they must nevertheless possess a universal validity [. . .][85]

Hegel argues that poetry is a form of art particularly capable of the expression of the universal and transcendent spirit (*Geist*: the ineffable, or the 'really real').[86] Crucially, such transcendent aspirations are demarcated as distinct from a specifically religious poetry, which Hegel sees as belonging to a separate tradition of contemplation of God.[87] My decision to exclude such poetry from this study is an acknowledgement that within it comes into play a different idea of poetic 'transcendence'.

In the rest of this book, my tripartite exploration is motivated by three 'problems' that a 'transcendent' Romantic formulation of lyric encountered in the context of the late nineteenth century. First (and this is the governing issue of Part I), the quest for the eternal, transcendent moment risked looking evasive and out of touch with the urgent temporalities of modern life and changing models of temporality. Second (reflected in Part II), the emphasis on introspection (perhaps crystallised in Romantic apostrophe) was a dangerous one in an urbanised context more and more aware of the threat of isolation – a threat explicitly theorised aesthetically by Walter Pater. Third (explored in Part III), the idea of a poet being a 'man speaking for men' – or a universal voice found through the individual – was increasingly difficult to imagine in expanding urban populations whose experience was often characterised by deracination and heterogeneity. Indeed, it is no coincidence that my period of study is one characterised by the reign of the self-defined 'minor' poet, who felt that professions of poetic authority were outdated. My claim is not that aestheticist poetry necessarily, or even typically, responded to all of these worries at the same time, but that it can frequently be seen to be engaged with one or another of them. Each of these problems relates to a different axis of lyric operation (broadly conceived here as time, space and subjectivity), along which aestheticist lyric's varied responses to the challenges of modernity can be followed; and these parameters structure the three parts of my book.

Of course, such concerns were recognised before 1860. David Lindley observes in his study of lyric that, after the ebb of religious conviction, Romantic poetry came under great pressure to fulfil a quasi-religious function, but from the start of the nineteenth century the 'subsequent history of lyric poetry down to the present day might be seen as exploring the premise, and doubting the conclusion'.[88] Shelley's 'Defence' was, of course, defending poetry against precisely the charge of its loss of relevance to the modern age – a charge made in somewhat arch fashion by fellow-poet Thomas Love Peacock. Indeed, English Romantic lyric poetry itself frequently explores its own failure to sustain its transcendent epiphanic moment. Keats's 'Ode to a Nightingale' represents the flight away from the world on the 'viewless wings of Poesy', but it also registers the return to earth and the admission that the 'fancy' is a 'cheat'. 'Ode on a Grecian Urn' concludes with a similar repudiation. Yet these experiences, if transient, are often seen as valuable, bringing not escape from 'the fever, and the fret' or, in the case of the Grecian Urn, the 'woe', but a productive poetic dialectic.[89] It was a rejection of such aspirations that became one of the underlying causes of the search for more 'objectively' anchored hybrid poetic forms over the middle part of the nineteenth century.[90] The dramatised pathology of Robert Browning's characters in his 'dramatic lyrics' is in part the sickness of the lyric subject itself: the inability of the duke to engage with his 'last duchess' as anything but an aesthetic ideal might be better seen as a parody of lyric when set alongside poems such as 'Christina' and 'Porphyria's Lover' (also published in the 1842 *Dramatic Lyrics* collection). The reinvention of the Petrarchan lyric subject as a stalker ('Christina') and a murderer ('Porphyria's Lover') highlights the collection's critique of a lyric heritage.[91] In the latter poem, the relation between lyric subject and object is parodied in the speaker's desire (similar to that seen in 'My Last Duchess') to kill his interlocutor to preserve, poetically, the beauty of the moment: 'That moment she was mine, mine, fair,/ Perfectly pure and good'.[92] Elizabeth Barrett Browning's critical engagement with a Petrarchan sonnet tradition has also been interestingly documented,[93] yet in her work we also find something of a more general indictment of the lyric genre. In 'A Musical Instrument', for example, she invokes (as did Selwyn Image in the poem quoted earlier in this chapter) the reed as a figure of poetry through her treatment of the myth of Syrinx, but for her 'lyric' is associated through this analogy with rape. Pan is described as wreaking havoc in the reed-bed, breaking and tearing, hacking and hewing, until he has the reed – 'poor dry empty thing' – notched with holes and ready for his music. More beast than god, Pan's divinity is, for Barrett Browning, eroded by his barbaric musical practice: 'The true gods sigh for the cost and pain,—/ For the reed which grows nevermore again/ As a reed with the reeds in the river'.[94]

Poetic commentary on lyric is, then, hardly scarce before 1860. My claim is not that a faith in lyric's transcendent aspirations failed or was questioned for the first time in the final third of the century, but that as a result of the aestheticist impulse in the later decades of the nineteenth century we can find a distinctive, and interesting, moment in this process. Jonathan Freedman argues that aestheticism is 'The moment in which the Romantic attempt to turn from antinomy to dialectic, from the emphasis on oppositions to the understanding of the potential reconcilability of such oppositions, is explicitly understood to be a necessary and inevitable failure.'[95] The enabling dialectic between the transcendent (the universal, the eternal and the introspective sublime) and the earthly (the individual, the temporal and material, and the social world) that powered much of English Romanticism was itself under suspicion. As Freedman shows, this was not the problem but the point of British aestheticism, and the impact of this on lyric will be central to my study. Moreover, I suggest it is in the final third of the century that the 'crisis' in lyric might be traced not through the search for ways to distance the poet from the genre (as it has been in the mid-century satirical and hybrid forms that have caught so much scholarly attention) – but through that quest for a more intense distillation of lyric and its forms that we see in aestheticist poetry. Because the dialectic Freedman discusses had become definitive of the lyric's structural negotiation with time, space and subjectivity, the acknowledgement of its failure could not be addressed purely by changing and modernising language, subject matter or even the mode of representation:[96] it became, in a fundamental way, also an issue of form. In the rest of this book I will explore the idea that aestheticist lyric has the potential to itself be engaged critically with its relationship with modernity through its apparently old-fashioned forms.

*   *   *

While this chapter has positioned aestheticist poetry briefly within a lyric trajectory, and set up key contexts for what follows, the rest of the book will introduce broader theoretical frames. These enable me to position readings of specific poems in relation to the three major 'problems' raised above in ways that help engage with deeper underlying philosophical shifts. To inhabit these broader epistemological trajectories of modernity *is* to engage with modernity and its material and social conditions, but, as my focus on form will suggest, not perhaps in the way we expect. My aim here is to engage with poetry in a way that is both historical and conceptual: to draw on a conceptual context that is historically relevant and philosophically inflected. The four main thinkers I draw on to achieve this are Hegel (whose early nineteenth-century work defining the 'modern' lyric provides something of a starting point for the study), Benjamin (who provides the main theoretical parameter for Part I), Merleau-Ponty (who does the same for Part II), ad Adorno (the main point of theoretical reference in the third part). With Hegel at one end of the nineteenth century and the rest at the other end, these commentators 'book-end' the period. Benjamin, Merleau-Ponty and Adorno theorise the experience of modernity in which I want to situate poetry of the period. While publishing in the early twentieth century, and frequently used as a context for high modernist poetry, these writers either explicitly look back to the last third of the nineteenth century as the locus of the crises of modernity they figure, or, as in the case of Merleau-Ponty, their thinking is a continuation of a nineteenth-century philosophical trajectory. In fact, all three theorists have Hegel as a major reference point, connecting them in ways that are crucial both to the historical positioning of this study and to the aesthetic trajectory in which the development of lyric is situated. Merleau-Ponty is the only one of the four not to have written specifically and substantially on the concept of 'lyric', but his work is important to this study because it captures a conceptual shift crucial for the aesthetics of modernity, and his dialogue with Hegel suggests that one might extrapolate from his work a response to or development of Hegel's position on lyric. The conceptual context these theorists provide for my study will be set up in the first chapter of each part, each of which aims to provide a brief frame for the following two case studies. The case studies, crucially, aim to recognise a characteristically aestheticist poetics that, while it responds to many of the same problems, is not simply a proto-modernism.

While early twentieth-century thinkers such as Benjamin, Merleau-Ponty and Adorno identified crucial cultural shifts rooted in the second half of the nineteenth century, I suggest we might see literary texts responding to and therefore marking these changes before they were articulated through twentieth-century theoretical and philosophical discourses. In this way, the poems discussed are critiques of modernity not so much in the sense of offering cultural commentary or satire within their content but rather through a formal response to their own shifting cultural remit. John Frow argues that genre is 'central to the different ways the world is understood';[97] it creates meaning by the forms and conventions it uses to think about experience. Poetry is not philosophy, but genre does, necessarily, respond to the same questions about how we experience and relate to the world. In reading genre we can perhaps read a narrative of cultural formation through poetry's forms.

Preliminary Case Study: Michael Field's Study in Lyric

Before setting up the first theoretical frame in Part I, however, I close this chapter with a reading of a poem that starts to introduce, poetically, some of the key issues described above. Michael Field's 1889 volume *Long Ago* ('Michael Field' was the joint pseudonym of Katharine Bradley and her niece and collaborator, Edith Cooper) provides both an important point of reflection on the conceptualisation of lyric in aestheticism, and a significant self-reflexive commentary on some of the key themes outlined. A volume in which Sapphic fragments are expanded by Bradley and Cooper into 'complete' poems, this is one of the most sustained poetic engagements with the newly available work of Sappho (edited and published by Henry Wharton in 1885), who was herself a central signifier of 'lyric' for the period. The project well represents the twin characteristics of an aestheticist conception of lyric described above as on the one hand a drive towards reduction and compression and on the other a recognition of lyric's 'totalisation' in print. Sappho's poetic fragments represent, among other things, an archetype of lyric's emotional distillation: a pure 'essence' of lyric. Yet in writing through the voice of Sappho, *Long Ago* incorporated, preserved and superseded (to echo Rowlinson's words, quoted above) one of the most significant predecessors in lyric history by literally completing her work for her. This volume demonstrates well how these ideas of lyric expansion, totalisation, distillation and compression are coexistent and interdependent.

The volume was certainly a focus for the discussion of issues of poetic genre by contemporaneous readers. John Gray's review of *Long Ago*, for example, first identifies the poems as dramatic monologues: quoting Robert Browning, he writes of them: 'while "lyric in expression" they are "dramatic in principle" [. . .] they are the imagined utterances of that one greatest poetess of antiquity'.[98] What Gray identifies in *Long Ago* is primarily a battle between excess and containment, and in his terms this is a pull between the lyric and the narrative or dramatic. 'Lyric' he defines as the 'most "free from baser matter"': a form that 'trembles on the border-line separating it from another form of art; in which it is ready to pass into music, to dispense altogether, for its effect, with the aid of words, and to employ sound alone as its minister'.[99] Lyric, for Gray, seeks to be free from narrative and even language. *Long Ago*, he asserts, is saved from the mere sound-music of lyric by its ability to embed the lyrical within dramatic and narrative momentum. Yet Gray also commends the volume for bringing the discipline of the shorter lyric form to control what he calls the 'extravagance' and the 'want of measure and of balance' that he finds in the more expansive narrative impetus of Michael Field's verse-dramas.[100] The significance to lyric of such discourses of containment and excess is, I will argue, a key point of reflection for *Long Ago* as a whole, and highlights a more self-reflexive commentary within the volume than Gray realises. After all, what does it mean for a poetic genre that seeks to be free even from language – to be pure soundscape – to become aware of its totalisation in print? This is surely the drama enacted in such a project as *Long Ago*.

Just after his location of the volume's poems within this generic space of the dramatic monologue, Gray presents Michael Field as a 'mouth receiving its song as though direct from the lips which for thousands of years have ceased to curve and quiver'. Yet surely this describes more of a passionate possession by Sappho than a dramatisation of her persona?[101] While the italics used throughout the whole of the original publication do suggest that Bradley and Cooper want to indicate that sense of speaking in another's voice, what they are performing here seems to be more Sappho as an embodiment of lyric, rather than Sappho as a historical personage, an individual persona or a disembodied aural echo. In his review, Gray notes that one of the key themes of the book is the 'overmastering power of passion' and it is this lyric force that Bradley and Cooper try to capture in Sappho's embodied song.[102] I will suggest here that *Long Ago* is an exercise in enacting the sublime excess of lyric that usually, by definition, lies outside of the linguistic entity of the poem itself and that risks over-spilling the boundaries of the print medium. In doing so, Michael Field might be seen to challenge the very idea of print 'totalisation' that underlies the project of textual 'completion'. In other words, Bradley and Cooper's drive towards completion reflects quite directly on what the printed lyric is in the late nineteenth century, what can and cannot be contained within and superseded by it, and how this might happen poetically.

Jonah Siegel's analysis of the growth of museum culture in the nineteenth century theorises the totalising impulse of nineteenth-century culture in ways that are highly relevant here. Symonds's description of poetry of the period as 'in large measure the criticism of all existing literature'[103] is echoed in Siegel's analysis of how, in the later part of the century, the critical impulse is 'an unavoidable manifestation of modernity'.[104] To be modern is to be forced to organise the past: 'The critical project is not optional; it offers the only way to be truly self-consciously modern: "he to whom the present is the only thing that is present, knows nothing of the age in which he lives".'[105] Yet, as Siegel notes, the drive towards summation and apparent containment also inevitably brings with it an awareness of uncontainable excess.[106] Similarly, I suggest, the 'totalisation' of lyric in print somewhat paradoxically served to highlight a key location of meaning outside the lyric's own language.

In their preface to the volume, Bradley and Cooper write:

> When, more than a year ago, I wrote to a literary friend of my attempt to express in English verse the passionate pleasure Dr. Wharton's book had brought to me, he replied: 'That is a delightfully audacious thought – the extension of Sappho's fragments into lyrics. I can scarcely conceive anything more audacious.'
>
> In simple truth all worship that is not idolatry must be audacious; for it involves the blissful apprehension of an ideal; it means in the very phrase of Sappho –
>
> Ἔγων δ' ἐμαύτᾳ
> τοῦτο σύνοιδα·[107]
>
> Devoutly as the fiery-bosomed Greek turned in her anguish to Aphrodite, praying her to accomplish her heart's desires, I have turned to the one woman who has dared to speak unfalteringly of the fearful mastery of love, and again and again the dumb prayer has risen from my heart –
>
> σὺ δ' αὔτα
> σύμμαχος ἔσσο.[108]

Both Michael Field's 'passionate pleasure' and Sappho's discourse on the 'fearful mastery of love' indicate something of the importance of the 'excessive' affect that makes Sappho an emblem of lyric itself; and the prominently repeated use of the term 'audacious' in this context is also striking. The term 'audacious' itself signifies a kind of excess. Defined by the *Oxford English Dictionary* as '1. Daring, confident, intrepid' and '2. Unrestrained by, or defiant of, decorum and morality; presumptuously wicked, shameless', the term's definition suggests, in various ways, a reaching beyond – whether that be the 'intrepid' venturing into new territories, or the 'unrestrained' surpassing of limits of various social kinds. It is a word particularly associated with aestheticism and Decadence because of its connotations of sensual and sexual adventurousness, yet it also refers to a textual audacity in this instance.[109] Michael Field's audacity is not only their voicing of Sapphic sexuality but also their attempt, textually, to master the boundlessness of the Sapphic fragment.

The surviving fragments of Sappho's poetry represented the sublimity of lyric through their gesture to that which lies beyond their textual bounds. As one essayist put it in 1863: to be sublime, something must convey a sense of 'magnitude, vastness, infinity'.[110] Crucial to Kant's distinction between beauty and the sublime is the association of beauty with form and the sublime with formlessness.[111] The surviving fragments of Sappho's texts gesture towards a much greater whole that exists outside any written record: a realm of infinite lyric signification. The interplay between part and whole has been central to the reception of Sappho at least since Longinus' inclusion of her in his treatise on the sublime. Neil Hertz's description of the dialectic throughout Longinus' work between the terms 'body' and 'fragment' inscribes this interplay in terms that are particularly relevant to an analysis of Michael Field's engagement with Sappho, as Yopie Prins's work has shown.[112] These are terms relevant also to my investigation, but I want to take a different approach to Prins. After all, it should be noted that Michael Field's expansion of the lyric fragments implicitly poses the 'audacious' question of which is more surpassing: Sappho's unbounded fragments, which are uncontainable and uncontrollable, or Michael Field's own elaborations of the fragments into fully formed (yet controlled and contained?) poems in print? Indeed, do Sappho's boundless fragments constitute an unknowable, uncontainable excess of meaning, while Michael Field's expansion of them in fact represents a limit: a taming of the sublimity in print? This volume poses important questions about the relationship between the print 'totalisation' of lyric and an inherited Romantic association of lyric with something that goes beyond its own purely textual significance. In Hertz's terms, Michael Field wants to represent the 'body', not just the 'fragment', but how do we read Michael Field's representation of the unrepresentable Sapphic body that lies outside of the fragment?

Poem LXIII in *Long Ago* reflects, I think, on exactly these issues, and enables us to see how the themes (of print totalisation and a crisis of lyric transcendence) outlined at length above were not only *reflected* in poetic practice, but were also *reflected on* poetically. Many of Sappho's surviving fragments are invocations to the muse (more often to her lyre) to give her song and voice. One of these is the fragment produced as number forty-five in Wharton's edition: 'Come now, divine shell, become vocal for me'. It is around this text that Michael Field's poem is based:

Grow vocal to me, O my shell divine!
　　I cannot rest;
Not so doth Cypris pine
To raise her love to her undinted breast
When sun first warms the earth, as I require
To roll the heavy death from my recumbent lyre.

O whilom tireless voice, why art thou dumb?
　　To-day I stood
Watching the Mænads come
From a dark fissure in the ilex-wood
Forth to the golden poplars and the light;
My tingling senses leapt to join that concourse bright.

Passed is the crowd, passed with his buoyant flute
　　The Evian King:
My plectrum still is mute
Of beauty, of the halcyon's nest, of spring;
Though deep within a vital madness teems,
And I am tossed with fierce, disjointed, wizard dreams.

Apollo, Dionysus passes by,
　　Adonis wakes,
Zephyr and Chloris sigh:
To me, alas, my lyre no music makes,
Though tortured, fluttering toward the strings I reach,
Mad as for Anactoria's lovely laugh and speech.

For thou – where, in some balmy, western isle
　　Each day doth bring
Seed-sowing, harvest smile,
And twilight drop of fruit for garnering,
Where north wind never blows – dost dwell apart,
Keeping a gentle people free from grief of heart.

Sun-god, return! Break from thine old-world bower,
　　Thy garden set
With the narcissus-flower
And purple daphne! To thy chariot get,
Glorious arise as on thy day of birth,
And spread illuminating order through the earth.

I scan the rocks: O sudden mountain-rill,
　　That sure hast heard
His footsteps on the hill,

Leaping from crag to crag to bring me word –
Lapse quiet at my feet; I hear along
My lyre the journeying tumult of an unbreathed song.

While Sappho is famed as the archetype of lyric song, Bradley and Cooper are more interested here in her silence. The divine shell in question is the lyre (originally a tortoise shell with cow gut stretched over it), and the fragment appears in the formulation of the first line of the poem: 'Grow vocal to me, O my shell divine!' The poem dwells throughout on the silence of Sappho's lyre and of her voice: 'tireless voice, why art thou dumb?'; 'My plectrum still is mute'; 'To me, alas, my lyre no music makes'. The poem ends with a listening to the silence of an 'unbreathed song': 'I hear along/ My lyre the journeying tumult of an unbreathed song'.

One might see here a parallel with the silence of a late nineteenth-century printed lyric that has lost any foundational affiliation with song. Is this a poem about a lost musical sublime? In part perhaps it is, but within this poem silence leaves space to bring to the fore an affective and bodily excess to which it does 'give voice' and which is dramatised in *Long Ago* through Sappho. The 'shell' is at once the lyre, but simultaneously the body of Sappho, which does indeed 'grow vocal' even as her lyre and voice remain silent. This dimension is expressed through phrases such as 'I cannot rest'; 'My tingling senses leapt'; I am tossed with fierce, disjointed, wizard dreams'; 'tortured, fluttering toward the strings I reach,/ Mad as for Anactoria's lovely laugh and speech'. While lyric's music may be silenced, its extra-textual sublime energy appears more performed than contained or muted in this 'totalised' print rendition. The poem finds in the body of Sappho a lyrical affect that is still, although in a different way from music, in excess of language. Representing the 'body' – the whole not the fragment – the Romantic transcendent spiritual sublime seems to have been replaced in this poem by an 'excess' of female sensuality – the body of Sappho representing a form of earthly lyric sublimity fitted for a newly material age. Sappho signifies at this time in one body the poet, the poem and the extra-linguistic excess of lyric: a bodily affective madness of passion, pain and love (hetero- and homosexual).[113] By the late nineteenth century, she is synonymous with the concept and practice of lyric poetry, but she is also an icon of an active female sexuality.

Kathy Psomiades has written eloquently and insightfully about the female form representing a site of conflict within aestheticism: particularly a tension between aesthetic and economic imperatives.[114]

Here I argue that femininity might also usefully represent for poets the tension characteristic of the totalised print lyric between containment and excess. Of course, the equation of woman and poem was current from much earlier in the century, but within aestheticism the image had morphed: no longer a chaste, beautiful and unobtainable creature, she became one whose availability and sexuality now had a different kind of poetic potential and one that might represent a powerful connective force. This newly sensual incarnation of lyric's extra-discursive dimension sat in opposition to any aspiration beyond the material realm. If concerns around lyric across the nineteenth century resulted in key part from the poor fit of an aspiration to spiritual transcendence with the reality of life in a highly materialised, urbanised and industrialised society, then female sexuality held an important role in figuring a new way to think about that extra-discursive lyric quest through the body – and that body was both corporeal and textual.

Crucially, one might see the restless fluttering, tingling and tossing in this poem communicated viscerally through the indented and abbreviated second line of each stanza which poses a rhythmical and visual disruption. Each second line contains just four syllables, which, although sewn into a rhyme with the fourth line, stand alone in the structure of each stanza in a way that echoes the nature of the Sapphic fragments: something at once part of a greater whole, but simultaneously separated and with some kind of independent existence. That physical intrusion of the curt second line of each stanza both conveys the affective passion whose expression is extra-textual, and also enacts the relationship of part to whole, of fragment to body, that is central to this project of audacious expansion. In this sense, Michael Field's project of 'completion' does not forestall the lyric sublime or contain the excess of Sappho's fragments, but reflects it in print and dwells on it, in many different ways – including, ultimately, through the form of the print poem on the page. Michael Field's 'completion' of the fragments dramatises a play around what it might mean for the lyric to be 'totalised' in print, and how it might reflect an uncontainable lyric energy. The idea of a lyric sublime is meditated on in the above poem through that awareness of what cannot be encompassed by language alone. Yet Michael Field's volume also reflects on how, in an age in which lyric is less firmly invested in an idea of aurality, the emotional sublime might be reimagined in relation to an affective corporeality that might find meaningful expression through the textual body of the printed poem on the page.

While this reading anchors in poetry of the period some of the foundational issues introduced above, and sets the scene for the negotiation of lyric in aestheticist poetry pursued in the rest of this study, it also implicitly poses the questions that will structure the three following parts. *Long Ago*'s profound interest in lyric history, and in the relationship of the late nineteenth century to a recently recovered past, raises the questions of temporality addressed in Part I. Indeed the very title of the volume, with its indeterminate gesture towards the past as another world, raises precisely the questions about the kind of historicism lyric can effect that I pursue in Chapter 4. In addition, the kind of somatic affect read through the body of Sappho in 'Come now, divine shell, become vocal for me' acts as a good introduction to the lyric phenomenology read in Part II. The nascent reading of a phenomenology of lyric form, above, begins to ask about the potential of lyric's formal presence on the page which I theorise much more fully in this second part. Equally powerfully, *Long Ago* raises the issues of lyric subjectivity that I explore in Part III. An introduction to Swinburne's Sapphic experiments explored in the penultimate chapter, Michael Field's volume raises similar questions about the potential of a lyric voice that speaks in chorus with voices from the past. For now it is enough for this preliminary short case study simply to raise these questions; they will be developed and explored in the nine chapters that follow.

Notes

1. Hegel, *Lectures on Fine Art*, p. 971.
2. Wellek, 'Genre Theory', pp. 251–2.
3. Letter, 27 January 1916. Quoted in Cunningham, *The Victorians*, p. 975.
4. Harrington, *Second Person Singular*, ch. 5 (see particularly pp. 163–4).
5. Radford, *A Light Load*, p. 23.
6. In contrast, Elizabeth Helsinger's *Poetry and the Thought of Song* does focus around the inheritance of song, thus following a different thread through the century and usefully filling in a different part of the picture. We are both interested in what happened to the ghost of aurality in lyric poetry encountered through printed text, but I am more concerned with what happened to 'lyric' poetry when an affiliation with song was lost, challenged or strained to the point of crisis. (Helsinger's book came out while mine was in press, but I am pleased to be able to include reference to it.)
7. Symonds, 'A Comparison', pp. 67–9.
8. Rowlinson, *Lyric*, pp. 59, 67.

9. See Stephen Arata's discussion of the importance of print mediation to Hardy's poetry in 'Rhyme, Rhythm, and the Materiality of Poetry', p. 519.

10. Jackson, *Dickinson's Misery*, p. 93.

11. Jackson, 'Who Reads Poetry?', p. 183.

12. Jackson and Prins (eds), *The Lyric Theory Reader*, p. 7.

13. Symonds, 'A Comparison', pp. 63–4.

14. On her twenty-first birthday Robinson was given the choice of two presents by her parents, and chose the publication of some of her poems in preference to a ball given in her honour. The result was her first volume of poems, *A Handful of Honeysuckle*, which appears in some sense a 'coming out' in print, with the material object strongly encoding the idea of the 'poetess' she wanted to project (Robertson, *English Poetesses*, pp. 377–8).

15. Bayne, 'Three Phases of Lyric Poetry', p. 627.

16. Bayne, 'The Poetry of Dante Gabriel Rossetti', p. 376.

17. Swinburne, 'The Poems of Dante Gabriel Rossetti', p. 85. In Rossetti's 1870 *Poems*, works appear grouped as 'poems', 'sonnets and songs', 'songs' and 'Sonnets for pictures', for example; the use of the term 'song' rather than 'lyric' for a sub-category of poetic type suggests that 'lyric' no longer refers to song (although, intriguingly, the term 'lyrics' as a sub-grouping does appear in the 1881 revised edition of *Poems*).

18. This is the kind of definition Jackson gives in 'Who Reads Poetry?', p. 183.

19. Anonymous, 'Mr Swinburne's Lyrics', p. 429.

20. Brewster, *Lyric*, pp. 1–2.

21. Ibid., p. 4. Alastair Fowler also observed in 1982 that the concept of the lyric genre subsumed almost every poetic form in the nineteenth century (*Kinds of Literature*, p. 206; see Brewster, *Lyric*, p. 72); and Mark Jeffreys argued in 1995 that 'lyric emerges as a dominant category from a "welter of shorter poetic genres", and it is only in the nineteenth century that it comes to be "mythologized as the purest and oldest of poetic genres"' (Jeffreys, 'Ideologies of Lyric', p. 197; see Brewster, *Lyric*, p. 10).

22. Abrams, *The Mirror and the Lamp*, pp. 84, 98.

23. Mill, 'The Two Kinds of Poetry', p. 719.

24. Garber, 'Address and Its Dialects', p. 375.

25. Duff, *Romanticism and the Uses of Genre*, p. 10. Duff gives many fascinating examples from commentators (see, for example, that of Hugh Blair and David Blair, pp. 54–6), all of which place 'lyric' as one genre among others such as 'epic', 'dramatic' and sometimes 'pastoral' or 'satirical'.

26. Lewis, *The Lyric Impulse*, p. 13.

27. Rowlinson, 'Lyric', p. 70.

28. Ibid., p. 77.

29. Ibid., p. 64.
30. FitzGerald, *Rubáiyát of Omar Khayyám*, ed. Decker, p. xli.
31. Guy and Small, *The Textual Condition*, p. 85.
32. Ibid., p. 75.
33. Ibid., p. 74.
34. Symonds, 'A Comparison', pp. 64–5.
35. Ibid., p. 59.
36. Ibid., p. 70; Tennyson, 'To the Queen' (published 1873), line 56, *The Poems of Tennyson*, ed. Ricks, p. 1756.
37. Tucker, 'Dramatic Monologue', pp. 238–9, 236–9.
38. Ibid., p. 239.
39. Ibid., p. 238.
40. Custance, *Opals*, p. 31.
41. Hardy, *The Complete Poems*, p. 416.
42. Wilde, *Poems*, epigraph (n.p.).
43. D. G. Rossetti, *Ballads and Sonnets*, p. 161; Douglas, *The City of the Soul*, p. 21.
44. Symons, 'On the Stage', *London Nights*, p. 15.
45. Image, *Poems and Carols*, p. 18.
46. Monkhouse, 'Review of *Ballades and Rondeaus, Chants Royal, Sestinas, Villanelles, etc.* by Gleeson White', p. 247
47. Rogers, *The Three Genres*, p. 36.
48. So, for example, Thomas Hardy's verse drama 'The Dynasts' is generally not considered 'lyric' by reviewers of the period even though it has elements of lyrical writing within it: 'But the subject of our present study, the lyrical poetry of Mr. Hardy, is not largely illustrated in "The Dynasts," except by the choral interludes of the phantom intelligences, which have great lyrical value, and by three or four admirable songs' (Gosse, 'Mr Hardy's Lyrical Poems', p. 293).
49. Freedman, *Professions of Taste*, p. 11.
50. Leighton, *On Form*, p. 41.
51. Symonds, 'A Comparison', p. 61.
52. Ibid., p. 60.
53. Ibid., p. 58. Here Symonds fascinatingly describes the proliferation of the commodity in space and time that critics such as Stephen Kern have since named the 'crisis of abundance' (*Culture of Time and Space*, p. 9).
54. Symonds, 'A Comparison', p. 55.
55. Ibid., p. 62.
56. Ibid., p. 63.
57. 'Lyrical has been here held essentially to imply that each Poem shall turn on some single thought, feeling or situation. In accordance with this, narrative, descriptive, and didactic poems – unless accompanied by rapidity of movement, brevity, and the colouring of human passion – have been excluded' (Palgrave, *The Golden Treasury*, p. ix).
58. Perloff, *The Dance of the Intellect*, pp. 177–8.
59. See Covey, 'The Decline of Poetry and Hardy's Empty Hall', p. 71.

60. Stuart Curran writes about the insatiable appetite for poetry in the first half of the nineteenth century in *Poetic Form and British Romanticism*, p. 5.
61. Pound, 'How to Read Part One: Introduction', p. 32.
62. Covey, 'The Decline of Poetry and Hardy's Empty Hall', pp. 61, 68.
63. Benjamin, '*Charles Baudelaire*', pp. 109–10.
64. Ibid., pp. 25, 152.
65. Ibid., p. 152.
66. Mallarmé, 'Crisis in Poetry', p. 40.
67. Hulme, 'A Lecture on Modern Poetry', p. 59.
68. Ibid., p. 63.
69. Although Peter Howarth has pointed out that Hulme does not and cannot reject Hegel's link between poetry and transcendence as easily as he thinks he can (*British Poetry in the Age of Modernism*, p. 35).
70. Adorno, 'On Lyric Poetry and Society', pp. 38, 37.
71. Baudelaire, *Selected Writings on Art and Literature*, p. 403.
72. Something that is apparent not only in *Le Peintre de la vie moderne* but also in *Salon de 1846* and *Salon de 1859*.
73. Baudelaire, *Selected Writings on Art and Literature*, p. 402.
74. Smith, ' "Le Peintre de la vie moderne" and "La Peinture de la vie ancienne" ', p. 87. See also Prendergast, *Paris and the Nineteenth Century*, pp. 144–52.
75. Baudelaire, *Prose and Poetry*, p. 99.
76. Baudelaire, *Prose and Poetry*, pp. 99–100.
77. Halpern, 'Baudelaire's "Dark Zone" ', p. 2: the comedy of the poem 'registers an awareness that the traditional artwork or poem could no longer claim a unique value, and that aesthetic authenticity – in this case, the elevated status of lyric poetry – had become incompatible with modern experience'.
78. Stephens, *Baudelaire's Prose Poems*, pp. 39–40.
79. This is a debate I have neither space nor remit to enter here, although I will point to both Scott Brewster's claims that the Romantic lyric constituted 'an evolution rather than a revolution in poetics' (*Lyric*, p. 72), and to David Duff's analysis of 'Tintern Abbey', and *Lyrical Ballads* more generally, as marking a poetic revolution (Duff, *Romanticism and the Uses of Genre*, p. 210). Paul Allen Miller suggests that lyric is not a new genre that arises out of late Romanticism, but the textual lyric genre that has existed since the Romans modified to exist 'under modern conditions of subjectivity' (*Lyric Texts and Lyric Consciousness*, p. 6).
80. See, for example, Coventry, 'What Makes the Perfect Lyric?', p. 1150.
81. 'Preface' to the *Lyrical Ballads*, p. 255.
82. Freedman, *Professions of Taste*, p. 4.
83. It is Hegel's account of lyric transcendence that Adorno echoes quite precisely at the other end of the century when asserting its incompatibility with modernity (Adorno, 'On Lyric Poetry and Society', pp. 38, 37).

84. Hegel, *Lectures on Fine Art*, p. 1112. The lectures were published posthumously in 1835, but delivered during the 1820s and 1830s.
85. Ibid., p. 1111.
86. Ibid., p. 1035.
87. Ibid., p. 1139.
88. Lindley, *Lyric*, p. 74.
89. *The Complete Poems of John Keats*, pp. 344–8.
90. See, for example, Stephen Gill's discussion of J. S. Mill's rejection of the 'transcendental' aspects of Wordsworth's poetry (Gill, *Wordsworth and the Victorians*, pp. 44, 48, 63).
91. This is a position I explore in more detail in Thain, 'Victorian Lyric Pathology and Phenomenology', passim.
92. Browning, *The Poems*, Vol. 1, pp. 380–1.
93. See, for example, Marianne Van Remoortel's article, '(Re)gendering Petrarch: Elizabeth Barrett Browning's "Sonnets from the Portuguese"', which reflects on much of the previous scholarship in this area.
94. Barrett Browning, *Poetical Works*, pp. 537–8.
95. Freedman, *Professions of Taste*, p. 31.
96. By the latter I refer to the shifts between Symbolism, Imagism and Impressionism that have been interestingly explored in recent critical discourse (see Hughes, *Imagism and the Imagists*, Chapter 1; Thacker, 'A Language of Concrete Things'; and Matz, *Literary Impressionism*).
97. Frow, *Genre*, p. 2
98. Gray, Review of *Long Ago*, p. 356.
99. Ibid., p. 357.
100. Ibid., pp. 359–60.
101. Ibid., p. 356.
102. Ibid., p. 357.
103. Symonds, 'A Comparison', pp. 64–5.
104. Siegel, *Desire and Excess*, p. 252.
105. Siegel, quoting Oscar Wilde's 'The Critic as Artist', *Desire and Excess*, p. 252.
106. 'Two pressures start to weigh on the museum, however, from the moment it is first conceived as a structure for education rather than pleasure: excess and incompleteness': Siegel, *Desire and Excess*, p. 275.
107. 'And this I feel in myself'. Wharton, *Sappho*, fragment 15.
108. 'Be thyself my ally'. Wharton, *Sappho*, fragment 1.
109. See, for example, Symons's description of Mallarmé as 'experimenting more and more audaciously' ('The Decadent Movement in Literature', p. 142); and Cosmo Monkhouse's description of Dobson's poetry as having a 'spontaneous audacity' (Review of *Ballades and Rondeaus, Chants Royal, Sestinas, Villanelles, etc.* by Gleeson White, p. 246).
110. Anonymous, 'The Sublime and Beautiful', p. 159.
111. Crowther, *The Kantian Sublime*, pp. 80, 100.
112. Hertz, *The End of the Line*, pp. 1–20; Prins, *Victorian Sappho*, pp. 74–111.

113. For discussion of the multivalency of Sapphic desire at this point in history, see Flint". . . As A Rule, I Does Not Mean I" ', p. 157 (she concludes that it is only in Michael Field's hands 'that Sappho's lesbianism is reasserted'); and Prins, 'A Metaphorical Field', pp. 136–7.

114. For Psomiades, femininity – a concept itself fissured, for the Victorians, beneath the surface into multiple dichotomies – 'allows for the difficult and vexed relation between the categories of the aesthetic and the economic in bourgeois culture to be represented and covered over by erotic relations'; Psomiades, *Beauty's Body*, p. 3.

Part I: Time

Part I: Time

Chapter 2

Metre and Temporality: Between Hegel and Benjamin

For the outpouring of lyric stands to time [. . .] in a much closer relation than epic narrative does.

Hegel, *Aesthetics*, p. 1136

It's not that what is past casts its light on what is present, or what is present its light on what is past; rather, image is that wherein what has been comes together in a flash with the now to form a constellation.

Benjamin, *Arcades*, 462, N2a, 3

Changes in the conception of temporality and history in the final decades of the nineteenth century have been documented fascinatingly by scholars, notably Stephen Kern, who shows how inventions such as the telephone (1876), the electric light and the cinema, not to mention the introduction of standard time or Einstein's theory of special relativity, all altered the way time was experienced.[1] Aestheticist poetry does not often reflect on such matters directly in content at any level of technological specificity. Yet metre is poetry's self-conscious awareness of its existence in time – it is what inscribes or maps poetry across time, and within time – and I suggest we might think about the broader history of the lyric genre and its key developments in metrical *form* as responsive to such changes. I suggest here that the very generic conventions of the lyric were brought into crisis by larger-scale theoretical shifts in the conception of time (that were, in turn, born out of many more specific events and technological innovations). Poetry had to respond to these larger-scale shifts, no matter what its concerns in content, because they shaped the very nature of the genre, both formally and theoretically.

So, my aim in Part I is to explore metrical responses to concerns about the relationship between lyric and modernity prior to the explicit attempt to 'modernise' poetic form through the use of free verse. The following two chapters will examine, particularly, responses to what I termed in my previous chapter a Romantic lyric dialectic between the transcendent and the earthly, exploring how it was negotiated in relation to the modern world towards the end of the century. I suggest that at the heart of what I trace in poetry of the period lie fundamental shifts in the conceptualisation of time that might be characterised through a development from Enlightenment to post-Enlightenment thought. In this chapter I will sketch a broad theoretical backdrop for the two case-study chapters that follow, with reference to Hegel and Benjamin: two thinkers whose work chronologically frames the theorisation of nineteenth-century lyric.

Hegel's conception of time was based on Newtonian physical principles and posits a theory based on linear temporal progressiveness in dialectic with an opposite 'atemporal' standpoint: the latter being a position outside the diachronic progression of time, and a kind of secularised spiritual space of eternity. Yet, as Ronald Schleifer has shown in *Modernism and Time*, towards the end of the nineteenth century post-Enlightenment theories of time challenged this conception, calling into question 'the self-evidence and universality of these assumptions':

> for Benjamin – and for many living within the enormous changes in wealth, knowledge, and experience at the turn of the twentieth century – time is inhabited by 'constellations' of historical events, meaning, and consciousness, 'collisions' of the Then and the Now. [. . .] Such constellations, collisions, and subjectivity suggest a different arrangement of the relationship between past and present and different modes of representation from the hierarchical reductions of Enlightenment science, the progressive continuities of political economy, and the enlightened consciousness of Hegelian metaphysics.[2]

Schleifer charts the distinctions between Hegel's Enlightenment theories of time which respond to the 'first Industrial Revolution' of the late eighteenth century, and modernist responses to the 'second industrial revolution' of the late nineteenth century.[3] Modernism's theorisation of time was, he argues, crucially transformed by the new 'abundance of *things*' that resulted from the proliferation of consumable commodities in the second industrial revolution (but not the first), and which dislocated experience of time and space. I will return to this idea in more detail in Chapter 4, but for the moment I will simply note that this leaves radically inadequate the experience of time that Hegel takes as self-evident in his dialectic of linear, progressive time and the atemporal standpoint.[4] What results is an experience of time that was not characterised by continuous stretches of the measurable, or by a hierarchy of past and present, but which positioned the present instead as the moment where past and present collide: 'the present inhabits the past as much as the past inhabits the present'.[5]

This post-Enlightenment theory of time can be characterised by Benjamin's 'dialectics at a standstill': 'It's not that what is past casts its light on what is present, or what is present its light on what is past; rather, image is that wherein what has been comes together in a flash with the now to form a constellation.'[6] Here, past and present are not in a linear and progressive relationship, but in constant complex interplay. Of course, Benjamin's very term 'dialectic' invokes Hegel, to whom he refers in the *Arcades Project* if only to push off against both his method and his theories.[7] Benjamin suggests that, under capitalism, time and history were experienced in ways falsified by the Hegelian narrative, and tries to capture a key shift in the *experience* of time in the later decades of the nineteenth century, rather than a theorisation of it. What Benjamin gives us is a way of thinking about the emergence of a new experience of temporality in the later decades of the nineteenth century that results from the revolution of the commodity. This new temporality rejects the dominant theorisation of time as continuous in favour of a recognition of time experienced as interrupted, disturbed and characterised by moments of discontinuity and repetition.

The key question for me is what effect this had on poetry, given that the nineteenth-century concept of lyric was founded on an Enlightenment understanding of time in the late eighteenth century. If lyric is (as Mallarmé had it) in 'crisis', the above is, I suggest, one of the key philosophical-cultural shifts that threatened to make lyric untenable in the modern world. Schleifer undertakes, as part of his study, significant literary analysis contrasting, for example, the Hegelian conception of time as continuous narrative in Victorian texts such *The Mill on the Floss* with the Benjaminian concept of time as a moment of collision of past and present in the modernist work of writers such as Woolf, Joyce and Lawrence. Noticeably, Schleifer rarely considers any poetry, choosing not to include Yeats, Eliot and Pound. He recognises that what he describes in his book is only half the story of literary modernism and its experience of time. Yet his rationale for splitting modernism ('the comprehension of Modernism in terms of two experiences and comprehensions of time') does not recognise the significance of genre within that division.[8] I suggest that what he finds might reflect not simply two strands within modernism, but rather the greater difficulty in applying Benjaminian ideas about time to a poetic genre heavily indebted to the Hegelian mould. It is precisely the shift Schleifer notes in *Modernism and Time* that I will use to think about that lyric revolution *prior to* high modernism. Crucially, Hegel and Benjamin are particularly productive theorists of time with which to frame my study not only because they are positioned at either end of the nineteenth century, but because both reflected profoundly on the operations of poetry, and of 'lyric' poetry specifically. Indeed, I will devote the rest of this chapter to thinking about how their ideas on time might be relevant to nineteenth-century concerns about the lyric genre when read in relation to poetry's metrical structure.

*   *   *

Since Plato and Aristotle insisted on poetic metre as a kind of drug that threatens one's rationality, scholars have debated its effects on the body and soul, asking whether it is part of the excitement of the passions that results in poetry's ecstatic flight, or whether rhythm in fact anchors poetry, grounding it in a regulatory pulse. Such discussion was particularly characteristic of the early nineteenth century. It is metre that, for Wordsworth, defined poetry when in 1800 he argued for the necessity of metre particularly for the regulation of the passions: poetry excites the imagination, and the dynamic between this ecstatic impulse and the regulating pulse of metre is key to the operation of lyric.[9] Coleridge too wrote of metre as a force for measure and containment in the onslaught of passion.[10] Constitutive of nineteenth-century lyric, then, is the idea of a productive tension between its metrical temporal grounding and its aspiration to transcendent flight. While Wordsworth and Coleridge may be the theorists more familiar to us in relation to English literature, it is Hegel, above all others, who thinks most deeply and systematically about the 'modern' lyric (and its definitive investment in metricality) as formed from this tension between its temporality and its aspiration out of time,

Hegel's detailed work on the lyric genre, in the *Lectures on Fine Art*, provides the most substantial statement about the concept of lyric in the period in which the modern understanding of the genre emerged. Although coming out of a German idealist tradition, Hegel's work was taken up in British literature from the 1830s and was influential across the nineteenth century, with a particular revival in the thinking of intellectuals such as Pater towards the end.[11] (The effect on British nineteenth-century aesthetic theory has been traced in detail by scholars including Bernard Fehr, Anthony Ward and William Shuter.)[12] Within Hegel's systematisation of the history of the arts as a gradual development away from sensuous form and towards a higher, more intellectualised, art, poetry ranks highly as one of the more transcendent art forms. Metre, however, is lyric's one remnant of the tie to the material: 'its one and only sensuous fragrance'.[13] For Hegel, as for Wordsworth, metre is what grounds poetry in the body, in the sensual world and in time. As for Wordsworth, metre grounds poetry in diachronic structures.[14] Throughout his lectures, Hegel worries around the conundrum of metre as simultaneously a necessary and central characteristic of poetry and a potential 'fetter' to its transcendent ambitions to the atemporality of the spiritual realm.[15] Yet when he turns to 'lyric' in particular (the form of poetry that for him comes closest to representing pure *Geist*), metre becomes constitutive also of something that pulls away from the external and material into something internal and transcendent ('the subjective movement of the poet's own heart').[16]

Many have articulated this productive tension at the core of lyric through a distinction between the rule of metre ('regular pattern of stressed and unstressed syllables') and the ecstatic movement of rhythm (the irregular 'sway and flow' of verse):[17] it is only by having the grid of a regular metrical pulse that a rhythmic lifting out of time can be framed and felt. In his writing on music, Zuckerkandl asserts the pre-eminence of rhythm over time in poetry: ' "Time" and rhythm [. . .] appear even to exclude each other: rhythm resists regular time; "time" appears to suffocate rhythm.'[18] For Zuckerkandl, 'Meter [. . .] draws boundary lines, interrupts, and separates. Rhythm is the unbroken continuity of a flux, such a continuity as the wave most graphically represents.'[19] Rhythm represents the lyric's aspiration out of diachronic time even as metre marks its passing. This is a useful terminological distinction to mark what Hegel recognises as central to the lyric: the difference between metre as lyric's one remaining element of the sensuous realm – a potential 'fetter' to its aspiration towards the transcendent realm of spirit – and lyric's rhythmical marking of an 'internal time' that is always in some sense out of time. Crucially, this distinction between metrical temporality and rhythmic atemporality is one naturally affiliated with regular verse forms in which the play of rhythmic variation over a steady beat can best be worked.

But what happened to lyric's aspiration to temporal transcendence when that Enlightenment conception of time to which it was so firmly linked came under pressure in the later nineteenth century? If the nineteenth-century lyric is a genre pulled between its insistent sensuous metrical inscription in linear time, and its aspiration to an atemporal transcendent realm, what happens to the genre when, as Schleifer shows us, that binary is rejected by post-Enlightenment theorists? It is this issue I want to explore in the case studies of the following two chapters. The lyric poet's loss of his 'halo', described in Chapter 1, marks among other things a scepticism around lyric's relationship with the temporal transcendence that is associated with an eternal realm. In place of the Hegelian dialectic between linear time and the atemporal, Benjamin finds in Baudelaire a connection with the past that is not linear, that does not cordon off the past into a separate realm, but that sees the past intruding upon the present. Through this theory of the '*correspondances*' Benjamin finds a moment that is not primarily connected contiguously with the day before and the day after, nor, significantly in Benjamin's reading, with the eternal, but with a particularly resonant moment in the distant past.[20] In this way, Benjamin connects poetic technique with the 'dialectics at a standstill'.

One obvious place to look for the poetic manifestation of this in the English tradition is in the turn to 'free verse' in the early twentieth century. While T. S. Eliot was right to be sceptical of the magnitude of the claims for the 'innovations' of free verse, the writings of those who made such claims reveal an interesting discourse on poetry, metre and transcendence around the turn of the century.[21] Those who embraced *vers libre*, 'free verse' or *verse libéré* were often rejecting what was seen as the prettiness and naivety of regular verse forms: forms that seemed untenable within the disorder, ugliness and horror of the modern mechanised world. Freer verse forms also signified a turn to the natural rhythms of everyday language in opposition to the heightened artificiality of the regular lyric form.[22] Crucially, free verse was seen as more authentic: a giving up on what were considered by some the pretensions of the transcendent aspiration central to an earlier conception of lyric poetry.[23] In Chapter 1, I quoted T. E. Hulme's rejection of the idea of lyric transcendence ('philosophers no longer believe in absolute truth'); this is immediately followed by an assertion of 'free verse' as a concrete marker of this new accommodation of poetry to modernity:

We shall no longer strive to attain the absolutely perfect form in poetry. Instead of these minute perfections of phrase and words, the tendency will be rather towards the production of a general effect; this of course takes away the predominance of metre and a regular number of syllables as the element of perfection in words. We are no longer concerned that stanzas shall be shaped and polished like gems, but rather that some vague mood shall be communicated.[24]

The turn to the freer forms of verse of high modernism, then, might be seen in part as a giving up on the patterning that gives the illusion of synchronicity.

D. H. Lawrence articulates such thoughts explicitly in 1919 when he advocates a poetic voice that aspires not to the '[p]erfected bygone moments' or the 'perfected moments in the glimmering futurity', which he sees as the 'treasured gem-like lyrics of Shelley and Keats', but a voice that is viscerally of the present moment.[25] Lawrence's poetry of the present is a literature that aspires to flux and not stasis: to mortality not eternity. He writes of an 'ever-present' that 'knows no finality':

Give me nothing fixed, set, static. Don't give me the infinite or the eternal: nothing of infinity, nothing of eternity. Give me the still, white seething, the incandescence and the coldness of the incarnate moment: the moment, the quick of all change and haste and opposition: the moment, the immediate present, the Now.[26]

This definition of the 'unrestful, ungraspable poetry of the sheer present' deliberately uses terms associated with Romanticism but inverts them, to associate 'transcendent loveliness', for example, not with a stilling of time but with vital movement; likewise he finds the 'very permanency' of poetry of the Now 'in its wind-like transit'.[27] He even imitates a Shelley-esque prose to write of the 'One realm we have never conquered: the pure present': 'One great mystery of time is terra incognita to us: the instant. The most superb mystery we have hardly recognised: the immediate, instant self. The quick of all time is the instant.'[28] Unsurprisingly, given what I have said above, Lawrence associates this conception of lyric poetry with free verse: 'free verse has its own *nature*, that it is neither star nor pearl, but instantaneous like plasm'.[29] Although the essay was used as an introduction to the American edition of the *New Poems*, Lawrence writes that it should have formed a preface for *Look! We Have Come Through!* (1917) – the first volume in which he makes extensive use

of free verse. Such a poetics of the present results in the final state-
ment of the poem 'Manifesto':

> We shall not look before and after.
> We shall *be*, now.
> We shall know in full.
> We, the mystic NOW.[30]

Carried through in poems such as 'Craving for Spring', the connec-
tion in Lawrence's work between free verse and a rejection of a lyric
ambition to transcend the material and mortal world can be seen
again to invoke something of the very language of Romantic lyric
transcendence:

> The gush of spring is strong enough
> to play with the globe of earth like a ball on a fountain;
> At the same time it opens the tiny hands of the hazel
> with such infinite patience.
> The power of the rising, golden, all-creative sap could take the earth
> and heave it off among the stars, into the invisible; [. . .][31]

Here the earthly realm contains within itself something equivalent to
divine power in its 'infinite' potential.

Yet how do we approach aestheticist poetry, which turned to ever-
stricter verse forms at a time when the concerns to which modernist
poetry responded were already articulated? If, as I have suggested,
the interplay of lyric's own metrical temporality and its aspiration
to an eternal (atemporal) realm is central to the nineteenth-century
conception of lyric poetry, then the fashion for ever stricter and
shorter verse forms towards the end of the nineteenth century might
be thought to intensify this central potentiality. I alluded above to
the idea that the high degree of internal patterning and complexity
in these forms offers the potential for an illusion that, at a formal
level, no time passes over the course of the poem. These short, strict-
form structures seem to depend on holding together many images
synchronically within the poem even though they appear textually in
diachronic sequence. Rhyme, as well as rhythm, is often a key com-
ponent in achieving this illusion, with end-rhymes across the length
of the lyric asserting temporal identity. D. G. Rossetti's 'The Sonnet' –
that 'moment's monument', an altar to the eternal and 'Memorial
from the Soul's eternity' – might be the most iconic statement of
this, exploring what it might mean to aspire to an escape from the
determinedly diachronic and metrically time-bound form to seek

the atemporal essences that characterise Hegelian transcendence. But why do we see a particular focus in aestheticist poetry on short, intricate forms and an aspiration to temporal transcendence at a time when both were starting to seem out of step with modernity?

A closer reading of T. E. Hulme's essay reveals that while he dismisses the Parnassians as writers who, in his eyes, left nothing of consequence, he does acknowledge that Parnassianism and free verse come from the same impetus: 'as a reaction from romanticism'.[32] In general, as T. S. Eliot points out in 'Reflections on *Vers libre*', poetry's interest in metre is the tension between fixity and flux;[33] to move to forms of lyric that aspire to be all fixity or all flux is clearly a sign that something is up. Parnassianism and free verse may seem to pull in opposite directions, but, as I will explore further in Chapter 4, whether a move to ever more intricate verse forms or a desire to oppose pattern in rhyme or metre, both are manifestations of a concern about the nature and status of lyric in relation to modernity.[34] The late nineteenth-century formal and metrical responses I trace here (like those better-known innovations of the modernists) recognise the problem of relevance of a lyrical aspiration to temporal transcendence, but they did not see a retreat to the more 'authentic' rhythms of every day to be the solution. In fact the aestheticist poems I examine seem deeply suspicious of the notion of poetic 'authenticity' – an issue to which I will return throughout this study.

To recognise in the intricate fixed forms of aestheticist poetry something other than nostalgia is to read in line with our current understanding of late nineteenth-century culture more generally. In my previous chapter I quoted Freedman's influential characterisation of aestheticism as the moment when the Romantic desire to reconcile oppositions 'is explicitly understood to be a necessary and inevitable failure';[35] and this is particularly relevant to aestheticist temporality and its negotiation of the Hegelian dialectic which I have been exploring in this chapter. Through Pater's image of the 'hard gem-like flame', a flickering symbol of transience is stilled into a freeze-frame in which the light appears not waxing and waning but solid, hard and eternal. Through this image, Pater holds the transient and the eternal in a paradoxical relationship of identity. Yet, as scholars have noted, such apparent reconciliations cannot be sustained and 'rapidly move toward an acceptance of dichotomy and irresolution'.[36] Because of the importance of its metrical incarnation, the lyric genre was particularly well placed to explore this process. The questions I explore in the next two chapters are simultaneously central to an understanding of aestheticism *and* have a particular and profound importance for a conceptualisation of the lyric genre specifically. Much nineteenth-century poetry is elegiac, mourning the losses of a rapidly industrialising society, but towards the end of the century this elegiac quality perhaps in some sense becomes a formal one as lyric enacts, and meditates on, its own generic 'failures'; mourning its continual failure to still time while simultaneously unfolding across time, it laments its own passing as it passes.

Elaine Scarry has noted the increased interest in poetic metre that seems to accompany the lead-up to the end of a century: 'the etymological identity of *meter* with *measure*, the intimacy between poetry and the act of counting, and hence the heightened poetic attention to numbers at the moment when the calendar turns over'.[37] It is no coincidence that ekphrasis is a focus for aestheticism, reflecting in some sense the increase in anxieties around time and history as 1900 approaches. One of the most influential theorists on the different artistic modes, G. E. Lessing distinguished literature from painting by recognising painting as a medium of spatial organisation, while language is distinguished by temporal organisation and action across time.[38] It is worth noting at this point that the diachronic nature of lyric poetry is central even after print came to dominate the audience's experience of the genre:[39] verse has duration even when read from a page. As Derek Attridge describes, even when reading in silence from the page the act of reading a poem is a viscerally experienced event whose very physicality determines that it is a process that unfolds over time:

> Reading poetry requires *time*; each word needs to emerge and fulfil itself before we go on to the next. A poem is a real-time event. Our habit of skimming for sense when we read a newspaper or a novel . . . doesn't stand us in good stead when it comes to poetry, which simply cannot work *as* poetry if it is read in this way.[40]

Crucially, it is the fixed division of lines on the page, determined irrespective of physical spatial constraints or of syntactical closure, that is both central to the identity of poetry as a literary form and that ensures poetry is read (whether silently or out loud) metrically. Whether it is in irregular verse or strict iambic pentameter, the specified line length packages the poem into metrical units, highlighting its metrical structure across the page as well as across time and dictating the poem's reception in and through time.

Lessing posits ekphrasis as a combination not of the content of the painting and the poem, but of the properties of the two distinctive modes of representation. Literature is temporal because it presents us with items in a specific order that we have to access diachronically: no matter what temporal content a poem represents, it will always exist for the reader as a medium bound to its own time and rhythm. Painting, on the other hand, is based around spatial rather than temporal organisation, and so does not restrict or dictate the temporal order in which items can be accessed. So, the point of ekphrastic poems is that they bring something of the perfect, still moment of art into a world of language governed by temporality. In Jonathan Freedman's words, they seem 'to create timeless icons in the very medium that seems bound most irrevocably to time'.[41] But, more than this, I suggest it is the very impossibility of this combination of timelessness and temporality that makes ekphrasis such an appealing motif for aestheticist lyric poetry. Ekphrasis is an aspiration to atemporality that is doomed to failure: for Lessing, however far one tries to achieve such a combination in terms of *content*, it will never be possible to discover an ekphrastic *mode* of depiction. In other words, any attempt at ekphrasis will turn out to be either literature or painting, but it will never form that elusive intermediate mode of representation.[42] The vogue for ekphrasis within aestheticist poetry was (as I will go on to argue) not so much about trying to transcend the temporal nature of verse as about recognising the problems of such aspirations. That enabling Romantic dialectic between controlling metre and transcendent ambition might often be seen to be recast in aestheticist ekphrasis as a paradox ultimately defined by failure. This ekphrastic meditation on lyric is a significant current within aestheticist poetry, and provides the starting point for the following chapter.

Yet the conditions of late nineteenth-century culture described by Benjamin also offered new opportunities for the remaking of lyric. What I propose in the following two chapters not only recognises this moment of failure, and the ability of aestheticist writers to riff playfully and inventively on it, but also a fresh experimentation with ways of thinking about time and metre.[43] Above all, however, the following two chapters enable me to explore that conundrum central to aestheticism: how should we understand this vogue for intricate fixed forms that intervenes between the more narrative, hybrid and dramatic poetic experiments of the mid-century and the turn to free verse in the early decades of the next century? Why the intense interest in the Parnassian at just the moment when strict metrical forms and the aspirations they encode were being challenged by the new realities and new temporalities of modernity?

Notes

1. Kern, *The Culture of Time and Space*, pp. 69, 29, 8, 19.
2. Schleifer, *Modernism and Time*, p. 3.
3. Ibid., p. 4.
4. Ibid., p. 13.
5. Ibid., p. 50.
6. Benjamin, *Arcades*, 462, N2a, 3.
7. Ibid., 867, Q. 21.
8. Schleifer, *Modernism and Time*, p. 23.
9. Wordsworth, 'Preface', pp. 262, 263–4.
10. Coleridge, *Biographia Literaria* II, p. 50.
11. See W. David Shaw's analysis in *The Lucid Veil*, Chapter 7, on 'Hegelian Aesthetics', in which he traces the influence in Britain, noting initially that 'When Jowett introduced Hegel's philosophy to Oxford in the late 1840s, Hegel had already been studied in England for at least a decade' (p. 234); see also Jerome Hamilton Buckley's *The Victorian Temper*, which discusses the importance of J. H. Stirling's *Secret of Hegel* (1865) to late nineteenth-century thought.
12. Ward traces Hegel's influence within British culture generally, noting that '*The Philosophy of Art* was translated by W. Hastie in 1886' (*Walter Pater*, p. 44), and Shuter notes that Pater and other admirers of Hegel read the works in German before that date ('History as Palingenesis', p. 415).
13. Hegel, *Aesthetics*, p. 1011.
14. Ibid., pp. 1011–14.
15. Ibid., p. 1012.
16. Ibid., p. 1136.
17. Eagleton, *How To Read a Poem*, p. 135.
18. Zuckerkandl, *Sound and Symbol*, pp. 158–9.
19. Ibid., pp. 169–70.
20. Benjamin, *Charles Baudelaire*, p. 141.
21. Eliot, 'Reflections on *Vers libre*', p. 31.
22. See Beasley, *Modernist Poetry*, p. 115.
23. As Mallarmé wrote, free verse represents 'finding the true condition and possibility not only of poetic self-expression, but of free and individual modulation' ('Crisis in Poetry', p. 154). Peter Howarth also comments: 'free verse allows the poet to be natural, at one with himself, his individuality never compromised by convention' (*British Poetry in the Age of Modernism*, p. 30).
24. Hulme, 'Lecture on Modern Poetry', p. 63.
25. Lawrence, 'Poetry of the Present', p. 182.
26. Ibid., pp. 182–3.
27. Ibid., pp. 182, 183.
28. Ibid., p. 185.
29. Ibid., p. 185.

30. Lawrence, *Complete Poems*, p. 268.
31. Ibid., p. 272.
32. Hulme, 'Lecture on Modern Poetry', p. 61. ('Modern lyrical verse' is, for Hulme as for so many others in the period, a Romantic formulation.)
33. Eliot, 'Reflections on *Vers libre*', p. 33.
34. Interestingly, Peter Howarth notices something similar when he writes of early twentieth-century poetry that 'the Imagist justifications for free verse based on direct transmission of the impulse sound remarkably similar to Georgian justifications for metre' (*British Poetry in the Age of Modernism*, p. 30).
35. Freedman, *Professions of Taste*, p. 31. More recently, Angela Leighton reads Pater as presenting a failed 'art for art's sake' because the aesthetic 'does not exist in his work as a thing apart, protected, and immutable'; instead it is 'known only in time' (*On Form*, p. 98).
36. Freedman, *Professions of Taste*, p. 19.
37. Scarry, 'Counting at Dusk (Why Poetry Matters When the Century Ends)', p. 8.
38. This fundamental difference in artistic mode has, Lessing believes, consequences for what is depicted. Because painting is a medium defined by spatial organisation it is more suited to representing visual impressions at a single moment in time. Literature, on the other hand, is more appropriate for depicting actions and events across time (Lessing, *Laocoön*, passim).
39. See, for example, Stewart, 'Preface to a Lyric History', p. 215 ('Lyric by definition appears in the unfolding web of memory, perception, and expectation so continually described in lyric theory from Augustine to Benjamin. The vaunted spatiality of lyric after the advent of print is only in fact an exaggeration of this position of ephemeral, yet significant, enunciation.')
40. Attridge, *Poetic Rhythm*, pp. 2–3.
41. Freedman, *Professions of Taste*, p. 19.
42. Lessing, *Laocoön*, passim.
43. To define nineteenth-century lyric as 'a suspended moment that stops the time of narrative and focuses on the "now" of composition and reception' might be, I suggest, to miss something of the potential of lyric poetry's self-analysis in this period (Morgan, *Narrative Means*, p. 4).

Chapter 3

Painting, Music, Touch: D. G. Rossetti's Ekphrasis and Competing Temporalities

Dante Gabriel Rossetti's 'Superscription' comments on precisely the precariousness, discussed in the previous chapter, of the search for a moment of painterly atemporality in poetic form. Invoking in its title the physical relationship between poem and painting, the poem meditates on artistic mode. This poem was written in 1869 and published in a sequence of sixteen sonnets in the *Fortnightly Review* (March 1869), before being included in the 'sonnets and songs' of 'House of Life' in the *Poems* of 1870.[1] The octave starts by invoking a portrait: 'look in my face'. This figure seems to represent time or death: 'might-have-been', 'no-more', 'too-late', 'Farewell'. The 'dead-sea shell' and mirror held by the figure give intimations of mortality and of 'life's form' reduced to 'shaken shadow intolerable'. The sestet mirrors the opening with the command to look at the figure ('mark me'), but this time the figure seems to represent the stillness and calm of the Mona Lisa ('still', 'lulls', 'peace'), rather than the temporal movement of the octave. The shift between octave and sestet suggests that, however much the painting depicts the ravages of time and death, a picture is ultimately a still moment, governed by spatial organisation and not temporal movement. By implication, however much the text tries to take on the qualities of the painting, it is still ultimately governed by temporal movement. The lyric cannot transcend time, even through ekphrasis. This message is in the metre as the iambic pentameter figures the relentless swell of the sea, and the poem itself becomes the sea-shell held to the reader's ear to give the sound of time passing, of mortality. 'Life's foam-fretted feet', cast up between the shell and ear, are the toes that feel the fret, or lap, of the continual advance of the foam-tipped waves as a constant reminder of mortality; but they are also the metrical feet, themselves undulating in iambic waves to convey to the ear the irrepressible momentum of time. However much the painting embodies stillness, the poem's metrical structure marches on in time, marking the creep of mortality with every foot.

The poem might be seen to highlight, then, the impossibility that Lessing saw as inherent in the ekphrastic project, but in doing so it highlights the nineteenth-century lyric's own impossible struggle with being both in time and out of time. For this reason it forms a good introduction to the issues I want to explore in this chapter. The poems I go on to examine are from Rossetti's 1870 volume *Poems*, but by virtue of having been drafted much earlier in the century the material in this first case study also has some claim to being the earliest work that I cover. Indeed, the very production history of this volume – a manuscript exhumation from the coffin of Rossetti's first wife, Lizzie Siddal – signifies, as noted earlier, something of the more general reconsideration of lyric in the period and therefore provides a fitting starting point. In fact, Rossetti's own writing about the exhumation is rather interesting in relation to discourses on time and poetry. In several letters to friends and relatives Rossetti allays their potential horror by repeatedly using the same euphemistic phrase to indicate that the corpse disinterred in the coffin was without decomposition: 'All in the coffin was found quite perfect'.[2] This, in contrast to the manuscript, which although not destroyed was significantly decayed. Rossetti dwells at length only on one poem: 'The poem of "Jenny" which is the one I most wanted, has got a great worm-hole right through every page of it in this proportion: [here he sketches a page of text with a large hole through it, which dominates half of the page]'[3] A dichotomy appears here between the 'perfect', unsullied Lizzie and the prostitute Jenny, the latter now signified by a hole. Yet in a strange twist on Rossetti's own assertion of the sonnet as a literary 'memorial', a creation that ensures a form of posthumous survival in contrast to the mortal body, his narrative also offers a dichotomy between the freshness of the physical body and the decomposed text. Lyric poetry, in Rossetti's version of the history of the 1870 *Poems*, is of the temporal, rather than atemporal, sphere. In this chapter I explore the centrality of temporality to ekphrastic poetry, suggesting that close engagement with the role and workings of metre should complicate and change any understanding of these poems as aspiring to a painterly atemporality. Taking just two poems for close attention, I argue first (in relation to 'For a Venetian Pastoral by Giorgione') that Rossetti's ekphrastic poetic reflects on and interrogates Hegelian ideals. Secondly, I suggest (through close engagement with 'For an Allegorical Dance of Women, by Andrea Mantegna') that one might find in such poetry models of temporality more associated with Benjamin and early twentieth-century modernism. Thinking about aestheticist poetry as negotiating a shift between different notions of lyric temporality provides a way to recognise poetry's engagement with the new contexts of cultural modernity even when it appears most wedded to the past. I end the chapter with a reflection on W. B. Yeats's work in order to provide another perspective on some of the issues discussed.

*   *   *

'For a Venetian Pastoral by Giorgione' poses the temporal ambition of ekphrasis particularly forcefully. It appears in *Poems* 1870 in the section titled 'Sonnets for Pictures, and Other Sonnets' after the opening piece: 'For Our Lady of the Rocks, by Leonardo da Vinci'.[4] That first poem introduces the centrality of temporality to the ekphrastic sonnet through its overt invocation of personified 'Time' and through the almost absurdly temporally rich concept of 'Infinite imminent Eternity'. Such concerns, I suggest, set the tone for 'Sonnets for Pictures, and Other Sonnets' and are maintained throughout the subsequent two poems, which I take as my examples in this chapter. The 'Venetian Pastoral' that forms the subject matter for the first of these two is a 'concert champêtre', now thought to be by Titian, depicting, centrally, two young men, one dressed in courtly attire with a hand raised about to strum a lute, the other dressed more simply. The two are turned towards one another, although their mouths are shut, suggesting that while they may have been sharing a song, or be about to do so, they are silent in the moment of depiction. They are seated on the grass in a pastoral landscape. The two men are at the centre of the painting but there are also two nude women, one on either side of this pair: the one to the left is standing, possibly pouring water from a glass pitcher into a fountain; the other sits in front of the men, with her back to the viewer, and holds a flute just away from her lips. Another figure can be seen in the background, which appears to be a shepherd with his sheep. The strange combination of clothed men and nude women has been a central conundrum in interpretations of this painting over the course of the twentieth century. While a painting such as Manet's *Déjeuner sur l'herbe* gives a clear narrative for its depiction of nude women (involving a heap of discarded clothes in the foreground), there is no such 'natural' narrative to explain the nudity of the women in the Titian. Indeed, Titian's nudes are not intended to be human; they are nymphs who have been attracted by the men's music but are invisible to those men. They serve an allegorical function, representing Poetry itself and the inspiration for the men's lyric (the flute and pouring water are symbols of lyric).[5] The painting, then, lends itself well to thinking about that dichotomy – characteristic of a Hegelian temporality – between temporal and eternal realms, in this case depicted side by side in the figures of the men and the divine spirits.[6]

Yet as well as playing within a visual space around what is visible and invisible, this painting might also be thought to play across the line of what is heard and not heard. Strikingly different interpretations exist of this painting, particularly in terms of its representation of music. When Dante Gabriel Rossetti first saw the picture in the Louvre in 1849 he described the scene like this: 'There is a woman, naked, at one side, who is dipping a glass vessel into a well; and in the centre two men and another naked woman, who seem to have paused for a moment in playing on the musical instruments.'[7] Rossetti sees the painting as depicting a cessation of sound: a glass dipped into a well, not the music of water pouring from it; a momentary pause in the playing of the lute and the flute as the hand is raised as if about to strum the former while the flute is momentarily removed from the lips. When Pater published his essay on 'The School of Giorgione' in 1877 he referred briefly to Rossetti's 'delightful sonnet' but described the woman pouring water from the pitcher and 'listening, perhaps, to the cool sound as it falls, blent with the music of the pipes'.[8] For Pater it is a scene full of sounds heard, rather than a cessation. Indeed, contemporary scholars offer readings of various combinations of sounds heard and not heard in this picture. Elizabeth Helsinger suggests that the picture represents a pause in the music that is filled sonically with the sound of water pouring from the jug: 'the silence of music that has ceased made audible by a trickle of water';[9] John Hollander, on the other hand, reads the painting as a complete cessation of sound: 'in his poem, Rossetti moves to the heart of the pictorial matter here by pointing to the momentary suspension [. . .] of the sound of water and of wind-music in the recorder'.[10]

That the picture lends itself to varying interpretations of what is heard and not heard in its scene is probably why it appealed as an image of nineteenth-century lyric. It offers up a vision of poetry as both music (the lyric metre that Hegel saw as lyric's one 'sensuous fragrance') and a transcendent pause in the music (that desire articulated by Hegel to belong to a realm beyond the material, beyond the 'accidental externality' of poetry's metrical form).[11] Indeed, Pater's reference to the School of Giorgione's ability to capture the 'music or the musical intervals in our existence' also refers obliquely to this duality of music and silence. A musical interval might be either the distance between two notes (played simultaneously as a chord, or in sequence across time), but it might also be an interval in the play of music: a cessation. Pater seems to embrace this duality, writing of the musical interval as both a moment in time and a moment out of time: 'life itself is conceived as a sort of listening – listening to music, to the reading of Bandello's novels, to the sound of water, to time as it flies'.[12] Yet it is also an 'exquisite [pause] in time' that transcends the diachronicity marked by a sequence of musical notes.[13] The picture is read by Rossetti, and ultimately Pater, as finding, through a play of sounds, a still, silent moment of listening. As Rossetti states in the last line of his poem, it is a picture that represents the moment outside of time: a moment of 'immortality'.

> Water, for anguish of the solstice:—nay,
> But dip the vessel slowly,—nay, but lean
> And hark how at its verge the wave sighs in
> Reluctant. Hush! Beyond all depth away
> The heat lies silent at the brink of day:
> Now the hand trails upon the viol-string
> That sobs, and the brown faces cease to sing,
> Sad with the whole of pleasure. Whither stray
> Her eyes now, from whose mouth the slim pipes creep
> And leave it pouting, while the shadowed grass
> Is cool against her naked side? Let be:—
> Say nothing now unto her lest she weep,
> Nor name this ever. Be it as it was,—
> Life touching lips with Immortality.[14]

So, a painting of a scene that is both an actual musical moment shared between two men and an allegory of lyric (represented by the two otherworldly women) becomes, through the poem, a moment of silence in which lyric achieves its goal of connecting briefly with the transcendent realm, with immortality. In asking us to listen ('hark', hush!, 'silent', 'say nothing now', 'cease to sing'), the poem is ostensibly asking us to hear a moment of pause: a moment between notes that represents a moment out of time. A suitable image, perhaps, of a Hegelian lyric dialectic between the poem's own enabling metrical 'fetter' and its aspiration to pure *Geist*?[15] Indeed, what current scholars agree on is that the poem conveys a 'moment of supraverbal spiritual transcendence'.[16] In his analysis of the poem, Jonathan

Freedman sees it as taking on the silent, visual mode of representation from the painting and implementing it within the realm of the poem: 'In suggesting that poetry can exert its greatest power not by the speaking of a word but rather by its silencing, Rossetti plots poetry's invasion of the territory previously occupied by [visual] art.'[17]

Yet does it? After all, surely this scenario of ekphrastic success is complicated by the fact that when we 'hush' and 'hark' what we hear is not the picture's immortal moment of silence, but the poem's own metrical inscription of time passing. The music of the poem is mainly iambic pentameter, the most noticeable departure occurring when the poem is evoking the music of the men in the scene (who are imagined in a moment of pause from both playing the 'viol' and singing): 'Now the hand trails upon the viol-string/ That sobs, and the brown faces cease to sing'. It is as if the earthly sound of the human music is being contrasted with the iambic music associated with the women and therefore with the ideal of lyric itself. Yet while Rossetti describes the painting as representing a hiatus in the women's allegorical muse-music (as well as the men's mortal music), the poem's own rhythmical throb is foregrounded when we are asked to listen to the silence the poem depicts. In this way, the poem seems a deliberate attempt to open up a space in which form can work against content to dwell on the central dilemma of ekphrasis: whether the poem's metrical presence can lift the poem out of time, or whether it will always be the diachronic metronome that anchors it in time; whether it can ever find in itself the still and silent moment of the painting. This is a question Rossetti poses in many other poems, particularly, for example, 'The Vase of Life', a poem written in the tradition of Keats's 'Ode to a Grecian Urn', which similarly problematises (albeit in a different way) that Romantic ekphrastic aspiration.[18]

A closer reading of 'For a Venetian Pastoral by Giorgione' in relation to its composition history will help develop my argument about the metrical message of the poem. The poem was first written in 1849, and an earlier version was published in *The Germ* in 1850. It is included in my study of the final third of the nineteenth century because it was significantly rewritten in the proof process of 1869–70 that led up to its new publication in the 1870 *Poems*.[19] Only three lines remain without major changes. Specifically, aspects of the poem that force a direct relationship between the reader and the poem, and that demand the reader listen to the poem ('hark', 'hush!'), were added later. Moreover, the metrical music the later poem asks us to attend to is substantially different to that present in the earlier version. The 1870 version is much more consistently iambic than the

1850 copy, and it is noticeable that two of the three lines that stand without major changes in the 1870 version are the two lines I have already identified as the later poem's only major break with iambic pentameter: the lines representing the men's mortal music in viol and song. In giving the poem a much more consistent iambic pulse, these changes to the poem have the effect of turning up the poem's own metrical music – its own poetic intonation – at the same time as Rossetti newly commands the reader to hear nothing but silence. Elizabeth Helsinger has wryly noted that 'Rossetti's insistence that the modern poet begin by listening to silence might have produced a more minimalist poetry than he himself practiced'.[20] And interestingly, between 1850 and 1870 we see changes to this poem that move it further towards an insistently *poetic* iambic regularity. For example, lines 3–4 of the 1850 version of the poem break the iambic pentameter (perhaps to become metrically full of the 'gurgle' of the water filling the vessel dipped into the basin):

> Listlessly dipt to let the water in
> With slow vague gurgle [. . .]

In the 1870 version lines 3–4 become broadly iambic:

> And hark how at its verge the wave sighs in
> Reluctant. Hush! [. . .]

While in content the gurgling of the water is replaced with that gentle 'sigh', the metre has become more insistent in its beat: the irrepressibility of the poem's own diachronic metricality becomes more apparent even as the iambic pentameter is used to better represent the poem's increased emphasis on silence.

The other point at which the 1870 poem departs significantly from its iambic underpinnings is in the final line ('Life touching lips with Immortality' /oo/o/o/oo): the line that makes explicit what it is that the poet finds so compelling about the painting.[21] Yet, presented within a rhythmical structure that connects this statement to the non-iambic music of the earthly men with their viol-strumming and singing, one wonders how much this final line contains a touch of divinity and how much an acknowledgement of its impossibility. Is the poem as far from transcending the world of time and change as are the men from meeting lips with the beautiful naked women who exist alongside them but in a completely different plane? Although Rossetti's interest in the painting is in its ability to depict a still, silent moment through which the mortal world was transcended,[22] the metrical changes in the 1870 version of the poem suggest that Rossetti became more self-conscious about the tension with the poem's own temporal diachronicity. The introduction of a more regular iambic pentameter appears, particularly when taken with the changes in content, to be trying to silence the poem, but it also foregrounds the poem's own rhetorical structure and the tension between content and form noted within the final line.

Isobel Armstrong's reading of the sonnets of Dante Gabriel and Christina Rossetti offers an analysis of their concerns and technique in light of visual technologies, and claims for the sonnet a particular affinity with the visual: in an age in which 'The eye dominates the sensorial', 'The peculiar Victorian modernity of the sonnet lay frequently in the coordinated action of sight and light.'[23] Armstrong's privileging of the visual within D. G. Rossetti's sonnets acknowledges the necessary connection between vision and touch, and vision and sound, but in a way that subordinates these other senses to the eye because of the primary experience of the modern sonnet as a visually received textual form: 'the eye releases the full plenitude of sensory experience in the interpretative act – visual, tactile, oral, aural'. Armstrong continues:

> Sound in the sonnet is, under this reading, a corollary of the visual, appended to it: sound [. . .] follows from the visual as the cadences of a soundscape become apparent in the linguistic landscape greeted by the eye. The visual becomes vocal.[24]

This kind of synaesthesia is a key part of the ekphrastic project (as the poet Herbert Horne says with some irony of Rossetti in 1887: 'the mannerisms of his verse correspond to the distressing colour of his flesh painting'), yet it is striking how far from dominant sight often appears to be in Rossetti's poems.[25] While the mode of accessing the lyric text might be predominantly visual, *and* D. G. Rossetti's picture sonnets are fundamentally concerned with the visual image, the poems frequently focus on other senses, and artistic modes other than the pictorial (sound and music, particularly). The effect is to draw attention to the poem's own metrically incanted form. It seems as if lyric became particularly aware of the ghost of an aural echo, of its origination in song, at the moment when, in Armstrong's terms, it acknowledged its own status as primarily a visual form.

'For a Venetian Pastoral by Giorgione' is a poem that plays on the tension between an ambitious, and painterly, aspiration to an eternal moment, and the recognition, through its own insistent music, of lyric's own inevitably diachronic nature. This study in ekphrasis is a study in failure: it highlights the impossibility of lyric's metrical struggle with being both in time and out of time. Ekphrasis enabled a formal expression of the difficulties in holding on to that enabling Romantic dialectic when claims for the status of the poet as prophet or seer of the transcendent realm were no longer tenable. This vogue for ekphrasis has various motivating forces, but it might be recognised as, in part, an expression of concern about the temporalities of the lyric genre and an interrogation of its own Romantic heritage.

*   *   *

In the 1870 *Poems*, the following sonnet appears as a pendant on the facing page of the book: 'For an Allegorical Dance of Women, by Andrea Mantegna':

> Scarcely, I think; yet it indeed *may* be
> The meaning reached him, when this music rang
> Clear through his frame, a sweet possessive pang,
> And he beheld these rocks and that ridged sea.
> But I believe that, leaning tow'rds them, he
> Just felt their hair carried across his face
> As each girl passed him; nor gave ear to trace
> How many feet; nor bent assuredly
> His eyes from the blind fixedness of thought
> To know the dancers. It is bitter glad
> Even unto tears. Its meaning filleth it,
> A secret of the wells of Life: to wit:—
> The heart's each pulse shall keep the sense it had
> With all, though the mind's labour run to nought.[26]

The painting that inspired this poem (more usually called *Parnassus*) depicts Mars and Venus, with Cupid, their son, nearby. At the centre of the scene is a dance of the Muses in their grove on Mount Helicon. They move to the music of Apollo who, seated, plays the lyre to the left-hand side of the grouping. To the right of the Muses is Mercury, with Pegasus. Vulcan, at his forge, can be seen in the background on the left side of the scene.

Being able to 'read' the picture in this way is all well and good, but it is not enough to unlock the meaning of its internal riddle. The image is famous for the speculation and uncertainty as to what encoded allegorical or symbolic meanings it holds: understanding the meaning of the picture requires the key, lost in history, to its specific allegory. The picture was painted for Isabella d'Este on her marriage to Francesco Gonzaga. It was done for her private quarters and there is strong reason to believe that it held a particular meaning for her.[27] Lawrence Gowing notes that Cupid pointing a pea-shooter at Vulcan's genitals, and Mars standing on Venus's foot, are both veiled pornographic references that Isabella would have understood.[28] Yet it is not known what the full significance of the picture's content was for her. William Michael Rossetti comments that his brother was not aware of either the title of the painting or the mythological references it contained.[29] Yet titling the poem 'An Allegorical Dance of Women', rather than 'Parnassus', looks more like a deliberate choice to highlight the fact that the interest of the painting is its hidden meaning, what lies behind those easily identifiable mythological references.

This painting, with its centrally mysterious and historically 'lost' allegory, foregrounds problems of interpretation, and, particularly, of knowing history. Of course, Rossetti's conclusion, in the last four lines of the poem, is that it doesn't matter that this allegory is lost to history; this is not, after all, where the picture's meaning lies. He uses the allegorical unknowability of this picture to draw attention to other ways of knowing art and history, advocating a more 'felt' approach: an understanding by feeling aesthetically, in an unreflective, unmediated way, through the heart, not the head. This meaning is, as McGann has noted, both one that is hidden and one that presents itself very directly: it is both a secret at the bottom of a well, and it 'wells up' or bubbles up to the surface.[30] As McGann has explored at length, the poem's conclusion is that meaning in art is not divined through 'hermeneutic operation[s]' but 'is present and manifest': 'It is the act and eventuality of the work itself'.[31] The advocated method is one that, I suggest, relies on the physical encounter with the artwork rather than an intellectual decoding of it, but what might that mean, and how does it work?

The poem begins with a sense of the problem of interpreting the painting and of finding what is, in the penultimate line, called 'the sense it had' (the past tense stressing the search for a historical meaning now lost to us): 'Scarcely, I think; yet it indeed may be/ The meaning reached him, when this music rang/ Clear through his frame'. Usually interpreted as imagining the moment of Mantegna's own understanding of the significance of his painting, these lines emphasise how the only way of overcoming the problem of historical knowledge is to inhabit that moment simply and immediately. The core of the historical experience in the poem lies in the possibility of

the immediate, sensory impression of the swish of the dancing girls'
hair across the face as they dance by:

> [. . .] he
> Just felt their hair carried across his face
> As each girl passed him; nor gave ear to trace
> How many feet; nor bent assuredly
> His eyes from the blind fixedness of thought
> To know the dancers. [. . .]

Again the subject of this sentence is 'to know', to divine meaning. But
the odd syntax gives a useful double ambivalence to 'just felt'. The
brush of their hair is 'just felt' as a delicate caress, but this phrase also
suggests that the presence of the dancers is only '*felt*', because their
footsteps are not *heard*, nor are they *seen*. This foregrounds the phe-
nomenological nature of the encounter in the poem. Indeed, women's
hair carries important freight throughout Rossetti's work, signifying
sensuality in his poetry as well as in his painting, and lending, in con-
text, additional emphasis to the physicality of the central encounter
in this poem.[32] The centrality of the sensation of the swish of hair in
'For an Allegorical Dance of Women', then, represents an attempt to
gain an immediate and sensuous connection with a subject matter
otherwise historically distant and beyond the grasp of knowledge.

Yet who is the 'he' who discovers meaning, who feels the swish of
hair against his face, at the centre of this encounter? Richard Stein
identified 'he' as Mercury (who stands to the right of the dancers).[33]
It seems likely that John Barclay's analysis of the 'analogy between
the figure beside the dancers and the beholder of the painting' also
refers to Mercury. Mercury holds the position of an onlooker, viewer
or 'bystander' as Barclay terms him, within the picture.[34] Much more
recently, Catherine Maxwell suggests the 'he' who feels the swish
of the hair is more likely to 'represent the artist [Mantegna], imag-
ined as he beheld the visionary scene that became the painting'. It is
Mantegna who, for Maxwell, in turn mediates between the scene and
Rossetti (and the reader of Rossetti's poem), the 'frame' ('The mean-
ing reached him, when this music rang/ Clear through his frame')
referring both to his own body and to his painting.[35] Indeed, Leonee
Ormond and McGann both agree that 'he' is Mantegna and that this
poem is about the artist's exploration of the meaning of the scene of
his painting.[36] Another study of this poem, by Elizabeth Helsinger,
again asserts the identity of the 'he' as Mantegna, feeling the vibra-
tions of Apollo's music ringing through the frame of his painting.[37]

What if the poem's central mystery (like the painting's) is both simpler and more complicated than this? The only 'he' capable of hearing the music and leaning forwards to feel the swish of the girl's hair across his face is Apollo. It is Apollo who is not hearing their steps ('nor gave ear to trace/ How many feet') because he is listening to his music; and it is Apollo who is not seeing the dancers, not looking at them, because his gaze is averted to the 'blind fixedness of thought'. But this 'just felt' encounter – an encounter that is about finding meaning, about 'knowing' the dancers – is not just between Apollo and the dancers. 'He' takes on a treble meaning throughout this poem to signify a multi-layered phenomenological connection between Apollo, Mantegna and Rossetti, as the search to 'know' the meaning of the dancers (their dance symbolising the central riddle of the painting) is one that happens across time as well as space. 'The meaning reached him, when this music rang/ Clear through his frame': as with the previous sonnet, music is central to this endeavour to discover meaning, to this attempt to attain a moment outside of time (a 'musical interval'). Here we find Apollo with his music ringing through the frame of his lyre; Mantegna, with the music of the scene reverberating through the frame of his canvas; and Rossetti, and/or the current reader of the poem, with the metrical music of the poem felt phenomenologically through the body, through his physical frame. This multifaceted 'he' enables a connection across time, in a synchronic moment of aesthetic experience, through which Rossetti inhabits not just the point at which Mantegna understood the full meaning of the picture he created, but the picture itself; he experiences the fullness of its meaning from within the scene through the 'inner standing point' of Apollo.

As with the previous sonnet, I suggest it is no coincidence that the features I find particularly significant to this reading were added in 1869–70, for publication in *Poems*. While this poem, too, was first published in *The Germ* in 1850, it is only in 1870 that it acquires the meaning and form that interests me in terms of the lyric's response to modernity. The 1850 version has 'when this music rang/ *sharp* through his *brain*' (my emphasis), not yet establishing that multiple meaning of 'frame' that forms the link between Apollo, Mantegna and Rossetti as the focus of the poem's phenomenological encounter ('when this music rang/ Clear through his frame').[38] Similarly, the 1850 version was concerned not with what it might mean to 'know' the dancers, but to 'see' the dancers. Again Rossetti's revision stresses a broader phenomenological comprehension that is not located in vision – which separates the locus of seeing from that seen – but in an 'encounter' with the world in which it is experienced through its contiguity with the perceiver. Likewise, 'But I believe he just leaned passively,/ *And* felt their hair carried across his face' is changed to 'But I believe that, leaning tow'rds them, he/ *Just* felt their hair carried across his face' (my emphasis). I have already discussed the significance of that added 'just', and it is, again, no coincidence that this radically changes the reader's sense of the type of contact with the world that is represented in the poem.

These two poems make a fascinating pendant pair. Both are ekphrastic lyrics devoted to musical scenes, creating a three-way exploration of the artistic modes of art, poetry and music. Yet they enact, formally, two different ways of knowing the past and of existing in time. Far from any ekphrastic ambition to enter into the definitively still and silent moment of painting, the second poem animates the painting, asking us to feel the movement of the scene. While the first poem appears both to aspire to a static, frozen, eternal moment and to critique that aspiration, the latter is invested in a dynamic moment of connection between the present and the past. In this way, the second poem posits an understanding of history and lyric temporality radically different from that Hegelian dichotomy explored (and challenged) in the previous poem. While 'For a Venetian Pastoral by Giorgione' appears primarily engaged with pictorial silence, asking the reader to listen to its 'hush', 'For an Allegorical Dance of Women' takes its cue more from the sonic arts, asking the reader to listen to the music of the scene. However, the latter poem advocates nothing as simple as a return to lyric 'song'. It might aspire to the condition of music, but for Rossetti that means finding a method by which both the painting and this poem itself are known through direct sensuous engagement: through the vibrations of form rather than through the intellectual 'reading' of visual symbols and language, respectively. Both the painting and the poem become apprehended through their rhythmic effects on the body – they become pure pulse. The reader is invited to experience the poem as Apollo experiences the dancers: not visually, nor through intellectualised metrical analysis (Apollo, punningly, does not 'give ear' 'to trace how many feet'), but through that more visceral experience expressed by the 'just felt' swish of hair.

In offering an epistemology based on the human body – a way of finding meaning through the 'frame' or the form rather than through the disembodied, otherworldly, allegorical nudes that represented poetry in the previous poem – this sonnet seeks not an eternal moment out of body and out of time, but an inhabitation of history through a shared physical sensation. What we see here is something like Benjamin's 'collision' of past and present; that temporal 'constellation', in which, as Rolf Tiedemann puts it, 'the past coincides with the present to such an extent that the past achieves the "Now" of its "recognisability" '.[39] This, I suggest, is that profoundly anti-Hegelian awareness of historical time that Benjamin describes in his early essay 'The Life of Students' as 'a particular condition in which history appears to be concentrated in a single focal point'.[40] Gone is the notion of a historical continuity: an understanding of the past – in this case the lost allegory – is not passed down through a historical line. What we find in this poem is something more like what Benjamin calls a 'Telescoping of the past through the present'[41] or, elsewhere, the 'tiger's leap into the past'.[42] The three figures involved in this synchronic moment of history are not stepping stones along a linear trajectory of history, passing on knowledge that would otherwise be lost; they simply share a 'touch' across time. To quote Benjamin again, 'In order for a part of the past to be touched by the present instant, there must be no continuity between them'.[43] The historicism I have explored in 'For an Allegorical Dance of Women' resonates strongly with the language of 'touch' Benjamin uses. As Rolf Tiedemann comments, Benjamin believes 'the historian should no longer try to enter the past; rather, he should allow the past to enter his life'; 'A "pathos of nearness" ' is the engagement with history worked out through the 'dialectics at a standstill'.[44] This is a method as alien as Rossetti's affective method to any intellectualised attempt at 'understanding' the past.

In reading these two poems in relation to conceptions of lyric temporality we can see the difference between the ekphrastic interest in temporal transcendence (albeit subject to Rossetti's critique) and an experience of a moment of collision of past and present. Although equally distant from any inhabitation of time as linear and progressive, the latter represents a very different mode of experience; and these differences are central to shifts in the conceptualisation of time over the course of the later nineteenth century that I traced in the previous chapter. While I suggest that we see in the first poem a dramatisation of the failure of lyric's aspiration to the atemporal, and in the second an exploration of a more Benjaminian method of lyrical engagement with history, I am not, of course, suggesting that these two poems themselves mark a key moment of transition in literary history between a Hegelian notion of lyric time and a new post-Enlightenment method of lyrical historicism. Nor would I want to argue that these poems mark that point in Rossetti's own individual understanding of time and history in lyric form. However,

I am suggesting that we might consider lyric's understanding of its own remit at this time as influenced by shifting conceptualisations of time, and that this effect might be worked out metrically in poems whose content is not necessarily concerned overtly with the motifs of modernity.

What I am proposing is that 'For an Allegorical Dance of Women, by Andrea Mantegna' presents a method of historical engagement approaching 'messianic time':

> He [the materialist historian] grasps the constellation into which his own era has entered, along with a very specific earlier one. Thus, he establishes a conception of the present as now-time shot through with splinters of messianic time.[45]

Benjamin differentiates this way of knowing from a historicism that concerns itself with gathering facts about the past. He advocates rather a knowing of the past through a 'moment of its recognizability' that flashes upon us as 'the true image of the past flits by'.[46] Such an engagement with time and history is, for Benjamin, 'prefigured in art', not in the critical prose of the period.[47] Moreover, when Benjamin writes that 'Historical materialism must renounce the *epic* element in history' (my emphasis) in order to 'blast[] the epoch out of the reified "continuity of history"', he invokes something that might be seen to offer possibilities particularly relevant to a newly configured 'lyric'.[48] The 'felt' approach to history in this poem is conveyed particularly through changes made to the work around 1870: changes, I have suggested, that reflect a cultural and intellectual context very different from that in which Rossetti produced the earlier version.

*   *   *

D. H. Lawrence's manifesto for free verse quoted in the previous chapter demanded a poetry of the present – 'There must be mutation, swifter than iridescence, haste, not rest, come-and-go, not fixity, inconclusiveness, immediacy, the quality of life itself, without dénouement or close' – in opposition to and in rejection of the forms of a Romantic tradition that prized 'the qualities of the unfading timeless gems'.[49] Those 'gems' were, of course, not only the gems of Keats and Shelley but also the 'gem-like' intricate fixed forms of aestheticist and Decadent poetry which modernism found so prissy. For Lawrence, metrical form and theories of temporality are bound together in the configuration described in my previous chapter: he broadly associates strict form with what we might call Enlightenment theories of time, and free verse with post-Enlightenment temporalities. It is this opposition that I have questioned through my reading of Rossetti's sonnets, suggesting that aestheticist strict-form ekphrasis was not simply a nostalgic valorisation of the lyric quest for the still, atemporal moment, but a vogue that could, and did, focus and confront concerns about the relevance of that formation of lyric to the contemporary world. I will end with a brief comparison with another writer whose work is particularly interesting in relation to the issues discussed above: W. B. Yeats. A poet who came into his own after my focal period, and therefore is not a figure for extensive study here, Yeats is nonetheless relevant because he appears to take forward into the twentieth century a late example of what Lawrence and other modernists deride.

Yeats is a poet obsessed by 'timeless gems', retaining an interest both in lyric atemporality and regular metre. He writes in 1900 that poetry has 'done with time, and only wishes to gaze upon some reality, some beauty'.[50] Rhythm in the poetry of Yeats seems to lead to symbolic representation of a spiritual realm.[51] 'Symbolism of Poetry' presents 'the purpose of rhythm' as a hypnotic one that allows the reader to transcend the earthly realm in favour of 'a subtler enchantment'.[52] I have already referred briefly to Schleifer's omission of Yeats from his study of Benjaminian concepts of time and high literary modernism. Peter Howarth also struggles with Yeats in *British Poetry in the Age of Modernism*. In a study that traces the 'poetry wars' between two separate traditions of modernist poetry (the avant-garde and the more traditional), Howarth notes that Yeats should figure as the key writer who 'transcend[s] the division', offering 'the best hope for common ground'.[53] Yet, as Howarth goes on to acknowledge, he does not. In spite of his friendship with Pound, Yeats disliked his use of free verse, and defended traditional forms because their artifice and impersonality offered access to something that transcended the writer's own realm of flux and contingency.

In fact, Yeats himself offers an explanation for his 'lack of fit'. In a lecture given on 19 May 1893 ('Nationality and Literature'), he discourses upon the relative 'stages' of English and Irish literature at the present time, arguing that they are at quite different points of growth. He proposes a developmental narrative of literature, supposedly applicable to the literatures of any country, in which there is first a period of narrative poetry, then the epic or ballad period, followed by the dramatic period, and finally the period of lyric poetry.[54] In England, the lyric period began with the Romantics:

> In a lyric age the poets no longer can take their inspiration mainly from external activities [. . .] for they must express every phase of human consciousness no matter how subtle, how vague, how impalpable. With this advancing subtlety poetry steps out of the market-place, out of the general tide of life and becomes a mysterious cult, as it were, an almost secret religion made by the few for the few.[55]

The age of lyric is clearly associated with a kind of spiritual transcendence. But while 'the older literatures of Europe are in their golden sunset, their wise old age', the Irish are 'at the outset of a literary epoch': 'a young nation with unexhausted material lying within us [. . .] Look at our literature and you will see that we are still in our epic or ballad period.'[56] Yeats sees this marked by the fact that 'All that is greatest in that literature is based upon legend – upon those tales which are made by no one man, but by the nation itself through a slow process of modification and adaption.'[57] His final rallying cry is for Irish writers to follow those nations with more advanced literatures and learn from them. So, pulled between an Irish pre-lyric context and the lyric Decadence of late nineteenth- and early twentieth-century England, Yeats does not fit easily within models of literary modernism.

Angela Leighton's reading of Yeats's rhythm finds a 'dispute with time' in his metrical stilling of time. In 'The Wild Swans at Coole', she reads the rhythmical paddle of the swans' feet 'bring[ing] everything almost to a standstill' as a rhythm of 'continuity and quiet' that keeps 'the possibility of something unchanged in spite of what has changed'.[58] This apparent aspiration to Romantic notions of lyric temporality fits with the idea that Yeats was engaging 'younger' models of lyric (and this may be part of the reason why Yeats did not, in an age of modernism, use free verse).[59] Yet even Yeats's work is not as committed to a transcendent model of lyric as this suggests. As for Rossetti, an alternative presents itself in the form of embodied rhythm, what Yeats calls 'organic rhythms'.[60] The bodily experience of his metre is something conveyed in the importance of references to 'feet' and 'footsteps' throughout his poetry.[61] There is in Yeats, as in Rossetti, a 'felt', bodily and organic connection with the past that seems to offer an alternative to the temporal transcendence one can also find in his poetry. In other words, what if the rapid paddle of the swans' feet beneath the water which keeps the swan apparently motionless is indicative not only of the metrical hum of the poem that keeps 'the possibility of something unchanged in spite of what has changed', but of the underlying diachronic nature of the lyric that itself troubles its transcendent vision? This, I suggest, might be read in the same way as that iambic pentameter in Rossetti's 'For a Venetian Pastoral by Giorgione': as much a troubling of the still and silent moment as a depiction of it. Indeed, the dualities between movement and stillness, and power and grace, that swans symbolise seem to hold a particular significance for Yeats in his thinking about lyric temporality. Using the example of 'Leda and the Swan' (from Yeats's 1928 collection *The Tower*) in his essay 'Time in Literature', J. Hillis Miller describes time, for Yeats, not as a linear progressive movement creating a 'seamless continuum between past, present, and future', but rather as a 'flow punctuated rhythmically by violent instantaneous interruptions, as well as by innumerable smaller events, such as his poems often register'.[62]

There is, then, something of the Benjaminian messianic time in Yeats's work. This is much more characteristic, perhaps, of his more mature and better-known work, but we can see something of it in his poetry of the 1890s. In 'He Remembers Forgotten Beauty' (from *The Wind Among the Reeds*, 1899), for example, the act of embracing another – with the emphasis on the very physical experience of 'wrap[ping]' and 'press[ing]' – unleashes a wealth of images from a medieval world that flood into the present moment. Rather than enabling a connection with the stillness of eternity, physical touch channels dynamically a connection with a moment of beauty located within the perishable realm (one 'That has long faded from the world'):

> The jewelled crowns that kings have hurled
> In shadowy pools, when armies fled;
> The love-tales wrought with silken thread
> By dreaming ladies upon cloth
> That has made fat the murderous moth[63]

Not dissimilar to the 'felt' connection with the past that Rossetti presents in 'For an Allegorical Dance of Women', this poem depicts an encounter with a historical moment that intrudes with a physical immediacy upon the present. These are experiences of history that are gained through the body and that can be linked to Benjamin's language of 'touching' history in an exchange that is dynamic, in contrast to that desire for a static moment outside of time.

Recent studies of Rossetti's work tend to stress his negotiation of that newly opening fissure between high and mass culture, between art and mass production. As John Barclay has pointed out, 'For an Allegorical Dance of Women, by Andrea Mantegna' offers a discourse on the consumption of art objects that reflects on the position of art in a commodity culture. He finds in Rossetti's approach to the visual objects he contemplates both a complicity and a critique 'of the commercial culture from which he sought to separate himself'.[64] Jessica R. Feldman also notably reads Rossetti in relation to the commodity, this time the world of 'things' that Rossetti surrounded himself with. She argues that his 'revisionary art turned to the private, interiorized and feminine as a way of countering the pressures of modernization'.[65] In reading a formal, metrical and bodily response to a profound shift in the philosophical basis of the lyric genre, I suggest a very different way of exploring the 'modernity' of his work. However, the conception of time I have explored here is also crucially linked to the world of 'things' that scholars such as Barclay and Feldman invoke, and my next chapter will continue a Benjaminian approach to metre, time and lyric form, but with a particular emphasis on lyric in the age of the commodity. I turn next to the decades subsequent to Rossetti's 1870 *Poems*, and to the poetry of the period that perhaps most pressingly raises both the issue of lyric's resistance to the modern world and its relationship with the commodity: the work of the 'minor' Parnassians.

Notes

1. Rossetti, *Poems* (1870), p. 234.
2. Letter from D. G. Rossetti to William Michael Rossetti, 13 October 1869, *Correspondence* 4.II, p. 302.
3. Letter from D. G. Rossetti to William Michael Rossetti, 15 October 1869, *Correspondence* 4.II, p. 304.
4. Rossetti, *Poems* (1870), p. 259.
5. Fehl, 'The Hidden Genre', pp. 153–68.
6. Such nymphs may or may not be immortal themselves, but certainly represent a link between the temporal and eternal realms.
7. Letter from D. G. Rossetti to William Michael Rossetti, 8 October 1849, *Correspondence* I, p. 114.
8. Pater, *Three Major Texts*, pp. 162, 166.
9. Helsinger, 'Listening: Dante Gabriel Rossetti and the Persistence of Song', p. 411.
10. Hollander, 'The Poetics of *ekphrasis*', p. 215.

11. Hegel, *Aesthetics*, pp. 1011, 964.
12. Pater, *Three Major Texts*, p. 166.
13. Ibid., p. 165.
14. Rossetti, *Poems* (1870), p. 260.
15. Hegel, *Aesthetics*, p. 1012.
16. See Fontana, 'Dante Gabriel and the Interrogative Lyric', p. 265.
17. Freedman, *Profession of Taste*, p. 23.
18. Carolyn Austin suggests that the conundrum of that poem turns on the fact that 'neither urn nor vase exist outside of their respective poems', and so the work is ultimately not one of ekphrasis, of longing for the properties exhibited in a work of art outside the poem, but one of mastering the vase's 'atemporality, its mystery, its alienness to poetry' by showing it to be a poetic creation (Austin, 'Mastering the Ineffable', p. 171).
19. 'Sonnets for Pictures', *The Germ* 4 (30 April 1850), p. 181.
20. Helsinger, *Poetry and the Pre-Raphaelite Arts*, p. 27.
21. The final line retains the same meter as the 1850 copy – 'Silence of heat, and solemn poetry': /oo/o/o/oo – even though the words in the line have changed completely (*The Germ* 4 [30 April 1850], p. 181).
22. In a letter to his brother of 1869 discussing the relative merits of the old and new versions of this line, Rossetti comments that it 'gives only the momentary contact with the immortal which results from sensuous culmination and is always a half conscious element of it' (letter to William Michael Rossetti, 27 August 1869, *Correspondence* 4.II, p. 253).
23. Armstrong, 'D. G. Rossetti and Christina Rossetti as Sonnet Writers', pp. 462, 463.
24. Ibid., p. 463.
25. Horne, 'Thoughts Towards a Criticism of the Works of Dante Gabriel Rossetti', p. 101.
26. Rossetti, *Poems* (1870), p. 261.
27. See Martineau, *Andrea Mantegna*, p. 421.
28. Gowing, *Les Peintures du Louvre*, p. 146.
29. W. M. Rossetti, ed., *The Works of Dante Gabriel Rossetti*, p. 665 (note to p. 188).
30. McGann, *Textual Condition*, p. 151.
31. Ibid., p. 149.
32. In the surrounding poems in the section of 'Sonnets for Pictures' it is noticeable that, while Rossetti refrains from comment on the hair of chaste subjects such as Mary (In 'Mary's Girlhood'), the hair of more physically embodied female subjects is prominent: not only does he draw attention to Angelica's 'loose hair' ('For Ruggiero and Angelica, by Ingres'), but often poems about images of female subjects begin with comment on their hair: 'For The Wine of Circe, by Edward Burne Jones'; 'Mary Magdalene, at the door of Simon the Pharisee (for a drawing)'; and 'Cassandra (for a drawing)'. All references to Rossetti, *Poems* (1870), pp. 259–82.

33. Stein, *The Ritual of Interpretation*, p. 137.
34. Barclay, 'Consuming Artifacts', p. 7.
35. Maxwell, *Second Sight*, pp. 63–4
36. Ormond, 'Framing the Painting', n.p.; McGann, the Rossetti Archive, http://www.rossettiarchive.org/docs/38-1849.raw.html: 'Depending on how one takes that word, we will read the lines as saying that (a) the unheard music that governs the dance rang through Mantegna's body and resulted in this great picture, the execution of which involved him in an experience of profound conceptual awareness; (b) Mantegna embodied the unheard music that governs the dance in this picture, and when he himself saw what he had painted he experienced an understanding of ultimate meaning.'
37. Helsinger, *Poetry and the Pre-Raphaelite Arts*, p. 32.
38. *The Germ* 4 (30 April 1850), p. 181.
39. Tiedemann, 'Dialectics at a Standstill: Approaches to the Passagen-Werk', p. 942.
40. Benjamin, *Selected Writings* 1, p. 37.
41. Benjamin, *Arcades*, N7a, 3.
42. Benjamin, 'On the Concept of History', XIV, p. 395.
43. Benjamin, *Arcades*, N7, 7.
44. Tiedemann, 'Dialectics at a Standstill: Approaches to the Passagen-Werk', p. 935.
45. Benjamin, 'On the Concept of History', Addendum A, p. 397.
46. Benjamin, 'On the Concept of History', V, p. 390.
47. Tiedemann, 'Dialectics at a Standstill: Approaches to the Passagen-Werk', p. 945.
48. Benjamin, *Arcades*, N9a, 6.
49. Lawrence, 'Poetry of the Present', p. 183.
50. Yeats, 'Symbolism of Poetry', p. 22.
51. See Lenoski, 'The Symbolism of Rhythm in W. B. Yeats', p. 205.
52. Yeats, 'Symbolism of Poetry', p. 19.
53. Howarth, *British Poetry in the Age of Modernism*, pp. 8–9.
54. Yeats, 'Nationality and Literature', p. 269.
55. Ibid., p. 271.
56. Ibid., p. 273.
57. Ibid., p. 273.
58. Leighton, *On Form*, p. 162.
59. Linda Dowling has traced in detail the development of Yeats's poetic voice and its commitment to, alternatively, the Irish peasant voice and more highbrow literary or aristocratic idioms (*Language and Decadence*, pp. 244–84).
60. Yeats, 'Symbolism of Poetry', p. 22.
61. As Leighton remarks: 'It is interesting, then, to notice how often that poetry imagines feet'; 'The sound of feet, then, is everywhere audible in Yeats. They tread, measure, pace, plunge, wander, dance, pass' (Leighton, *On Form*, pp. 156, 158).

62. Miller, 'Time in Literature', p. 96.
63. Yeats, *Collected Poems*, pp. 69–70.
64. Barclay, 'Consuming Artifacts', p. 19.
65. Feldman, *Victorian Modernism*, p. 73.

Chapter 4

Parnassus and Commodity Time

The really embarrassing bodies of aestheticism and Decadence are
not those infected by syphilis or ravaged by opium use, but those
poetic forms that in their quaint archaisms were seen by the modern-
ists to offer a chintz-like pattern thoroughly out of tune with twenti-
eth-century notions of modernity. A generation of modernist writers
gave this poetry a lambasting from which it has still not recovered,
and I suggest that reading these forms is still a, if not *the*, major
problem in approaching late nineteenth-century poetry for today's
readers. T. E. Hulme's attack in 'A Lecture on Modern Poetry' is typi-
cal: 'they were not very fertile; they did not produce anything of great
importance; they confined themselves to repeating the same sonnet
time after time, their pupils were lost in a state of sterile feebleness'.[1]
In a retrospect on the early years of the twentieth century (written
in 1920), Ford Madox Hueffer writes that in 1914 the modernists
'plotted the blowing of Parnassus to the moon'.[2] In my introduc-
tion I noted the recent critical impetus that has sought to redeem the
relationship between late nineteenth-century poetry and modernity
under what one might think of as a modernist set of values. While
this might be possible through an emphasis primarily on content and
context, one is still left with the 'problem' of the poems' intricately
patterned forms. In this chapter I focus on English Parnassian poetry,
whose ornate medieval French forms, often archaic language and the
nostalgic, antiquated tropes of its subject matter appear to leave no
room for such a redemptive reading. English Parnassianism poses, in
its purest form, the question of how we should read the 'gem-like'
forms of the late nineteenth-century lyric (what de Banville calls the
'precious treasures');[3] and current scholarly answers to this question –
asserting the nostalgic twilight of Decadence, or the art for art's sake
emphasis on formal craft – do not do enough to explain the cultural
work of those forms in relation to modernity. In this chapter I argue

that even in the 1880s it was impossible to read the Parnassian vogue as simply a nostalgic retreat from the modern world. More specifically, I will ultimately be asking what kind of historicism or notion of time is attendant on the strict and compact rhythmical repetitions of Parnassian forms. If not a nostalgia for a simpler age and a more secure and orderly poetic response to it, what kind of engagement with medieval France do they offer?

While Dante Gabriel Rossetti's sonnets of 1870 are located at the start of what we think of as English 'Parnassianism' – and he did bring many of the strict *Parnasien* forms to prominence in England – he was opposed to the trend and was not concerned with fidelity to the original models.[4] Other, much less well-known writers became more direct champions of Parnassianism. LaPorte calls for more attention to be paid to genre in Victorian studies, suggesting that 'lending more attention to genre and to Victorian theory will free us from the habit of presenting little-known poets in primarily biographical terms', a benefit I hope to reap in this chapter.[5] Ultimately it was the likes of Andrew Lang, Robert Bridges, Graham R. Tomson, Austin Dobson, May Kendall and John Payne who popularised the use of such forms. Journal articles such as Gosse's 1887 'A Plea for Certain Exotic Forms of Verse', which promoted the crafted forms of the Parnassians, also made the case outside of verse. Théodore de Banville's *Petit traité de poésie française* (1872) formed a central text for the English Parnassians, stressing form over subject matter.[6]

While in British aestheticism, the 'art for art's sake' impetus did not lead to any simple rejection of spirituality, just as it was never a simple rejection of morality, it did push those poetic rationales to the extreme as if to explore their breaking point. I argue that the vogue for Parnassianism marks a testing of lyric in relation to modernity by pushing formal repetition to an almost parodic extent; in the strict and obsessive repetition of Parnassianism we might see something of a *reductio ad absurdum* of the association between the lyric genre and a quest for transcendent meaning. There is no doubt that the relevance of lyric to the modern age is, under all that medieval nostalgia, an important question for Parnassianism. Take, for example, John Payne's poems that address specifically the relationship of the English Parnassian poet to the modern age. In 'Ballad', Payne asks:

> What do we here who, with reverted eyes,
>   Turn back our longing from the modern air
> To the dim gold of long-evanished skies,
>   When other songs in other mouths were fair?[7]

Stanza three elaborates:

> Songs have we sung, and many melodies
>   Have from our lips had issue rich and rare;
> But never yet the conquering chant did rise,
>   That should ascend the very heaven's stair,
>   To rescue life from anguish and despair.
> Often and again, drunk with delight of lays,
>   'Lo!' have we cried, 'this is the golden one
> That shall deliver us!' – Alas! Hope's rays
> Die in the distance, and Life's sadness stays.
>   Why, but because our task is yet undone?

This stanza meditates on the hope for lyric transcendence and its repeated failure. Payne's 'Double Ballad. Of the Singers of the Time' ('double' because it has six stanzas rather than the usual three of the ballad form) further reflects on this theme, taking as its refrain, in italics, '*Songs and singers are out of date*'. The italics signal that this is the current charge against lyric with which the poet struggles: the potential irrelevance of lyric to modern society. Again a poem full of questions, the central problem posed here is that of the subject matter of modern poetry. Stanza two begins 'What shall we sing of?' Doubting whether the modern capitalist world offers suitable poetic subject matter ('Shall we sing of the sordid strife for gain'), the poem ends with the problem of writing lyric poetry in an age that deeply problematises poetry's transcendent aspirations:

> Song is a flower that will droop and wane,
>   If it have no heaven toward which to grow.
>   Faith and beauty are dead, I trow
> Nothing is left but fear and fate:
>   Men are weary of hope; and so
> *Song and singers are out of date*.[8]

Both of these poems appear in Gleeson White's 1887 anthology, *Ballades and Rondeaus, Chants Royal, Sestinas, Villanelles, &c.*, the key text explored in this chapter, and a major marker in the history of English Parnassianism. White's volume provides plenty of evidence to show that there was a strong awareness in Parnassian poetry of the importance of its transaction with modernity and, more specifically, an awareness of its position as out of kilter with the times in its turn to 'old-fashioned' forms. His introduction to the volume establishes Parnassian poetry as 'lyric' in no uncertain terms, beginning with an assertion of its origins in 'the intricate rhyming of the Troubadours' and their songs.[9] But even White posits the problem of the credibility of the modern lyric poet, naming 'our modern substitute for the troubadour – the popular novelist'.[10] The 'crisis' in lyric poetry is posed and framed in White's anthology in relation to Parnassianism, making it a crucial document for my study. Yet in this chapter I question whether these lyrics are as esoteric as they may at first appear. I will be suggesting something similar to what Walter Benjamin asserts of Baudelaire's works when he says that the social experiences reflected there are 'nowhere derived from the production process – least of all in its most advanced form, the industrial process – but all of them originated in it in extensive roundabout ways'.[11] It is such an indirect connection that I seek to reflect on in this chapter by thinking about the vogue for Parnassian forms in relation to modern modes of production and commodity form.

Work on Pre-Raphaelite art and literature, particularly, has addressed the tension between the return to old-fashioned 'craft' and the newly mechanised modes of production. William Morris's carefully fashioned furniture and hand-printed wallpapers are well known as representing a rejection of the newly alienated forms of mass production while being motivated by them – thus constituting a key response to industrialised modernity. Elizabeth Helsinger acknowledges that Pre-Raphaelite work was not simply a rejection of the sphere of mechanised and industrialised production, arguing that it 'sought to define itself as both like and unlike the manufactured objects whose primary and default status was the commodity among repeatable commodities'.[12] Yet ultimately she sees the Pre-Raphaelites as finding an alternative to the alienation of modern methods of production and consumption, and finds this a motivator for Rossetti's poetic production. Helsinger's book concludes that 'at a time when the future of poetry as a central cultural practice seemed seriously threatened', Morris and Rossetti found an 'affirmative recentering of poetry as a practice, one that stressed the value of pattern and repetition in lyric utterance as an alternative to the disintegrative and disruptive forces of modernism'.[13] Yet to recognise *Poems* as a response to nineteenth-century concerns about the relationship between the lyric and modernity must be to problematise this interpretation. The Rossetti who wrote 'The Woodspurge' was a poet not afraid to confront directly the failure of lyric's quest for transcendent meaning and order in the modern world.[14] British Parnassian poetry is similarly underestimated, and has been so by many scholars, if its emphasis on strict formal patterning is seen as merely part of a retreat from the chaos of modernity.[15] Payne's lyrics, already quoted, may be heavy-handed, but they make it clear that a retreat into the past is not the aim of, or even a possibility for, those taking part in the resurrection of fixed forms. I suggest that this poetry offers a much more knowing reflection on the nineteenth-century poetic tradition. There is no doubt that the relationship with a 'burgeoning materialism' is central to Parnassianism, but I think it is a more energising tension than critics admit.

Gleeson White's 1887 *Ballades and Rondeaus, Chants Royal, Sestinas, Villanelles, &c.* is taken here as a key statement of the fashion for fixed-form poetry in the late nineteenth century. The volume was compiled by White, but encouraged by the literary biographer and poet William Sharp (also poetically known as Fiona MacLeod), who was general editor of the series in which this volume appears, and it was planned as the definitive edition of English Parnassianism.[16] While it makes little sense, beyond the instances of a few devotees, to nominate individual poets as specifically 'Parnassian', there is undoubtedly a strong sense in the late nineteenth century that when a poet used these fixed forms he or she was working in relation to a Parnassian revival. The vogue was fond of cataloguing and mapping itself and its medieval French sources (as one can see in John Payne's 1878 efforts to produce the first complete unexpurgated English translation, in the original metres, of the poetical works of François Villon),[17] and it is not an accident that White's volume was, as he notes in his preface, intended to be a 'complete' edition of English Parnassian poems, even though the sheer quantity of material dictated that it would end up a 'selected' edition. White notes that the selected volume pulls poems from varied original contexts, representing works from around two hundred different authors. The metrical impetus signified by Parnassianism is best comprehended by looking at these poems in this edition rather than in their individual contexts, because the collective iteration is so important to its identity and to the engagement of individual writers with these forms. Charles LaPorte has noted that in Victorian criticism 'new generic territory is plotted by literary critics as quickly as British naturalists might name tropical flowers or shellfishes'.[18] The very format of White's large collected edition, divided as it is into discrete and precise formal categories, is evidence of this tendency, and the replication of forms that results from this urge for a totalising collection is central to my reading of the book.

The collector is, of course, a key motif of modernity for Benjamin; unlike the rag-picker who amasses the city's detritus for use and financial gain, the collector of beautiful objects 'made the glorification of things his concern'.[19] He reifies objects by amassing them: 'To him fell the task of Sisyphus which consisted of stripping things of their commodity character by means of his possession of them. But he conferred upon them only a fancier's value, rather than use-value.'[20] Parnassian poetry evokes something of the duality of the commodity and the reified art-object. In her sustained analysis of the significance of Dante Gabriel Rossetti's domestic bric-a-brac, Jessica Feldman writes: 'a conservative count of items in the catalogue reveals twenty-five cabinets, chests, and cupboards, and thirty-one glasses and mirrors'. Moreover, she notes that 'Most of these cabinets [. . .] have interior shelves and drawers enclosed by highly decorated folding doors in various arrangements: within cabinets are smaller enclosures, themselves holding discrete items, repetition within repetition.'[21] Parnassian poems are very like these cabinets, containing within each an infinity of repetitions: of previous sources, of translations, of set forms, of their own internal rhythms and rhymes, and of the very act of repetition itself. When amassed in a 'collection' such as White's, the similarity with Feldman's Victorian 'bric-a-brac' is even sharper. I suggest that this Victorian penchant for collecting objects, in a period of mass commodification, could not but have had an impact on the reading and reception of White's compendious 'collection' of poems. Indeed, White's volume was itself the product of a series that capitalised on the Victorian commodification of books, encouraging readers to see them as collectors' items.

To offer this context for reading Parnassian poetry may seem perverse. Looking through White's volume, there is no doubt that the turn to medieval French strict forms *was* in one sense, as many have it, a self-consciously nostalgic gesture: Parnassian poetry turns for inspiration to a pre-modern literature, and it embraces intricately patterned forms after such self-conscious poetic 'artifice' has been challenged and often rejected in favour of more socially outward-looking forms. Moreover, it invites us to see its turn to 'old-*fashioned*' form as a way of stressing the 'craft' of its 'gem-like' form in opposition to the cheap mass-produced goods of the industrial age. This is a recurring refrain, from Swinburne's 'A roundel is wrought./ Its jewel of music is carven of all or of aught' to Andrew Lang's meditation on 'Arnold's jewel-work' and Browning's 'iron style' smiting 'gold on his rude anvil'.[22] Yet simultaneously, and perhaps rather paradoxically, the experiments of Parnassianism seem to flirt knowingly with what looks very much like a commentary on art in the age of the machine. Tight patterns of rhythm and rhyme emphasise visual and sonic structures in a way that highlights not semantic meaning but a decorative, or perhaps mechanical, repetition. Helped by subject matter that is often entirely formulaic in its tropes, Parnassian poetry might be seen to have more of an affinity with the repeatable commodity of the machine age, and the incessant repetitious rhythm of the machine itself, than with the craftsman's tap of the hammer. Intriguingly, Ford Madox Hueffer made the association between Parnassianism and materialism in 1920, in the retrospective quoted earlier. Here he notes, 'We, as a Nation, are too inclined always to be commercial, and a Nation that becomes over-materialist in its views is destined to decay – or to obliteration', and he explicitly associates this with the 'stodginess and Academicism' of Parnassianism, which 'at the fount of a nation's intellect mean tenfold Materialism in the race that is content to endure them'.[23] This sits in direct opposition to claims for a Parnassian eschewal of a 'burgeoning materialism',[24] and offers something of the connection that I pursue here (albeit that I pursue it in much less damning terms).

Take, for example, 'Rondeau Redoublé' by Graham R. Tomson, a poem fairly typical of the more accomplished Parnassian works, for which I will give just the second stanza:

> The rose-wreaths fade, the viols are not gay,
>   That which seemed sweet doth passing bitter prove;
> So sweet *she* was, she will not say me nay
>   I will go hence and seek her, my old Love.[25]

This demonstrates the typical subject matter of the Parnassian poem, with motifs of lost love, 'rose-wreaths' and 'viols' (and later on, lutes): a timeless, although medieval-tinged, world of 'romance'. Yet although without any reference to the modern world, when read in the context of publication in this 1887 volume, is it possible for its insistent iambs and its alternating end-rhymes across twenty-eight lines to avoid putting the reader in mind of the rhythmical throb and clatter of the machines that had become such a dominant presence in urban life? This may seem a less fanciful assertion in light of the following villanelle by W. E. Henley:

> In the clatter of the train
>   Is a promise brisk and bright.
> I shall see my love again!
>
> I am tired and fagged and fain;
>   But I feel a still delight
> In the clatter of the train,

Hurry-hurrying on amain
   Through the moonshine thin and white –
I shall see my love again!

Many noisy miles remain;
   But a sympathetic sprite
In the clatter of the train

Hammers cheerful: – that the strain
   Once concluded and the fight,
I shall see my love again.

Yes, the overword is plain, –
   If it's trivial, if it's trite –
In the clatter of the train:
'I shall see my love again.'[26]

Parnassian poems such as this one that engage directly with the modern world in their content may be a small minority, and atypical in subject matter, but they reflect on the point, purpose and effect of Parnassianism in the modern world, and as such we can find in them a way of reading the vogue as a whole. The poem plays on the similarity of the steady clattering of the steam engine ('Hammers cheerful') with the rhyme and rhythmic momentum of the poem. The sound of the train evokes for the poet the pattern of the villanelle, singing of – as well as enabling on a practical level – the reunion with the poet's beloved. The use of trochaic metre is central here, but the villanelle's use of just two different end-rhymes is also crucial to emphasising the insistence and lack of modulation of the machine. The two refrains of the villanelle enable Henley to emphasise a juxtaposition of the age-old, timeless and tropic subject matter of Parnassianism ('I shall see my love again!') with the modern rhythms of the machine age ('In the clatter of the train'). In so doing, the poem draws into intriguing likeness the depersonalised tropes of Parnassianism with the depersonalised momentum of the machine: indeed, the final stanza admits the triviality or triteness of the 'overword' (meaning refrain). Parnassian poetry may return to the timeless and nostalgic themes of old, but its very rhythms and texture, when situated in the age of the machine, deracinate these themes and do not allow them to provide a retreat or haven from the modern world. No matter how it was intended, nineteenth-century Parnassianism conveys, one might say, a surface play of images and themes to the tune of the machine.

Brander Matthews, the American poet, also finds the rhythms of strict poetic form in the steam engine. His poem 'En Route' hears in the rhythm of the train a trochaic stress, as did Henley in the previous poem, but it also plays on the similarity between the string of coupled carriages of the train and the form of the 'Pantoum'. In this form an exact repetition of the second and fourth line of one four-line stanza is used as the first and third of the next, linking each of the fourteen stanzas to their neighbours. The poem abandons traditional Parnassian tropes in favour of a reflection on the niggles and irritations of rapid modern machine travel. To quote the first two stanzas:

> Here we are riding the rail,
>   Gliding from out of the station;
> Man though I am, I am pale,
>   Certain of heat and vexation.
>
> Gliding from out of the station,
>   Out from the city we thrust;
> Certain of heat and vexation,
>   Sure to be covered with dust.[27]

The very side-to-side swaying motion of the train is mirrored in the Pantoum form in which lines indented to the right in one stanza are repeated exactly but lined up to the left in the next. The irritations of human proximity with machine continue in subsequent stanzas: 'Heat and the dust – they are choking/ Clogging and filling my pores'. The human irritations within the train are also itemised as babies cry and old men snore. The text in quotation marks below gives the poet's voice as he fends off the vendors of the commodities which found a new captive market in the train carriage:

> Just by a wretched old hovel,
>   Small speck of dust in my eye.
> 'No! I don't want a new novel!'
>   – Babies beginning to cry. –
>
> Small speck of dust in my eye,
>   'I will not buy papers or candy!'
> – Babies beginning to cry –.
>   Oh, for a tomahawk handy!
>
> 'I will not buy papers or candy!'
>   Train boys deserve to be slain;
> Oh, for a tomahawk handy!
>   Oh, for the cool of the rain![28]

The 'train boys' selling the new novels, newspapers and sweets question the status of the strict-form poem not just in the age of the machine, but also in the age of the mass-produced commodity. The 'new novels' refers to so-called railway fiction – the cheap-to-buy and quick-to-write stories that had become possible as a result of several revolutions in print production. Implicitly, the poem raises the question of whether there is something that we might think of as an equivalent 'railway poetry': a poetry resulting from the same forces of modernity. Although not a medieval French form, the Pantoum was imported to England from France, where it was originally introduced from Malaysia by M. Ernest Fouinet.[29] While the title of the poem is a satirical gesture towards the love of all things apparently French by the English Parnassians, one wonders quite where this poem is 'en route' to. Where is this poetry of modernity taking the lyric? Fittingly enough for a poetry that I claim is 'deracinated' – and in line with the rules of the form – the poem ends exactly where it starts with the last stanza taking as its second and fourth line the third and first line (in that order) of the first stanza. The first line of the last stanza ('Ears are on edge at the rattle') suggests that the poetry of the age of the machine is no transcendent lyre-music. This is true not just of the very few, and unusual, 'Parnassian' poems, such as those above, which engage in content with the mechanisation of modernity; when piled up in Gleeson White's 300-page anthology, the very many nostalgic or timeless addresses to the beloved or to nature cannot help but evoke the rhythmical repetitions of the machine through their very forms, regardless of subject matter – and perhaps even more so when the subject matter is such generic, repetitious stuff. So what happens if we read the Parnassian impulse more generally as manifesting, at least at one level, the meeting point of art and the machine age, even if, or as, it might attempt to escape it?

In describing White's collection as a whole I earlier compared it to the culture of 'bric-a-brac' collection. To pursue this way of reading the Parnassian vogue is to find a dialogue not just with the methods of the machine, but with the resulting commodity culture and the new iterability of mass-produced goods. Theodor Adorno famously positioned late nineteenth-century aestheticism as the moment at which art simultaneously becomes autonomous and decontextualised, separate from everyday life, yet increasingly involved with commodity culture and consumerism. *L'art pour l'art* is to some extent 'the opposite of what it claims to be'.[30] The various critical narratives of aestheticism – most notably those by Freedman, Gagnier, Schaffer and Psomiades – recognise its ambivalent relationship with the marketplace, '[w]hether aestheticism is seen as a claim for the absolute autonomy of art, a critique of that claim, or the moment at which art abandons itself wholeheartedly to the world of commodities while pretending not to'.[31] The material volume of aestheticist poetry, more specifically, had to negotiate self-consciously its own double-sided nature of both commodity and aesthetic value. In Parnassian poetry, I suggest, we find a form of aestheticism that not only demonstrates awareness of its own resonance with the commodity, but, moreover, finds within it a new lyric aesthetic. In 'Double Ballade of the Nothingness of Things' W. E. Henley writes of the vanity of earthly things: 'What is the worth of all/ Your states supreme urbanities?'; 'Well might the sage exclaim:–/ 'O Vanity of Vanities!'[32] Yet to sing of the 'nothingness of things', particularly twice over, in the supreme age of 'things' might, at some level, highlight the 'thingness' of Parnassian poetry itself.

When reading White's *Ballades and Rondeaus, Chants Royal, Sestinas, Villanelles, &c.,* one cannot help but notice that even the piling up of poetic templates in the title signals more the mass production than the one-off. White's anthology, with its long section of seventy-three pages of Ballades by various authors, followed by shorter, but similarly collected, sections of 'Chants Royal', 'Kyrielles', 'Pantoums', 'Rondeaux Redoublés', 'Rondels', 'Rondeaus', 'The Sicillian octave', 'Roundels', 'Sestinas', 'Triolets', 'Villanelles', 'Virelai', 'Virelai Nouveau' and 'Burlesques, Etc', cannot help but leave the reader (after nearly 300 packed pages) with the sense of an industrial-scale operation. Indeed, even that final sub-heading, ending in an open-ended 'etcetera', signals the iterability of the art forms reproduced in the volume. In his long 'Introduction' White outlines the 'rules', or templates, for the various different forms represented, but he also gives a philological and historical context within medieval France for the song-origins of these lyric forms, and an overview of their adoption within English literature (acknowledging the Pantoum to be an anomaly in its Malay origins, but asserting that it has come to hold a place in the group of 'Parnassian' forms).[33] He quotes from various critics who write about the original French medieval forms, citing both those who admired them and those, like James Russell Lowell, who did not. From the latter, he quotes the following:

> Their poetry is purely lyric in its most narrow sense, that is, the expression of personal and momentary moods. To the fancy of the critics who take their cue from tradition, Provence is a morning sky of early summer, out of which innumerable larks rain a faint melody (the sweeter because

rather half divined than heard too distinctly) over an earth where the dew never dries and the flowers never fade. But when we open Raynouard it is like opening the door of an aviary. We are deafened and confused by a hundred minstrels singing the same song at once, and more than suspect the flowers they welcome are made of French cambric, spangled with dew-drops of prevaricating glass.[34]

The criticism here is the iteration not just of a repeated refrain within a poem, but of repetition between poems, with each poet working to the same template. Moreover, the meditations on the beauty of nature are seen as worked artifices of fabric and glass. This criticism already begins to make the connection between Parnassian poetry and consumer objects. Indeed, a poetry review of 1875 is not unusual in its presentation of Parnassianism as a 'fashion', currently in vogue, but whose time will pass ('already there are some signs that the tide is turning').[35] Although mocking Parnassianism, the terms in which this review does so are interesting. Quoting a Parnassian poem of medieval subject matter by Edmund Gosse, with the refrains 'peach and apple and apricot', 'apple and filbert and nectrine', the reviewer notes:

A lady to whom these stanzas were read naively inquired, in our hearing, whether their burden were intended to imitate the cry of an itinerant fruit-seller, or the *sotto voce* of a waiter handing round the dessert at a *table d'hôte*. Further comment would be surely superfluous.[36]

While intended as an indictment of the triteness and triviality of the poem, this comment makes that connection between the medieval refrains of Parnassianism and the modern-day urban and urbane world that is rather crucial to understanding the cultural space occupied by these poems – poems that, I suggest, at one level cannot but court such resonances. Indeed, when this reviewer terms Edmund Gosse's work a *'reductio ad adsurdum'* of the Parnassian fashion, he gestures towards something of the nature of Parnassianism as itself a *reductio* of the lyric genre.[37]

The context of mass reproducibility that revolutionised both the consumption and production of 'things' could not leave artworks unchanged. In Chapter 2 I suggested that Benjamin can be useful in giving us a way of thinking about the nature and temporality of lyric in relation to this late nineteenth-century revolution in commodity culture, and it is to such a reading that I will now turn. In 'The Work of Art in the Age of its Technological Reproducibility', Benjamin is of course writing about the visual image and the particular revolution in our consumption of it effected by the new technologies of film and photography, but the rise of Parnassianism as a literary vogue in the 1870s and 1880s should perhaps provoke some of the same questions and issues. British Parnassian poetry, granted, is mostly concerned with medieval, or timeless, subjects of love, nature, ladies and their lovers – in contrast to the new poetry of the city and Baudelaire's specifically modern experiences – but its apparent nostalgia might nonetheless signal a particular concern with modernity. In his essay, Benjamin writes: 'the technology of reproduction detaches the reproduced object from the sphere of tradition. By replicating the work many times over, it substitutes a mass existence for a unique existence.'[38] I have already observed that the proliferation of rondeaux, of ballades, or of Chant Royal from multiple print contexts that are brought together in Gleeson White's anthology give a sense of mass rather than unique existence; of the iterability of the commodity. Yet not only do they repeat over and over the same strict forms among themselves, and on a micro level echo that with a high degree of repetition of rhyme or refrain; they also take part in a broader cultural iteration. Many of the poems are translations from the original medieval French poems that inspired the fashion, enabling a printed (and therefore endlessly reproducible) version of earlier manuscript texts. Take, for example, Villon's 'Lay ou Plutost Rondeau', whose first line is 'Mort, j'appelle de ta rigeur'. This poem was translated by Dante Gabriel Rossetti, John Payne and Swinburne. The original and Payne's translation are included in White's anthology, whose introduction laments the impossibility of including Rossetti's translation and other 'noteworthy examples' ('for reasons beyond my control'), thereby situating the echoes within the anthology in relation to a continuing chain of repetitions that overspill its boundaries.[39] I will return to this particular series of poems in a later chapter. Here I simply want to draw attention to the fact that the interplay between these three late nineteenth-century versions (and their medieval source) compounds the repetition that already defines the 'Rondeau' form, and produces a sense of the endless repeatability of Parnassian templates over time and history as well as across culture.

Benjamin notes in Section II of his essay that text and image have different histories of reproduction. He acknowledges the 'enormous changes brought about in literature by movable type, the technological reproduction of writing', but his real concern is the photographic reproduction of the image that completely changed its consumption around 1900.[40] Yet English Parnassianism, with its play on endless iteration, perhaps marks something not of a newly reproducible text but of a new era of mass textual circulation and commodification. The richly bound, expensively crafted volumes of aestheticist poetry have been recognised to constitute a response to and rejection of mass forms of publication, yet it is telling that even these were often immediately pirated and reprinted by publishers such as the American Thomas B. Mosher, in cheap imitation editions. With the revolutions in print over the course of the nineteenth century, the poem had became a commodity among a newly proliferating mass of commodities. Parnassianism's play around sameness and difference resonates with a culture of mass reproduction which, in Benjaminian terms, 'extracts sameness even from what is unique'.[41] Each villanelle, each rondeau, while presenting a 'unique' poetic creation, cannot but be aware of simultaneously being a repetition of a form among many iterations – with the well-worn tropes of its subject matter exaggerating this effect. Susan Stewart's theorisation of lyric notes how,

> the temporal impossibility of any pure repetition is emphasized in lyric by the creation of redundancy on the level of the somatic, where sensual information offered to sight and sound appears to be the same. Lyric synesthesia emphasizes that figuration is accomplished by sound and that spatial interval makes sound intelligible and subject to measure. And because that measure does not fade as the semantic burden increases, any semantic transformation remains inseparable from the somatic.[42]

Parnassian poetry seems perfectly poised to interrogate the *aesthetic impossibility* of 'pure semantic repetition' in lyric in light of the *inevitability* of 'pure' repetition in both production and product in the age of mechanical reproduction.

We might usefully find here a textual commentary on what Benjamin calls the loss of 'aura', even though the printed literary text had long since lost the kind of object status that Benjamin posits for the image prior to the nineteenth century. Benjamin argues that aestheticism, or '*L'art pour 'l'art*' ('a theology of art') was a regressive response to the threat technologies of reproduction posed to art's place in the ritual of beauty, to its 'aura'.[43] If one locates Gleeson White's volume in relation to the loss of that strange interweaving of locatedness in space and time that defines 'aura' for Benjamin,[44] one might recognise it as something of a pastiche of physical locatedness in space and time. The delicate gilt cover design of swags and bows recalls something of earlier book design, perhaps in order to appeal to an established readership, while the title appears in a font more associated with the aesthetic movement (echoes of the past updated with a modern twist), and the name of the book series that appears on the first page ('The Canterbury Poets') is determinedly medieval in font. This is a volume that appears to respond to the threat of technologies of reproduction in the regressive way Benjamin attributes to aestheticism. Yet ironically, particularly when presented in this vast collection, the poetry riffs playfully on its lack of uniqueness. Parnassian poems, with their plethora of echoes of other sources (whether medieval French poems or more recent examples), delight in being one among many in a way that questions the value of 'authenticity' and questions the artwork's sense of itself as a unique production with a unique history in time and space. As Benjamin notes, the photograph deracinates and enables an image to appear at any time and in any place. The artwork, in an era of mass reproduction, is no longer a single important event located in time and space. The simple fact of its proliferation means that poetry is dislocated from time experienced as continuous, progressive, linear narrative.

So, this formal flirtation in Parnassian poetry with the newly pervasive context of mass production and reproduction brings with it new ways of thinking about time: in this case, what we might call the transformation of historical time by commodity form. In Chapter 2 I cited briefly the importance to poetry of the 'crisis of abundance', and noted that it was at the core of what Schleifer calls the 'second industrial revolution of the late nineteenth century', which produced 'a world seemingly filled with abundances of *things*'.[45] The reification of the commodity had the effect of cutting things off from their own history and so changed the experience of time.[46] What the new era of abundance effected was a 'transformation of economic analysis from that of need to that of desire'.[47] 'Concomitant with the vast multiplication of commodities in the last decades of the nineteenth century', notes Schleifer, 'were vast multiplications of knowledge – enormous increases in data within the remarkable creation and professionalization of intellectual disciplines in the emerging system of research universities in the West.'[48] The abundance of commodity was matched by a vast increase in historical data – including that pertaining to medieval French literature – and what Gleeson White describes as a 'flood' of modern Parnassian poetry in France.[49] If the endlessly repeatable, and repeated, Parnassian poetic form puts poetry in tune with the culture of commodity abundance and opens it up to the same problems of deracination from its own heritage of production in a particular time and place, then it might constitute a challenge to the experience of time as linear progression.

One response to this unprecedented abundance of 'things' was the upsurge in collecting, touched on earlier in this chapter: an attempt to organise and contain, to make comprehensible and manageable. This might include the kind of personal bric-a-brac collection noted above, and the major collections of the Great Exhibitions – but it might also include volumes such as White's and its response to the proliferation of Parnassian poems. It is in this context that we might understand the 'deracination' that interests me here. A collection of things that share a form or likeness tends to decontextualise them spatially and temporally; it might give them new meaning in relation to the other things with which they are grouped, but this is often achieved at the expense of recognition of their embodiment of a particular heritage of production. It is no coincidence that the 'totalisation' of the printed lyric (and particularly the production of printed editions that attempted a compilation and summation of lyric heritage) coincided with the rise of the museum. Yet it might be worth considering how individual poems, as well as collections such as White's, reflected this cultural moment. To suggest that the lyric poem itself had become something of a reflexive museum of lyric history is to suggest that it might exhibit qualities of both recognising while also decontextualising key elements of its heritage.

This might help explain the very strange negotiation that Parnassian poetry effects with history: how even as it roots itself in a backward gaze to its medieval French heritage, it does so in a manner that emphasises a deracination and simultaneity, rather than a historical embeddedness. In fact, the Parnassian revival took as a major theme forgetfulness and loss. The 'lost loves' of 'A Ballade of Old Sweethearts' by Richard Le Gallienne is typical, as is A. Mary F. Robinson's 'A Ballad of Lost Lovers', with its refrain 'Half-remembered and half-forgot'.[50] Emily Pfeiffer's 'Rondel' takes as its theme the status of the 'modern' world as 'unfit' for song, and Charles D. Bell writes in 'The Sweet, Sad Years' that:

> Like echo of an old refrain
> That long within the mind has lain,
>   I keep repeating o'er and o'er,
>   'Nothing can e'er the past restore,
> Nothing bring back the years again,
>   The sweet sad years!'[51]

More gnomically, 'Ballade of a Garden' by Arthur Reed Ropes takes as its refrain 'In the Garden of Grace whose name none knows', while A. Mary F. Robinson's 'A Ballad of Forgotten Tunes' sum-marises the theme in its title.[52] Oscar Wilde's address to 'Theocritus' offers simply the refrain 'Dost thou remember Sicily?'[53] This poem addressed to the founder of the pastoral tradition uses the villanelle form which is itself a descendant of the pastoral poem, in which 'villa' refers to the farmhouse. In this poem Wilde draws attention to the detachment of the modern lyric from any original pastoral poem, and to the distance between the invocations of the modern urban poet and those of Theocritus in Sicily in the third century BC. One of the poems included in White's final short section of 'Burlesques and Pasquinadas' is a parody of the Parnassian focus on what is lost. 'A Ballade of Ballade-Mongers (After the manner of Master Francois Villon of Paris)' begins:

> In *Ballades* things always contrive to get lost,
>   And Echo is constantly asking where
> Are last year's roses and last year's frost?
>   And where are the fashions we used to wear?
>   And what is a 'gentleman,' what is a 'player?'
> Irrelevant questions I like to ask:
>   Can you reap the *tret* as well as the *tare*?
> And who was the Man in the Iron Mask?

The poem ends in the envoi with the statement: 'If you do not remem-ber I don't much care/ Who was the Man in the Iron Mask'.[54]

Indeed, these themes aid a re-reading of the 'Rondeau Redoublé' by Graham R. Tomson that I introduced earlier as typical of the more accomplished Parnassian poems, demonstrating a predictable the-matic occupation with the questing suitor seeking his love. Tomson herself (born Rosamond Armytage) was well acquainted with the nature and power of the commodity. Not only did she write news-paper columns on fashion, but one of her own poem collections, *A Summer Night*, raises interesting questions about the tension between the repeatability of the commodity and the individuality of the aes-thetic object. This book was subject to one of John Lane's reissuings in 1895, when it had the original title page torn out and replaced by a new one, enabling it to masquerade as a new edition.[55] Unusually, however, the key change to the title page fronting the 'new' work was the author's name. Linda Hughes explores how Graham R. Tomson became Rosamund [*sic*] Marriott Watson when she left her husband Arthur Tomson to live with H. B. Marriott Watson in 1894.[56] The rondeau redoublé form, like many Parnassian forms, emphasises inevitable return. In this six-stanza form the four lines of the first stanza become, in turn, the final lines of the next four stanzas, while the last, sixth, stanza takes as its final refrain the first half of the very first line of the poem. Add to this just two end-rhymes throughout the whole 25-line poem and the poem folds in on itself like origami. Yet within this formal enactment of inevitable return the poem is about the lover who goes back to his 'old Love' only to find her gone: 'Here lies her lute – and here her slender glove/ [. . .] But her he saw not, vanished was his Love'.[57] While the form is destined to end with a re-finding of the very same words with which it began, the woman herself is not to be rediscovered. The secure repetition within the room of the stanza is contrasted with the absence of the woman in her own dwelling: 'The house is desolate that held my Love'. The disappearance of the woman, who by way of the abandoned lute is in some sense the lyric poet, presages perhaps both Armytage's disappearance from her marriage with Arthur Tomson and also the later desertion of the title page of *A Summer Night* by its original authorial signature. The opposition between inevitable formal return and the failure of rediscovery in the content also signals something of that loss of aura: the aesthetic loss that comes unexpectedly as a corollary of the insistent reproducibility of the printed text. Armytage herself was continuously deracinated from her own history by her changes of name and the immense upheaval from one family to the next that those changes represented. The forgetting at the heart of the return is a theme well exemplified by her poetic corpus.

Much more generally within the Parnassian oeuvre, these themes alert us to the fact that for a poetry so inspired by the past, it appears remarkably free-floating from it. I suggest that the loss expressed in Parnassian poetry in part represents the loss of contact with a continuous thread back into history – the loss experienced by a poetry that cannot retrace a trail of breadcrumbs back to the world of medieval France even though it constantly reiterates and translates its forms. In other words, the sheer proliferation of repetition of medieval French forms in the late nineteenth century produces something similar to the disruption of the hierarchy of past and present generated by commodity abundance. What results instead is a surface interplay of past and present on the same plane. May Probyn's 'Villanelle' combines a classic Parnassian form with a newly modern urban landscape to offer a poem about love and loss, and their echo in poetic metre.[58] The poem reflects something of the metrical historicism of Parnassianism itself. The two refrains ('In every sound, I think I hear her feet'; 'And still I say, "To-morrow we shall meet"') speak of a presence, or the echo of a presence, that becomes audible through the 'feet' of the poem, but also of a loss never quite recovered. The conflation of the human footsteps in the poem with poetic rhythm is invited because the poem only ever imagines the lost woman as glimpsed sonically in the montage of noises of the busy city – never through sight or smell. Even in stanza four, although the flowers are sweet, it is not their scent that is wafted over on the breeze but the 'breath of sound'. The beat of the clock, the beat of the heart and her 'tender undertone' all speak of a rhythmical haunting. The villanelle is a form, I suggest, whose repetitious echo is well placed to register this as a condition of modernity.

Reading the Parnassian vogue in relation to the historical shifts described in Chapter 2 means thinking about it in relation to a revolution in commodity abundance and, consequently, in relation to the attendant changes in the experience of temporality. The Parnassian revival might be rooted in a new knowledge of medieval French literature, but the reproduction of its forms gives rise not to a sense of linear connection with the past, but rather to a synchronic moment, forgotten but half-heard within the present through the insistent repetition of its rhythmical forms. Through the act of repetition within a field of many other repetitions, an aural echo emerges through the present as medieval forms and thematic tropes appear palimpsestically within new poems. This resonates more strongly with Benjamin's lyric temporality than with Hegel's: a dialectics of collision between past and present rather than a quest for an eternal time out of time. Crucially, in the poems discussed above the rhythmical echo of the past is more of an affect than a memory: the past is forgotten but felt through the rhythmical pulse of these medieval forms. The relationship with the past here is, as in Rossetti's 'For an Allegorical Dance of Women, by Andrea Mantegna', in key part a somatic one. Far from a retreat into lyric history, it might be seen to engage with concerns about our ability to reach back for continuity with the past, offering instead a kind of deracinated, simultaneous, but not historically transcendent iteration of the past.

Perhaps more directly than Rossetti's poetry, Gleeson White's anthology forces us to confront the untenability of reading the insistent assertion of refrain and repetition that characterise these fixed poetic forms as purely naïve or nostalgic linguistic gestures. That final section of White's anthology devoted to 'Burlesques, etc.' shows an acknowledgement within the vogue (and by its own authors) of its own outrageousness, and suggests that we read it with a sense of its own self-reflexivity. Susan Sontag defines 'camp' as a strategy of perception, rather than a strategy of creation.[59] Yet in his substantial analysis of *fin-de-siècle* camp, Dennis Denisoff offers evidence for camp being a 'conscious undertaking' in this period.[60] This is not to say that the use of Parnassian forms was always satirical; sometimes it was, but 'camp' signifies, as Denisoff understands, a serious strategy, but one self-reflexive enough to recognise its own participation in a discourse. Using the idea of camp to read aestheticist poetic form enables us to recognise in the Decadent lyric values we might think of as post-Victorian – and to do so in a way that is very recognisably connected with the contemporaneous strategies of the Dandy. I suggest here a reading of Decadent literature that finds within poetic *form* something of the vertiginous, yet serious, textual playfulness that Jonathan Freedman has argued characterises aestheticism as a whole. For Freedman, these features were largely rejected and evaded by high modernism, only to be recovered much later in the twentieth century.[61] Similarly, I suggest, at the level of form: modernism's rejection of the Parnassian forms of Decadence seems to express a horror at the notion of an audaciously performative self *and* the proliferation of mass commodities to which it was linked. *Vers libre* signalled the quest for a more 'authentic' metrical self: 'clothes made to order, rather than ready-made clothes', as T. E. Hulme revealingly put it – part of the search for 'the maximum of individual and personal expression'.[62] Yet if we, as readers, recognise and free ourselves from modernist prejudices around metrical 'authenticity', we can perhaps read with less embarrassment the knowing performativity of Parnassian poetry, and consider that its apparently quaint forms might be read as a moment at which lyric tradition was deliberately thrust against modernity to test each against the other.

The turn to free verse by the 'men of 1914' marked a reaction against Parnassian verse that still colours, or rather discolours, our reading of poetry of the later nineteenth century. Writers such as T. E. Hulme present the modernist turn to free verse as a key marker of poetic modernity: a rejection of a Romantic model of lyric transcendence, and an indication of an 'authenticity' triumphing over the artificial patterning of regular forms. Yet in this chapter I have suggested that, by the later decades of the nineteenth century, the obsessive repetition of Parnassian forms reads more like the boundless iterability of the commodity than the nightingale's transcendent flight, speaking more of the material age than of a universal spiritual realm. In short, we might consider them as much a poetic response to the conditions of cultural modernity as was free verse. Indeed, Parnassianism and free verse sometimes share similar sources of inspiration, with Villon and Cavalcanti being crucial for Ezra Pound's theorisation of melopoeia, as I will explore in a later chapter.[63] Jessica Feldman has written interestingly on why, in the later decades of the nineteenth century, we need to look for the politics of pattern, rather than just seeing the 'merely decorative':

> ornamentation gradually becomes in Victorian Modernism a celebration of surface as well as depth, of the local and the individual as well as the universal, and of the possibilities of addition, arrangement and rearrangement that challenge the fixities of essential or ideal form.[64]

In the case of Parnassian poetry, I have suggested that the intricate pattern of its form is tied ultimately to an economic backdrop and to the major changes that commodity abundance brought to society. Both modernism's *free* verse and Parnassianism's '*gem*-like' forms stress the centrality of lyric's negotiation with the economic structures that had changed the experience of modern life, describing its pricelessness in two very different ways, but both, interestingly, in relation to a language of commercial value.

Notes

1. Hulme, 'A Lecture on Modern Poetry', p. 61.
2. Hueffer, 'Thus to Revisit. . . (iii)', p. 212.
3. Quoted in White, 'Introduction' to *Ballades and Rondeaus*, p. xlvi.
4. Robinson, 'A Neglected Phase of the Aesthetic Movement', p. 744.
5. LaPorte, 'Post-Romantic Ideologies and Victorian Poetic Practice', p. 523.
6. On the influence of French texts, Ronald E. McFarland notes that the movement brought to late nineteenth-century poetry a 'much-needed "literary cosmopolitanism"' ('Victorian Villanelle', p. 125).
7. White, *Ballades and Rondeaus*, p. 87, lines 1–4.
8. Ibid., pp. 88–90.
9. Ibid., p. xxiii.
10. Ibid., p. xxvi.
11. Benjamin, *Charles Baudelaire*, p. 106.
12. Helsinger, *Poetry and the Pre-Raphaelite Arts*, p. 10.
13. Ibid., p. 257.
14. Catherine Maxwell reads this poem in ways that interrogate and usefully complicate such assertions of the poem's meaning in ' "Devious Symbols": Dante Gabriel Rossetti's Purgatorio', pp. 19–40.
15. See, for example, Weir, *Decadence and the Making of Modernism*, p. 34.

16. White, 'Introduction' to *Ballades and Rondeaus*, p. xli.
17. Robinson, 'A Neglected Phase of the Aesthetic Movement', p. 751.
18. LaPorte, 'Post-Romantic Ideologies and Victorian Poetic Practice', p. 523.
19. Benjamin, *Charles Baudelaire*, p. 168.
20. Ibid., p. 168.
21. Feldman, *Victorian Modernism*, p. 98.
22. A. C. Swinburne's 'The Roundel', and Andrew Lang's 'Ballade for the Laureate' (White, *Ballades and Rondeaus*, pp. 199, 30).
23. Hueffer, 'Thus to Revisit . . . (iii)', p. 214.
24. Weir, *Decadence and the Making of Modernism*, p. 34.
25. White, *Ballades and Rondeaus*, p. 131.
26. Ibid., p. 253.
27. Ibid., p. 124.
28. Ibid., p. 125.
29. Ibid., p. lvii.
30. Adorno, *Aesthetic Theory*, p. 339.
31. Schaffer and Psomiades, 'Introduction', in *Women and British Aestheticism*, p. 5. See also Freedman, *Professions of Taste*; Gagnier, *Idylls of the Marketplace*; and Schaffer, *The Forgotten Female Aesthetes*.
32. White, *Ballades and Rondeaus*, pp. 82–4.
33. Ibid., p. lvii.
34. White, *Ballades and Rondeaus*, p. xxvi; quoting James Russell Lowell, *My Study Windows* (1871).
35. Hewlett, 'Modern Ballads', p. 979.
36. Ibid., p. 978.
37. Ibid., p. 978.
38. Benjamin, 'The Work of Art in the Age of its Technological Reproducibility', p. 104 (section III).
39. White, *Ballades and Rondeaus*, p. lxxix (Villon's poem and Payne's translation are given on p. lxiv).
40. Benjamin, 'The Work of Art in the Age of its Technological Reproducibility', p. 102 (section II).
41. Ibid., p. 105 (section IV).
42. Stewart, 'Preface to a Lyric History', p. 216.
43. Benjamin, 'The Work of Art in the Age of its Technological Reproducibility', p. 106 (section V).
44. Ibid., p. 103 (section III): 'In even the most perfect reproduction, *one* thing is lacking: that here and now of the work of art – its unique existence in a particular place'.
45. Schleifer, *Modernism and Time*, p. 4.
46. Ibid., p. 4.
47. Ibid., p. 47.
48. Ibid., p. 4.
49. White, 'Introduction' to *Ballades and Rondeaus*, p. xxxii.

50. White, *Ballades and Rondeaus*, pp. 32, 90.
51. Ibid., pp. 147, 153.
52. Ibid., pp. 53, 52.
53. Ibid., p. 275.
54. Ibid., p. 289.
55. Hughes, 'A Woman on the Wilde Side', p. 123.
56. Ibid., p. 113.
57. White, *Ballades and Rondeaus*, p. 131.
58. Ibid., p. 263.
59. Sontag, 'Notes on "Camp"', pp. 56, 58, notes 10 and 18.
60. Denisoff, *Aestheticism and Sexual Parody*, p. 100. Denisoff links the emergence of camp to the emergence of a homosexual identity (p. 98).
61. See Freedman, *Professions of Taste*, pp. 25, 77.
62. Hulme, 'A Lecture on Modern Poetry', pp. 62, 63.
63. Victorian poets were crucial mediators of this material for modernism; as Robinson notes, 'by 1877 French verse, medieval and modern, was a good deal better known than in the 1860s, when only Swinburne and Arnold had stood between it and oblivion in England' ('A Neglected Phase', p. 748).
64. Feldman, *Victorian Modernism*, p. 120.

Part II: Space

Part II: Space

Chapter 5

Form and Transaction: Lyric Touch

Touch is the paradigm for the reciprocal open-endedness of all art forms involving the representation of persons [. . .] Touch, like dizziness is a threshold activity – subjectivity and objectivity come quite close to each other.

Susan Stewart, *Poetry and the Fate of the Senses*, pp. 168, 178

Space is not the setting (real or logical) in which things are arranged, but the means whereby the positing of things becomes possible. This means that instead of imagining it as a sort of ether in which all things float, or conceiving it abstractly as a characteristic that they have in common, we must think of it as the universal power enabling them to be connected.

Maurice Merleau-Ponty, *Phenomenology of Perception*, p. 243

Part II explores aspects of lyric's response to modernity that fall under a broad dimension of spatiality. This part responds to two central problems and enables a sensitivity to issues that go to the heart of Decadent and aestheticist poetics. The first is the charge that the fashion for strict verse forms represented an ossification in print of an aural lyric energy, producing a poetry that appealed primarily as spatial patterns on the page. Indeed, the accusations often levelled at aestheticist poetry referred to it killing the music of poetry in the complex rhetoric of those intricate strict verse forms, forms that are themselves more readily appreciated visually. The Scottish scholar John Campbell Shairp, for example, is typical of the more conservative condemnations of this verse (Shairp was elected Professor of Poetry at Oxford in 1877 and re-elected in 1882; he was in his sixties when he wrote a piece for the *Contemporary Review* on 'Aesthetic Poetry' in the 1880s). He discusses its primary appeal to the eye, a marker, for him, of a degrading of the imagination in contrast with poetry written for the ear: 'The ear is a more spiritual sense, and so we find the spiritual poet making sound, not sight, ally itself to the finest beauty.'[1] The second problem motivating this part is what was outlined in Chapter 1 as the threat of solipsism bequeathed by a Romantic idea of lyric introspection, and connected with the fate of lyric in an age of mass print circulation: a threat to the idea of lyric as a transaction (a reaching out across space) between a framing 'I' and 'you'. Of course, these two problems are connected: it was the perceived loss of lyric's aural energy in a heavily mediated print culture that threatened the idea of lyric as a mode of verbal address. As I described in Chapter 1, it is the problem of a body of lyric poetry that at some level no longer recognises itself as the printed mark of an aural impetus, but as a fully reconstituted print genre. In this part, I suggest that an alertness to modes that might best be described as stemming from an extended conception of tactility – touch, the somatic and phenomenological modes of encounter and spatial inhabitation – might enable an exploration of aestheticist poetry's response to both of these issues.

This chapter outlines a context for the poetic issues that drive the analysis, and it introduces the discourses of tactility and phenomenology that I use as my method. The following two chapters argue that the remaking of lyric in aestheticism involved finding a new lyric energy to replace the loss of the affiliation with the aural, and show how this was discovered not necessarily in a disembodied visuality, but often in a sense of embodiment and somatic encounter. I argue ultimately that this sense of embodiment was connected with a textual phenomenology: the strong presence of those fixed verse forms on the printed page. This part aims to complicate and enrich our understanding of the central relationship between lyric and the senses at this time. Touch is perhaps the sense least obviously associated with the lyric genre. Indeed, isn't poetry often written as a substitute for touch? Isn't the Petrarchan-style love lyric motivated by the beloved being out of one's grasp? So long as the lyric poem is primarily associated in commentators' minds with a disembodied ear or eye, the significance of the encounter with its textual body is likely to be underestimated. Yet in a period characterised by the increasing availability of both the textual and erotic body, one might consider the possibilities that the body offers to a conceptualisation of lyric. My starting point for the following two chapters is J. A. Symonds's statement that 'the best lyrics of the Victorian age are not made to be sung';[2] I ask what this means for thinking about Decadent poetry – and particularly for the significance of embodiment, and the body, to the life of the text on the page.

* * *

First, as an important preliminary, it is necessary to note that in aestheticist lyric poetry, concerns about the genre's 'totalisation' in print engendered two very different responses – one that pushes towards the body and the textual phenomenology that interests me here, and one that calls for a reinvigoration of poetry's oral/aural culture. After all, the Decadent lyric poetry I explore in Chapter 6 must be situated in relation to both the vogue for archaic, strict poetic forms whose complex patterning was best appreciated on the page *and* Oscar Wilde's declaration that 'We must return to the voice. That must be our test.'³ The period witnessed the popularity of both the French *ballade* and the English *ballad* that, with their very different formal politics, together represent one of the key schisms in poetics of the period.⁴ William Sharp recognised and tried to capitalise on this in the series he edited with Walter Scott, stirring up controversy with his *Romantic Ballads and Poems of Phantasy* of 1888 by stating in the 'Dedicatory Introduction' to the volume that 'we are all tired of pseudo-classicism, pseudo-medievalism, pseudo-aestheticism'.⁵ Yet he also published Gleeson White's key aestheticist statement of the Parnassian revival of medieval French forms – *Ballades and Rondeaus* – in the same series just the year before, a book in which White notes the series editor's encouragement for the volume.⁶

Linda Dowling has explored the significance of those calls for a return to the living voice at the end of the nineteenth century, which arise, she argues, in opposition to the 'dead language' of written English.⁷ Tracing philological debates of the period, Dowling sees the English ballad as a vernacular form opposed, at this time, to the flowery 'rhetoric' of Parnassianism; a 'neo-Wordsworthian demand' for a literary language based on the vernacular speaking voice rather than high poetic language; a return to poetry designed to please the ear rather than the eye.⁸ Most notably, perhaps, the ballad was championed by *fin-de-siècle* poets who identified with a Celtic folk tradition and with indigenous oral cultures.⁹ Not unrelated is the work of John Davidson – a writer frequently identified as the most 'modern' of the *fin-de-siècle* poets because he specifically sought a return to the language of the common man, satirising (in his 1891 *In a Music-Hall and Other Poems*) an aspiring Parnassian poet in 'From Grub Street'.¹⁰ Yet it is too easy to associate the simplicity of the spoken voice – whether Davidson's voice of the common urban man, or the folk-inspired ballad – with poetic modernity in opposition to a complex Parnassian medievalism (and this narrative is in danger of being overdetermined retrospectively as a result of T. S. Eliot's experiments with poetic vernaculars). After all, Wilde's call for a 'return' to the voice acknowledges a nostalgia that must be recognised; the print condition of the late nineteenth-century published lyric had become formative for its very conceptualisation.

To take one important example: the Rhymers' Club (to which Davidson belonged, although he did not contribute to either of their anthologies)[11] had strong, self-defined Celtic roots, and members tested their poetry by reading aloud to one another at their gatherings in the Cheshire Cheese pub.[12] Yet they also devoted considerable attention to the print appearance of their poetry collections and its textual phenomenology.[13] This should help clarify that my interest in the phenomenology of lyric in print in this period is not a claim for a decline in the reading of poetry out loud – indeed, my claims do not touch upon any of the many popular vocal activities around poetry (many of which depended on printed texts).[14] Rather, my claims are for the significance of an engagement with poetry through a printed text, whatever the poet or his or her audience then did with the poem vocally. This is the significance of J. A. Symonds's claims quoted above; for Symonds, although the lyric poem could, of course, still be vocalised, it could no longer be defined through some latent generic resonance with song as its imagined mode of production and transmission (as he thinks it was for the Elizabethans, however much they may have circulated poems in textual form).

To think about the significance of a phenomenology of print in Decadent poetry is not, then, to deny the ongoing significance of voice and the aural to lyric of the period, but rather to recognise a different and perhaps more direct negotiation of its position in late nineteenth-century print culture. So my interest is not in a nostalgic turn to song or in a modernising vernacular, but in the ways in which aestheticist poetry exploited the possibilities of a perceived loss of implicit aurality/orality and rethought the potentiality of lyric within the contemporary mass-print medium. My interest is, in other words, in the phenomenological potential of what had been seen by John Campbell Shairp and others as the ossification of Decadent lyric on the page. It is worth noting at the outset that while Walter Pater's well-known observation of the aspiration of all art 'towards the condition of music' may lead him to privilege lyric as the most 'poetic' of verse forms, this is no call for a return to cultures of orality and song. Rather, what Pater has in mind here is a more abstract observation about the way lyric poetry makes meaning: 'lyric poetry, precisely because in it we are least able to detach the matter from the form, without a deduction of something from that matter itself, is, at least artistically, the highest and most complete form of poetry'.[15] Pater groups together lyric poetry and painting as the 'ideal examples' of the welding of content and form, in which 'the material or subject no longer strikes the intellect only; nor the form, the eye or the ear only; but form and matter, in their union or identity, present one single effect'.[16] Lyric poetry features so prominently in this analogy with music because of the importance of the *formal embodiment* of its meaning, and it is the importance of an embodied lyric within print publication that is my focus here.

*   *   *

The concerns in this part are motivated particularly by the crisis in lyric 'transaction' that this totalisation in print is thought to have generated. If the lyric is no longer made to be sung, then what happens to lyric address? The solipsistic turn within modern literature is usually charted as a response to 'the poets' growing sense of alienation from the urban, materialist world and the retreat to the solitary world of the mind'.[17] This is something J. A. Symonds described at first hand, as discussed in Chapter 1. Walter Pater articulates particularly eloquently an anxiety about the isolating bounds of individual subjectivity that haunted aestheticism,[18] and it is no accident that Pater's own response to this problem was in many ways a phenomenological one. Pater may have stated the problem of subjectivity (of each of us being enclosed within that 'thick wall of personality'), but he also indicated that the way out of this dangerous solipsism was sensitivity to bodily sensation, through sensory impressions of things.[19] However, such anxieties were not just thematic concerns for lyric poetry: they challenged the genre's core identity. A pervasive and persuasive narrative of lyric history sees poetry as progressively more and more isolated from its addressee – a process that has been seen to culminate in the nineteenth century.[20] In this critical narrative, classical lyric from ancient Greece is held up as an archetypal lyric mode, based around direct aural address to a real audience, while modern lyric poetry is defined by the loss of this potential, haunted by solipsism. This idea of modern lyric alienation is well demonstrated in W. R. Johnson's *The Idea of Lyric*, where he argues that the modern lyric genre is defined by, and profoundly troubled by, this sense of loss of connection with an audience.[21] He explores the consequences of this lyric 'isolation', arguing that poetry 'tends to be bereft of its singers and its audiences' in a way that haunted 'all modern lyric'.[22] Romantic apostrophe is, in Jonathan Culler's earlier influential work, a gesture definitive of the modern lyric, as 'an act of radical interiorization and solipsism'.[23]

It is important to recognise that such scholarly narratives tend to have embedded within them two different critical claims. One relates to what we might think of as the external lyric transaction, which, so the story goes, finds a progression from the direct presence of an audience listening to an aural song, through textual and manuscript circulation of lyric in various forms to increasingly larger and therefore less 'immediate' audiences, to, finally, in the nineteenth century, an established large-scale anonymous circulation in mass print. Alongside this, and reflecting it, there is another claim, this time about the internal lyric transaction, which is seen to progress from a more natural direct invocation of the lyric addressee ('you') towards a tendency, within nineteenth-century poetry, towards apostrophe and a failure of direct invocation of a lyric other.[24] In lyric there are always many nuanced and interesting relations between these two transactions, but they are nonetheless, in basic ways, distinct. They become aligned because the 'I/you' negotiation of the poem is in an important sense a reflection on the nature of all self/other relationships – the lyric is a reflection on the self in a rhetorical transaction. (It is for this reason that I think we do not need to agree on whether the primary identification for the audience of lyric is with the speaker or the lyric addressee.)[25]

Indeed, this distinction is crucial to reading John Stuart Mill's two essays on poetry, later published as the bipartite 'Thoughts on Poetry and its Varieties', which have come to be taken as an iconic statement of the isolation of modern poetry and its failure to connect with the modern world. Mill's formulation of poetry as a 'soliloquy' staged for the reader on 'hot-pressed paper' (in opposition to eloquence, which 'is feeling pouring itself forth to other minds, courting their sympathy, or endeavouring to influence their belief, or move them to passion or to action') is crucial evidence for a critical narrative in which the lyric poem is seen as undergoing a crisis of interiorisation in the nineteenth century.[26] Mill's claim that the lyric is spoken as a soliloquy entails two ideas. The first is that it is a musing to the self with no internal audience directly present. The second is about the actual audience of the soliloquy: not an addressee, but the third party who 'overhears' (rather than hearing directly) the musing of the character to him or herself. Crucially, Mill is identifying the disappearance of a projected auditor within the lyric as something attendant on the changes within culture that led to the modern poem being circulated in a mass-print format that distances the writer from the reader. The falling away of the internal addressee is a reaction to the alienation of the poet who writes with little direct contact with the 'external' audience of their work.

This narrative of poetry's introspection and alienation in modernity has been challenged by critics who suggest that too much weight has been placed on Mill's essay. For example, Matthew Bevis's study of nineteenth-century literature and eloquence has questioned Mill's core distinction on the basis that 'the most vibrant poetic development of the age – the dramatic monologue – blurred the dividing lines between poetry and eloquence further by creating an internalized speaker–auditor relationship within the form itself'.[27] It is, of course, true that much poetry of the period did not fit into the mould set out by Mill in this essay. However, in spite of his talk of 'poetry', Mill makes it clear that he is primarily writing about lyric poetry: 'Lyric poetry, as it was the earliest kind, is also, if the view we are now taking of poetry be correct, more eminently and peculiarly poetry than any other.'[28] And while contemporaneous reviewers questioned Mill's insistence on lyric's dominance within the field of poetry as a whole (linking this bias to his political affiliation with individuality), they by and large accept his characterisation of the aspirations, if not the realities, of lyric poetry.[29] So, the popularity of the dramatic–lyric hybrid forms invoked by Bevis might more usually be seen to mark a recognition of the problems presented by the ambitions of lyric, as it was coming to be characterised by Mill and others. The dramatic monologue *represented* the frame of the lyric transaction itself so that the poetic 'I' and 'you' became not just pronominal invocations framing the poetic transaction but implied characters within it. In this sense, the dramatic monologue offers as a solution to the crisis of lyric solipsism something closer to a representation of a functional transaction between characters.[30] It is, after all, significant that Robert Browning considers his 'dramatic lyrics' as hybrid in their generic identity, and certainly by the late nineteenth century reviewers received them as an alternative to a 'pure' lyric.[31]

A more sustained challenge to the narrative of lyric isolation in the period is Virginia Jackson's important study of Emily Dickinson. Jackson shows how, in fact, much of what is presented in anthologies as Dickinson's 'lyric' is taken originally from manuscript contexts that demonstrate very specific acts of textual communication; when presented independently in print it is 'lyricized' or 'abstracted', and the poems are 'revoked from their scenes or referents'.[32] The theorisation of lyric that results from reading these texts in isolated print formats inevitably ignores, Jackson insists, the many forms and methods of address for poetry in the nineteenth century that existed outside print culture. Indeed, Dickinson, with her hand-made fascicle editions of her poems, *is* a case to point. However, as I indicated in my introduction, my interest in this book is in writers who wrote for publication in print, and who shaped their work in light of the aesthetic and conceptual problems and possibilities that this context offered for lyric poetry at this time. Characterisations of lyric within the period based on printed sources cannot help but have an effect on the production of lyric when the authors are, unlike Dickinson, writing for print and with an awareness of the print circulation and review of their material. I am interested in the operations of lyric within that feedback loop.

Of course, modern lyric poetry written for print circulation did not abandon altogether the direct address to 'you', and in his book *Poetry's Touch*, William Waters takes as his topic an analysis of such address, thinking about what this might mean and how that transaction might operate in print transmission.[33] More recently, Emily Harrington's study, *Second Person Singular*, has argued that women's poetry has played a particular role in reflecting on the terms of lyric relationships. Returning to the nineteenth-century association between the women poet and silence, Harrington argues that the woman poet's awkward positioning within a lyric dialectic sometimes gives rise to an interest in 'a feminine lyric poetics' about relationality and duality.[34] Yet the poetry that interests me here, particularly, is that least able to invoke a direct addressee, and that most beset by worries about lyric isolation. Even in this work (indeed, particularly here), I suggest that we see poets and poems finding rhetorical strategies to re-make that connection in new ways. When Pater represents the self in glorious subjective isolation, he poses a problem that confronted lyric particularly acutely because of the genre's myth of origins in a 'rhetorical transaction'.[35] It is with this in mind that I offer an idea of a type of transaction that we might find inscribed textually in the late Victorian printed lyric that grapples with the problem of alienation. What is explored in this part of the book, through an appeal to phenomenology, is ultimately the potential for somatic lyric connection. I argue that the focal poetry offers a fresh emphasis on how lyric might figure a somatic transaction between the subject and the world. Such strategies, I suggest, refit the lyric 'transaction' at a time when a direct addressee might have become problematic. In a poetry greatly aware of the body, the lyric 'other' might be rediscovered not as an addressee, or as a separate character within the drama of the poem (as in the dramatic monologue), but as a necessary part of the poetic 'I': something felt as an extension of the self. While the mid-century interest in dramatic and hybrid poetic forms responded to the problems of lyric solipsism by turning away from lyric, the responses identified here from the later part of the century might be seen to seek new possibilities from within the print-lyric genre.

*   *   *

Discourses of embodiment and an extended tactile sense have been recognised as relevant to twentieth-century literature for some years now, resulting in works such as Santanu Das's *Touch and Intimacy in First World War Literature* and Abbie Garrington's *Haptic Modernism: Touch and the Tactile in Modernist Literature*. Yet according to the *OED* citations, the word 'haptic' was first used with this meaning in the late nineteenth century, and the previous generation witnessed the development of an array of new languages of touch. Indeed, Garrington's own study emphasises particularly the significance of the later nineteenth century as a key moment in the formation of the haptic discourses that she finds in modernist literature, citing the influence of art historians such as Alois Riegl (whose influence was established in the 1880s and 1890s) and Adolf Hildebrand (whose *The Problem of Form in Painting and Sculpture* was published in 1893).[36]

The growth of tactile aesthetics towards the end of the century is hardly surprising given the importance of a scientific discourse on touch that had developed much earlier in the nineteenth century. Charles Bell's 1833 treatise, *The Hand: Its Mechanism and Vital Endowments as Evincing Design*, was an important reflection on the taxonomy and significance of touch, and certainly in the middle of the century there was a strong sense of the relative importance of touch within a hierarchy of the senses. The year 1855 saw the publication of both Herbert Spencer's *The Principles of Psychology*, which subordinated all other senses to touch, and Alexander Bain's *The Senses and the Intellect*, which believed touch to be a more direct source of knowledge of the physical world than the other senses. The belief that touch was the most primitive of the senses was also the source of its primacy for these thinkers, and its location as the origin of knowledge.[37] Roger Smith's work on the history of psychology and science has charted an intense interest in the 'special character' of touch in the nineteenth century.[38] Smith details how mid-nineteenth-century thinkers were particularly invested in an extended sense of touch which foregrounded the awareness of the body in space and a kinaesthetic sense, making it 'the sense most directly important to knowledge of the physical world'.[39] Drawing on James Mill and J. S. Mill as well as Bain and Spencer, Smith describes how the 'phenomenal quality' of the movement of the body through space was, for many in the mid-nineteenth century, 'the basis of all we know about the world and our place in it'.[40] Smith connects this tradition of thought quite explicitly to the work of Maurice Merleau-Ponty, to whom I appeal particularly in this part of this book.[41] Doing so enables me here, as in Parts I and III, to read aestheticist poetry in light of responses to the experiences of modernity that did not emerge fully theorised until the early twentieth century, but that are wholly relevant to the period. One might, I think, see in poetry the possibility of an imaginative articulation of ideas not yet formally theorised or represented in other discourses. To only ever allow poetry to be a reflection of that which is already known in other discourses is surely to underestimate its creative ability, and to misunderstand its significance in culture and society.

Rooted in nineteenth-century science and psychology, phenomenology was also a product of the philosophical shifts across the nineteenth century that are at the heart of the development of lyric that I trace in this book. While not emerging fully theorised and with its current philosophical meaning until the first half of the twentieth century, it is more than simply a useful tool for the exploration of late nineteenth-century literature. Phenomenology is a philosophical response to some of the same problems and experiences of modernity with which lyric poetry itself was grappling. Phenomenology recognises, crucially, a point of fundamental contact with the world that is pre-reflective and happens prior to any formulation in language: once this experience is narrated in language it is distorted and incomplete, codified in a signifying system that cannot capture the experience as it was initially felt. To return us to the experience of direct contact with the world, untarnished by interpretation, it prioritises the experience of our environment gained directly through our bodies.[42] For Merleau-Ponty, our experience of the world is primarily one of physical locatedness:

> In so far as I have a body through which I act in the world, space and time are not, for me, a collection of adjacent points nor are they a limitless number of relations synthesized by any consciousness, and into which it draws my body. I am not in space and time, nor do I conceive space and time; I belong to them, my body combines with them and includes them.[43]

The primary experience here is not of *reflection* on physical locatedness but the '*feel*' of it: a fundamentally embodied, rather than reflective, experience of the world. For Merleau-Ponty, thought (or meaning) and doing (or being) are not separated in respective internal and external realms. Rather, those aspects usually associated with our internality are in fact constituted by our existence as participants in an external world. 'Consciousness is in the first place not a matter of "I think that" but of "I can"': 'Consciousness is being towards the thing through the intermediary of the body.'[44] In *The Phenomenology of Perception*, Merleau-Ponty describes the body as a framework of intentionality; it is through the body that we interact with the world; it is the point at which sensations are translated, but, more than this, it is also something that maps the world spatially for us. This conception of our 'being in the world' opens new avenues for reflection on the operation of lyric, and particularly lyric form, in the later decades of the nineteenth century. Although he did not write a phenomenological aesthetics, Merleau-Ponty offers a particularly rich body of work through which to think about poetry.

Phenomenological modes of experience are characteristic of aestheticist poetry, which often aims to render the poem as much a record of a sensory encounter as a reflection on that experience. Aestheticist poetry's interest in recording an immediate impression, and in expressing an experience of the world that exists prior to its formulation in conventional structures (whether those of society, religion or commerce, or even language itself), takes part in the same philosophical trajectory from which phenomenology was emerging. For this reason a phenomenological discourse is well suited to describing its aims.[45] Indeed, much philosophical work that was more closely contemporaneous to the poetry I study (for example, by F. H. Bradley, William James and Henri Bergson, among others) shares a concern with the problem of registering immediate experience. Poets and philosophers of the period both sought to reflect experience itself rather than the interpretative structures that we use to make that experience intelligible. A phenomenological method might enable us to see how the quest for a 'pure' lyric impulse, outlined in Chapter 1, might engage profoundly with philosophical modernity at the same time as it appears most explicitly to meditate on its own irrelevance to contemporary society. In short, I suggest that we might see a productive resonance between the operations of aestheticist poetry and a philosophy of phenomenology that grew out of currents of thought developing within the period.

For the phenomenologists, the key sense was one that might best be described as an extended sense of touch, or an awareness of the body in space (that foundational experience of embodiment described above) gained through the skin. This sensation is one fundamental to and enmeshed with other senses. In his essay 'The Intertwining – The Chiasm', Merleau-Ponty provides something of a taxonomy of touch, distinguishing 'three dimensions which overlap but are distinct':

> a touching of the sleek and of the rough, a touching of the things – a passive sentiment of the body and of its space – and finally a veritable touching of the touch, when my right hand touches my left hand while it is palpating the things, where the 'touching subject' passes over to the rank of the touched, descends into the things, such that the touch is formed in the midst of the world and as it were in the things.[46]

The first ('a touching of the sleek and of the rough') is the idea of touch as an act within the world: a transaction, a touching of something. The second ('a touching of the things – a passive sentiment of the body and of its space') is the idea of bearing the 'impress' of something: of being touched. The third (a touching of the touch) is the key for Merleau-Ponty to our understanding of ourselves as subjects in a reciprocal relationship with the world outside of our bodies – and it is with this idea that Chapter 7 culminates. Each of these types of touch is relevant to my investigation over the course of the following two chapters, and will be used to think about the ways in which late nineteenth-century poetry engages with the problems of lyric modernity. Crucially, drawing on phenomenological ideas enables me to think about hapticity in relation to literary form as well as content – something not yet much in evidence in the burgeoning field of modernist haptic studies.

While Part I of this study situated aestheticist poetry within the broad parameters of a shift, across the century, from Hegelian to Benjaminian theories of time, Part II frames it within J. S. Mill's reflection on lyric isolation, the aural and disembodiment, on the one side (chronologically speaking), and, on the other, with the development of new phenomenological modes of connection and embodied vision. Chapter 6 explores how our critical narrative of lyric's shift of affiliation from music to image over the end of the nineteenth century tends to miss something of the significance to the genre of the corporeal and the tactile within Decadent poetry. The older association of lyric with aurality is, I suggest, contested in ways that do not simply resolve into (or anticipate) modernist theories of the image. Recognising Decadent poetry's interest in the potential for the affective and erotic body to provide a phenomenological mode of engagement with the world, I consider the significance of this mode for the operations of lyric and of the textual body. Building on this, Chapter 7 moves towards a reconsideration of the fate of the lyric addressee within poetry's own meditation on its 'totalisation' in print. Again establishing the historical relevance of phenomenological ways of reading, I suggest that the lost lyric 'I/you' transaction was at times rediscovered through the phenomenology of the printed page. In a genre redefined by a culture of mass print and by its life on the page, a lyric 'you' might be invoked more through the spatial phenomenology of textual forms on the page than through the rhetorical conventions of vocal address.

Notes

1. Shairp, 'Aesthetic Poetry', pp. 20, 21.
2. Symonds, 'A Comparison', pp. 67–9.
3. Wilde, 'The Critic as Artist', p. 351.
4. The French *ballade* being a fixed-form lyric, while the English 'ballad' was a narrative poem (with strong associations with folk song), consisting of simple stanzas, often with a refrain.
5. Sharp, *Romantic Ballads and Poems of Phantasy*, p. vii.
6. White, *Ballades and Rondeaus*, p. xli.
7. Dowling, *Language and Decadence*, p. xv.
8. Ibid., pp. 181–4.
9. See Maureen McLane on the importance of Scotland to Romantic minstrelsy (*Balladeering, Minstrelsy, and the Making of British Romantic Poetry*, Chapter 3).
10. Davidson, *In a Music-Hall*, pp. 25–7.
11. See Harper and Beckson, 'Victor Plarr on "The Rhymers' Club"', p. 380; and Hughes, 'Ironizing Prosody', passim.
12. Harper and Beckson, 'Victor Plarr on "The Rhymers' Club"', pp. 379–80.
13. See Nicholas Frankel's astute analysis: ' "A Wreath for the Brows of Time": The Books of the Rhymers' Club as Material Texts', pp. 131–57.
14. Catherine Robson's analysis of the culture of recitation in schools, for example, touches on the importance of books of poetry published, and sold in large numbers, specifically for this purpose (*Heart Beats*, p. 48 and passim).
15. Pater, 'School of Giorgione', in *Three Major Texts*, pp. 156, 157.
16. Ibid., p. 158.
17. Lindley, *Lyric*, p. 69.

18. See the 'Conclusion' to *The Renaissance*, in *Three Major Texts*, p. 218.

19. Pater, 'Conclusion' to *The Renaissance*, in *Three Major Texts*, p. 218

20. John Henriksen writes of apostrophe in Romantic poetry as 'somewhere between address and non-address: Romantic apostrophe affirms the convention of poetic speaking-to-someone-else, even as it empties that same convention' ('Poems as Song: The Role of the Lyric Audience', p. 80).

21. Johnson, *The Idea of Lyric*, pp. 8–10.

22. Ibid., pp. 10, 19.

23. Culler, *The Pursuit of Signs*, p. 162.

24. See Waters, *Poetry's Touch*, p. 9.

25. Helen Vendler claims that identification of the reader with the poetic speaker is the norm ('the lyric is a script written for performance by the reader'), while Bonnie Costello (writing about John Ashbery) points out that 'it is difficult, when reading an unspecified second person pronoun, not to take it personally first, however else we might go on to take it' (Vendler, *The Art of Shakespeare's Sonnets*, p. xl; Costello, 'John Ashbery and the Idea of the Reader', p. 495).

26. Mill, 'What is Poetry', pp. 64–5.

27. Bevis, *The Art of Eloquence*, p. 146.

28. Mill, 'The Two Kinds of Poetry', p. 719.

29. See, for example, an anonymous review (Anonymous, 'Art. IX. – John Stuart Mill', pp. 495–6), where it is noted of his prizing of introspection and isolation in poetry that 'The excessive appreciation of "individuality" which was noticed in a recent review of our author's treatise on "Liberty," belongs to the same general tendency.'

30. Brewster notes: 'While standard accounts of modern lyric emphasise its progressive retreat from the world, it can be argued that, in fact, lyric in the nineteenth century becomes increasingly anxious to speak to others' (*Lyric*, p. 84). I suggest these might be two sides of the same coin.

31. See, for example, Anonymous, 'Art. VIII. –1 The Poetical Works of Robert Browning', p. 483.

32. Jackson, *Dickinson's Misery*, pp. 159, 3 and passim.

33. Waters, *Poetry's Touch*, passim.

34. Harrington, *Second Person Singular*, p. 12.

35. See Culler, 'Why Lyric?', p. 205; see Pater's 'Conclusion' to *The Renaissance*, in *Three Major Texts*, p. 218.

36. Garrington, *Haptic Modernism*, pp. 22–3.

37. Spencer, *The Principles of Psychology*, passim; Bain, *The Senses and the Intellect*, passim.

38. Smith, *Free Will and the Human Sciences in Britain*, p. 88.

39. Ibid., p. 88.

40. Ibid., p. 90.

41. See ibid., pp. 88, 170.

42. Importantly, this goal of describing the 'things themselves' is not an attempt at *faux* objectivity that thinks we can, through this method,

invoke a common objective world and bypass subjective processes. Phenomenologists acknowledge fully that their study of the experience of the world involves examining 'those intentional acts which are not merely cognitive but also involve caring, desiring, and manipulating, and are tied up with moods, emotions, and simple feeling' (Soloman [ed.], *Phenomenology and Existentialism*, p. 32).

43. Merleau-Ponty, 'The Body, Motility and Spatiality', p. 381.
44. Merleau-Ponty, 'The Body, Motility and Spatiality', p. 379.
45. Jesse Matz has detailed the relationship between the rise of literary Impressionism and philosophical phenomenology in the work of late nineteenth-century and early twentieth-century philosophers and writers (*Literary Impressionism*, pp. 25–9).
46. Merleau-Ponty, 'The Intertwining – The Chiasm', p. 166.

Chapter 6

Arthur Symons and Decadent Lyric Phenomenology

The threat of isolation outlined in the previous chapter might seem particularly relevant to Decadent lyric poetry. Paul Bourget's theorisation of Decadence as a relation between part and whole finds in it the isolation of the individual, disconnected from the greater social body: a Decadent society is one in which there are 'un trop grand nombre d'individus impropres aux travaux de la vie commune' ['too many individuals unsuited to the labours of communal life']. Bourget goes on to define a Decadent literary style as one in which there is a corresponding breakdown in subordination of part to whole:

> l'unité du livre se décompose pour laisser la place à l'indépendence de la page, où la page se décompose pour laisser la place à l'indépendence de la phrase, et la phrase pour laisser la place à l'indépendence du mot.
> [the unity of the book decomposes to make way for the independence of the page, where the page decomposes to make way for the independence of the sentence, and the sentence makes way for the word.][1]

Nowhere might this seem more true than in Arthur Symons's definition of Decadent poetry as characterised by the 'disembodied voice'. Yet in this chapter I suggest that within this process of decomposition and deracination, a new type of connection with the whole is being discovered. In what follows I develop a reading of Decadent lyric phenomenology along several different dimensions, taking the work of Arthur Symons as the central focus. Exploring the relevance of phenomenological ideas to the operations of first Impressionism and then Symbolism in Symons's poetic practice, the chapter complicates claims (notably Symons's own) for Decadent lyric's disembodiment. Moving on, in the third section, to outline the relevance of phenomenological ideas of the 'reduction', I suggest that we might witness in aestheticist lyric compression something similar to that stripping away of the social concepts by which we think we know the world in order to reveal a more fundamental connection. The chapter concludes with an extended reading of one of Symons's best-known poems, bringing together the phenomenological frames of reference built up in the previous three sections.

* * *

Impressionist poetry might be the best-recognised marker of the shift of lyric's affiliation from ear to eye in the later nineteenth century. Moving away from traditional associations with song, and Romantic-transcendent associations with the spiritual, towards a modernist science of the image, this association with sight has become central to an understanding of Decadent lyric. In 'The Decadent Movement in Literature' Arthur Symons outlines a lyric poetry that 'is the poetry of sensation, of evocation; poetry which paints as well as sings'.[2] For Symons, the lyric eye appears just as 'disembodied' as the lyric voice when he characterises the painterly poetry of the Decadents through the metaphor of the opera glass, suggesting an act of vision that foregrounds technologies of viewing rather than physical immediacy.[3] Indeed, Jonathan Crary's influential account of the 'dissociation of touch from sight' during this period has resulted in a particular emphasis on modernity and disembodied visuality. For Crary, this occurred as part of 'a pervasive "separation of the senses" and industrial remapping of the body in the nineteenth century': 'The loss of touch as a conceptual component of vision meant the unloosening of the eye from the network of referentiality incarnated in tactility and its subjective relation to perceived space.'[4] Isobel Armstrong's work on nineteenth-century poetry and the visual mode, such as that on the Rossettis explored in Chapter 3, resonates particularly interestingly with this agenda.

Yet, much as new technologies of vision and image-reproduction may have driven apart the body of the viewer and the object viewed, there was also an important late nineteenth-century counter-action valuing a return to more 'empathetic' experiences of perception that drew the two together. Influenced by earlier German aesthetic theory, thinkers including Vernon Lee and Bernhard Berenson articulated something much more phenomenological. Vernon Lee's 'gallery experiments' with Clementina Anstruther-Thomson between 1887 and 1897, for example, explored a mode of art criticism that involved the viewer's whole body in a physical response to the work (the importance of this to a history of *literary* criticism is just starting to be recognised).[5] The idea that the body receives from the work of art its 'impress' as well as its visual impression can be seen in, for example, Lee's 'Beauty and Ugliness' (published in the *Contemporary Review* in 1897). In these experiments Lee explored a somatic aesthetics in which Clementina Anstruther-Thomson's physical responses to works of art (the tensing and relaxing of muscles, the rate of her breathing, the shift of her balance) were carefully noted.[6] There is a powerful resonance, I suggest, between the aesthetics of 'empathy' and phenomenological methods of reading that followed later in the twentieth century in the work of thinkers such as Dufrenne: 'In poetry, sense is totally within the sensuous. The meaning carried by the discourse is not signified, it is expressed . . . If you prefer, the sense surges within the sensuous in the reciting body. . .'[7] In a different way, Berenson's theory of 'tactile values' also posited an embodied vision by finding a mode of representation in painting that appears to represent not the visual but the tactile appearance of its subject.[8]

These theorisations of an embedded somatic vision in the 1880s and 1890s arose in key part in reaction to a painterly Impressionism and were linked, at least in the case of Berenson, to post-Impressionist painterly modes. But this work was circulating at the same time as Decadent poetry was inspired to practise a poetic Impressionism. What happens if we explore Impressionist poetry – even that of Arthur Symons – in relation to these ideas of the senses as embodied and connected, and in relation to the kind of somatics that both Lee and Berenson were articulating? After all, for all his talk of the 'disembodied' within 'The Decadent Movement in Literature', Symons also articulates particular praise for W. E. Henley's volume *In Hospital* in which his 'lyric verse' invokes the physical sensations of the body: 'the ache and throb of the body'.[9] Similarly, while the 'Prologue' of *London Nights* ('My life is like a music hall') stresses the distance of the spectator from the spectacle – a body 'chained by enchantment to my stall' – he also projects himself bodily on to the stage in every stanza through his gaze. I argue in this section for the importance of the body, and particularly the embodied eye, to our understanding of Decadent Impressionist lyric by giving attention to the significance of tactility and skin (the most under-explored of all Decadent Impressionist senses and sense organs) and, more specifically, the combined sense of sight and an awareness of the body in space that is best recognised through a discourse of phenomenology.[10]

In Impressionist poetry, a range of senses are invoked, but the role of touch within this economy is perhaps least well recognised. For example, poems such as 'Le Chat', a translation of a poem by

Baudelaire, invokes the cat's diabolical harmonies as emblematic of a newly Decadent lyric song, but the smell and feel of the animal's fur also play a key role in the phenomenology of the poem, whose internal lyric transaction is premised on a fully embodied experience. Touch also takes an active, although much overlooked, part in the sensory translations of synaesthesia that are so central to Decadent poetry, and I will begin my reading of Symons with reference to a fairly well-known poem – 'Morbidezza' – in which the sense of touch is implicitly central:

> White girl, your flesh is lilies
> Grown 'neath a frozen moon,
> So still is
> The rapture of your swoon
> Of whiteness, snow or lilies.
>
> The virginal revealment,
> Your bosom's wavering slope,
> Concealment,
> 'Neath fainting heliotrope,
> Of whitest white's revealment,
>
> Is like a bed of lilies,
> A jealous-guarded row,
> Whose will is
> Simply chaste dreams:—but oh,
> The alluring scent of lilies![11]

Here touch is invoked synaesthetically, in order to play with the prohibition of the tactile. The lyric is addressed to a love object that appears to be a corpse: a woman whose prone body ('So still' in the 'rapture' of her 'swoon') is debarred from the narrator by a barrier of funeral lilies: 'A jealous-guarded row,/ Whose will is/ Simply chaste dreams'. The sentinel lilies provide a barrier against physical proximity between the poetic subject and the woman's body – a barrier against a potentially necrophilic touch. Yet when the stanza ends by invoking the power of the 'alluring scent of lilies!' more is at stake here than simply the smell of flowers. Scent acts as a synaesthetic expression of tactile desires, as this final exclamation cannot avoid referring back to the equation of the woman's corporeal body with the lilies made in the first line: 'your flesh is lilies'. There is no explicit discourse of touch in the poem at all – it appears to focus on vision and the olfactory – yet the Decadent transgression of the poem lies in the invocation of a forbidden tactile impression through the mediating language of other senses.

Indeed, the one-word title 'Morbidezza' suggests that we read the poem synaesthetically as a poem about touch. The word connotes 'morbid' – that unhealthy interest in death – which, together with the flowers and the prone body, puts us in mind of the laid-out corpse. The word is also a technical term in painting to denote naturalistic or life-like flesh tones, reinforcing the visual basis of Impressionism in this poetry that 'paints as well as sings'. Yet its literal meaning in Italian – soft or smooth – anchors the term fundamentally in touch, pointing us towards an embodied vision and projecting on to the poem a subversive tactile reading. Merleau-Ponty writes:

> every experience of the visible has always been given to me within the context of the movements of the look, the visible spectacle belongs to the touch neither more nor less than do the 'tactile qualities.' We must habituate ourselves to think that every visible is cut out in the tangible, every tactile being in some manner promised to visibility . . .[12]

So it seems with Symons's embodied eye in this poem. Read in this way, Symons's poem represents a phenomenological Impressionism, in which the eye operates as part of a body whose skin and haptic awareness mediates knowledge about its relations with the world. This is a formulation of Impressionism that, while perhaps not relevant to the classic Impressionist paintings, might be a useful context for approaching poetry that is written very much in light of post-Impressionist ideas (circulated by members of the same aesthetic community, such as Lee and Berenson) that articulate a newly embodied vision.

Indeed, faces and hands feature prominently in Symons's poetry: sometimes rather fetishised, but not, I argue, necessarily disembodied. Their isolation within his poetry at times emphasises their function as sites of intense tactile responsiveness, rather than relegating them to the realm of the spectral (even when, as below, they are distanced by memory). It is a part of the erotic charge of his verse that they can become the sensory focus of an 'impression' in his work. The poem 'Hands' is a case in point, and a good example of a phenomenological Impressionism:

> The little hands too soft and white
>   To have known more laborious hours
> Than those which die upon a night
>   Of kindling wine and fading flowers;

The little hands that I have kissed,
   Finger by finger, to the tips,
And delicately about each wrist
   Have set a bracelet with my lips;

Dear soft white little morbid hands.
   Mine all one night, with what delight
Shall I recall in other lands,
   Dear hands, that you were mine one night![13]

The focus on a meeting point of lips and hands in this poem draws our attention to touch at least as much as vision (notably using the interplay between 'morbid' and 'soft' that I suggested was operative as the basis of the tactile synaesthesia in 'Morbidezza'). This poem describes, in fact, a process of exploration primarily through touch: a knowing of another through tactile or bodily incorporation. The encompassing of the fingers and wrist in the circle of the lips invokes the kind of physical incorporation that Merleau-Ponty claims is involved in knowing the world phenomenologically: 'it is precisely my body which perceives the body of another person, and discovers in that other body a miraculous prolongation of my own intentions, a familiar way of dealing with the world'.[14] This same point seems to hold true of the other poem also titled 'Hands' in *London Nights*, which inhabits a world of the tactile, and again focuses on mouth and hand as the meeting point of lyric subject and object.[15] Here the poem stresses particularly the experience of feeling the pulse of the other's body on the lips: a bodily incorporation of the most essential somatic presence of the other body, and a knowing of the other through their physical 'impress'. I will return in more detail to this idea of phenomenological tactile knowledge and bodily incorporation in my next chapter, but for now it is enough to note that critical narratives of lyric's 'modernising' shift from ear to disembodied visualities might usefully be augmented and challenged by considering the importance of the phenomenological.

To consider the importance to Impressionist poetry of an embodied eye – one invested in lyric tangibility as well as visuality – is to posit a type of epistemology that helps explain the operation of a Decadent erotics. Knowing things as an extension of the body (knowing through touch), and finding the sense of sight dependent on, and inseparable from, the reach of the tactile, takes Impressionist poetry into markedly different territory from the typical Impressionist painting. Yet the term 'impression' itself holds this potential; having a meaning both visual and tactile (referring to an indentation), it suggests we might look for a vision cut out of the tactile, a seeing with the body rather than the spectral sight of modern technologies. At the end of the century we might consider further the relationship between not just music and image but also between the disembodied and the somatic: between song and shape, the aural and the tangible.

*   *   *

In fact, it is not just Symons's Impressionism that benefits from being read in relation to a developing strand of phenomenological thinking. 'The Decadent Movement in Literature' identifies Symbolism as Impressionism's twin impetus in Decadent poetry, and I suggest a sensitivity to phenomenological modes productively expands our understanding of Symbolism's operation in Symons's poetry too. In what follows I will suggest that recognising the significance of this impulse helps resolve some of the apparent tensions in his work. Symons's interest in the figure of the dancer is easily seen as a Symbolist manifesto. Indeed, his own critical essays term dance a 'living symbol':

> the dancer, with her gesture, all pure symbol, evokes, from her mere beautiful motion, idea, sensation, all that one need ever know of event. There, before you, she exists, in harmonious life; and her rhythm reveals to you the soul of her imagined being.[16]

The dancer symbolises, rather than represents, and it is specifically her 'rhythm' that conveys her soul. Yet this language of the transcendent is undercut by Symons himself through a connection with something much more primitive. In the same essay he portrays the dancer as signifying a form of communication in which 'there is no intrusion of words', and in which one can communicate 'primitive feeling' and the instinctual.[17] He values dance for its indifference to questions of morality, for its expression of some fundamental experience of the world, and for its viscerality. This has led scholars to chart a tension in Symons's work between dance as a quasi-religious transcendent ecstasy and as an animal expression of female sexuality. This is a critical debate that I wish to dwell on a little and engage with. After all, while Symbolism seeks a connection with the realm of soul and spirit that tends to transcend the material and the linguistic, phenomenology enables a recognition of the pull in the other direction, towards a materiality so immediate that it precedes language.

In relation to contemporary philology, Dowling reads Symons's interest in the dancer as one that celebrates 'a language even more "primitive" than the lower-class vernaculars for it was assumed that the more physically overt the linguistic sign, the cruder the mental capacity of the sign-maker'; but the philological and anthropological sources to which she refers do little to explain or capture the ecstatic nature of this experience as it is presented lyrically.[18] More recently, Chris Snodgrass has commented, in an account of Symons's connection with Beardsley, that 'Unlike the Symbolists and his friend Yeats, Symons could not avoid distinguishing the female dancer from the dance, or rather, emphasizing that the sanctity of the dance could never entirely cleanse the primitive animal sexuality of woman.'[19] This is an important observation. For W. B. Yeats, dance might often appear as pure symbol, but for Symons it was never so straightforward: in spite of his engagement with Mallarmé, dance was in key part a profound expression of physicality.[20] Critical narratives have therefore tended to see Symons's poetry about dance as ultimately expressing the failure of the symbol, and specifically its failure to enable a connection with something transcendent. For example, Jan B. Gordon's essay sees the dancer in Symons's poetry as aspiring to represent 'a mode of transcending individual isolation': an opportunity for 'freedom from the bounds of the self'.[21] Citing 'Nora on the Pavement', Gordon argues that the dancer also represents the aspiration to transcend time.[22] Yet for Gordon, Decadent poetry both articulates this aspiration and its failure: 'Symons terminates the work [*London Nights*] with a quiet acceptance of human mortality and isolation.'[23] As with lyric's ekphrastic ambitions, then, might one see this aspiration towards dance as a transcendent ambition entertained in key part to mark its failure in the modern world?

In comparison with the work of classic English Symbolists such as A. Mary F. Robinson, it is indeed tempting to read Symons's work as concerned with the failure of Symbolism. Robinson eschewed the body, embracing something beyond the material. Vernon Lee terms Robinson's poetry 'a negation of all that's of the flesh & blood . . . a quality of voice rare, aetherial [*sic*], singing in an altogether higher stratum of atmosphere, coming out of what seems an immaterial throat'. Lee aptly characterises Robinson's flight from the somatic when she writes to her:

> You are a stray creature, Mary, & I feel that were I to clutch you never so close, I should clutch you thus a phantom, or rather that the real thing would elude me, volatile, distant. I ask myself to what extent is all this real-real experience, like the flesh & blood experiences of my own heart as tangible, if I may say so, as hunger or a headache.[24]

Robinson's work offers what one might consider a more successful, or purer, form of Symbolism than Symons, as seen in her Symbolist manifesto 'The Idea', which opens as follows:

> Beneath this world of stars and flowers
>   That rolls in visible deity,
> I dream another world is ours
>   And is the soul of all we see.[25]

Robinson's Symbolism leads her away, in general, from the corporeal and more towards phantoms and ghosts. Her intense immersion in European Symbolist literature was in key part responsible for this, as well, perhaps, as the decorum involved in the idea of the 'poetess' on which she based her authorial construction.

Yet to read Symons's investment in the body as a failure of the Symbolist aspiration is, I suggest, at best only half the story. Symons's dancer poems emphasise something else: dance not, or not only, as a failed Romantic symbol of spiritual transcendence, but as an emblem of a lyric aspiration to represent something that is extra-linguistic not because it exceeds language, but because it precedes it. To think about these poems in relation to the phenomenological is to recognise the importance of what I described in the previous chapter as a fundamental experience of the world that is pre-reflective and prior to articulation: the inherently physical experience of the world that is direct and untarnished by language. In this sense there is no tension between the animal sensuality of dance and its aspiration to give voice to the 'soul', because phenomenology started from a point that rendered the mind/body problem somewhat redundant. In short, reading Symons's poetry phenomenologically leads us to see that the primitive element he finds in dance might be a force for escaping language rather than for transcending matter. When Symons describes dance as – like 'wantonness' and wine – one of those things in which 'energy passes into an ideal excess', that is not an ideal beyond the material but one in closer sensual connection with our material existence.[26] In other words, dance might figure the extra-linguistic dimension of lyric in a way that, through a strong association with sensuality, gives it a profoundly material meaning.

In 'Javanese Dancers', for example, the dancing woman is 'unintelligible' and 'mysterious'; she represents (along with a lot of obvious challenges, for our own age, in terms of race and gender politics) the embodied experience expressed through female sensuality.[27] Symons's women have long been read as 'mysterious in that they transcend discourse',[28] yet the dancer here appears more a poetic expression of base rhythmicality – her 'lingering feet that undulate' – than a symbol of a transcendent spiritual realm.[29] The experience invoked here is one not of reflection but of a phenomenological 'feeling': an experience of the world that is gained fundamentally through the body and the skin. Towards the poem's end the dancers fade to the spectral, like figures on a screen – a more conventional 'symbol' perhaps – but the poem primarily appeals to something more enticingly immediate. 'To a Dancer' also presents the physical embodiment of rhythmical musicality, from 'The rhythms of her poising feet' to 'Her body's melody,/ In silent waves of wandering sound'.[30] In this poem the poetic voice asserts a particular connection between himself and the female dancer in the repeated refrain, 'Her eyes that gleam for me!' (and in lines such as 'From her desire that leaps to my desire'). The dancer here remains no otherworldly symbol, but an emblem of sensuous experience of the world that defies, and precedes, linguistic articulation, an experience best described, I think, with reference to phenomenology, and one that locates meaning in excess of the linguistic content of the poem.

In 'Nora on the Pavement', the child-like qualities of Nora's insanity provide for Symons a location of primitive regression to pre-reflective sensual experience equivalent (and equally interesting and unsettling in terms of disability politics) to the 'primitivism' that he finds in dancers of other races.[31] Here the mad woman's dance on the pavement in the middle of the night becomes a shamanic twirling that results in a form of ecstasy; a centrifugal force powerful enough to release the 'the very Nora', spun out in one leap: 'Herself at last, leaps free the very Nora'. Lexical repetition within the poem links poetic form to the repeated twirling of the dance (the word 'circle' is itself repeated four times) generating a momentum out of which meaning spins almost in excess of the poem itself, and certainly in excess of its semantic content. The lyric here is able to 'get to the heart of things' and represent an authentic spirit:

> It is the soul of Nora,
> Living at last, and giving forth to the night,
> Bird-like, the burden of its own delight,
> All its desire, and all the joy of living,
> In that blithe madness of the soul of Nora.

Yet even in this poem, with all its talk of a 'soul', the liberation appears in equal parts sensual and spiritual: that interlocking of

'Life's capricious rhythm, and all her own' appears more an apprehension of her own physical connection with the world than a transcendence of it. If we see Symons's dancers as representing more an experience of the pre-reflective moment than a search for otherworldly transcendence, then the perceived tension in his poetry between the animalistic and primitive, on the one hand, and the 'spiritual', on the other, is resolved. For all Symons's talk of Symbolism being a communication of 'things unseen' to the 'soul', his own poetry often seems more concerned with an idea of a bodily communication in which body and soul are united.[32]

In recognising this as a phenomenological mode of engagement with the world, we might find in Symons's poetry not (or not just) the failure of a transcendent Symbolism but a different kind of poetics: perhaps the poetics of what he calls in 'Stella Maris' the 'embodied soul':

> When souls turn bodies, and unite,
> In the intolerable, the whole,
> Rapture of the embodied soul.[33]

Crucially, this somatic lyric energy presents an anti-dualist response to the spiritually transcendent potentiality of the Romantic conception of lyric. The invocation of the body as a route to an ecstatic phenomenological escape from language rather than a spiritual one offers the possibility of capturing experience prior to its codification in language, rather than a supra-linguistic transcendence. This, then, is an important way in which poetry of the period might be seen as responding to the 'crisis' in lyric transcendence outlined in Chapter 1 – an interestingly different strategy, I suggest, from those we see earlier in the century, and one that needs to take its place within narratives of lyric's engagement with modernity across the nineteenth and twentieth centuries.

*   *   *

The poetic impetus identified above might be likened to the phenomenological 'reduction'. Phenomenology's interest in one's own consciousness of the world relies on this method, which ensures that we focus simply on the immediacy of somatic experience, free from the prejudice of interpretation. The reduction asks us to abandon, at least temporarily, the theories we use to make sense of the world (including reflection and language) in order to gain a more direct connection through an experience of physical embodiment: 'to return to that world which precedes knowledge'.[34] Although dated and disturbing for a present-day audience, Symons's repeated choice of women, the insane and the 'primitive' is no doubt designed to focus on subjects whom he believes to be freer from the distorting lenses of culture, education and knowledge – subjects, in other words, more able to access the sought-after experiences of immediate embodiment. While the poems discussed above represent this connection internally (whether representing the tactile–visual impressions of the embodied eye, or a phenomenological connection with the world through dance), I will argue in this section that aestheticist lyrics not only *represent* that experience but might actually invite the reader to have that experience of the poem itself. One of the key poetic modes of the aestheticist lyric is a quasi-phenomenological one, in which the poem is, I suggest, itself akin to the phenomenological 'reduction'. (It should come as no surprise, of course, given the mirroring between lyric's 'internal' and 'external' transaction discussed in the previous chapter, that we might see such a connection.) It is not unusual for modern poetry to be thought of as an experience of the gap between the reflective and the pre-reflective, yet this is a feature of lyric that has a more precise historical instantiation in relation to a dislocation of inner from outer experience – the alienation of feeling from language in the late eighteenth century – which leads to the problems of isolating 'subjectivity' in the nineteenth century. The search for a 'pure' or intensified type of lyric from the 1860s combined in Decadent poetry with the kind of deconstructed Decadent text described by Bourget to produce what I am suggesting might productively be considered as a type of 'reduction'.

Certainly a characteristic of Decadent poetry is the paradoxical connection we often see between lyric and silence: a framing of the unexpressed and the unheard. It is as if lyric strives, through an intense process of articulation, to convey an impression that cannot be articulated. In this body of work we see an 'art for art's sake' poetry that, as intimated in the previous chapter, not only resists a positioning of art in moral, social or commercial discourses, but that seems almost to resist the contamination of language itself. Mystery and secrets are also frequently found at the heart of this poetry in a way that highlights something outside of the poem's linguistic structures (see, for example, Symons's 'White Heliotrope' with the word 'mysteriously' nearly at its centre; Wilde's 'Helas' with the secrets of the 'twice-written scroll' at its centre; and the 'secrets' of Olive Custance's 'Grey Eyes').[35] Such lacunae, within a Romantic transcendent tradition of lyric, might most naturally be thought to gesture towards a glimpse of the spiritual realm – 'participat[ion] in the eternal, the infinite, and the one', to quote Shelley's 'Defence'.[36] Poetry for Shelley is the expression of divinity in human beings, and is itself 'indeed something divine'.[37] In his essay, poetry is defined in opposition to the body and the physical and all of its perceived constraints: 'poetry defeats the curse which binds us to be subjected to the accident of surrounding impressions'.[38] Poetry distils and preserves the 'evanescent' flashes of 'the interpenetration of a diviner nature through our own', enabling the poet to flee the degradation and flux of the mortal realm.[39] Yet for many of the Decadent poets, the physical and mortal realm is often too compelling for any easy reversion to such transcendent ideals. Even in the case of Lionel Johnson – perhaps the Decadent most drawn towards the ideal[40] – 'The Dark Angel' represents the pull of the body and its 'aching lust' in his quest for a disembodied poetics. What interests me here is, again, the possibility that these silences, mysteries and secrets at the heart of many Decadent lyric poems might give way not to something otherworldly (a disembodied music and spirituality) but to the body – and to a bodily encounter with the world that might supply a credible phenomenological alternative to the transcendent spiritual experience.

For the reader to encounter a poetic preoccupation with not speaking, not telling and not representing is to have our attention turned away from content. With aestheticist poetry's intense investment in form, such silences inevitably invite attention to the printed poem's own textual body – its presence on the printed page. It is the potential this might offer for the reader's somatic encounter with form that I will explore further here. A consideration of the work of Ernest Dowson, with his injunction to 'give over words' because 'Silence is best' ('Venite Descendamus'), helps initially to think about the operation of Decadent silence in relation to the textual and corporeal body.[41] As has been noted, almost every poem in Dowson's *Decorations* (1899) 'ends on a note of disillusion, reaching nothing, silence'.[42] Dowson's is a poetry that seeks to detach itself from language. Such lyric silences might be seen to direct attention to the expressiveness of pure sound or image, and it is this direction that critical work by Stephanie Kuduk Weiner has taken.[43] Yet Weiner's own comments about Dowson's concern with a metricality and punctuation that can only be appreciated in print might lead us to consider an idea of lyric based not only on an absent aurality or image but on what is there to fill the silence for the reader of these poems: an encounter with print on the page. Weiner is at her most interesting, I think, when she describes the perfection of Dowson's poems as lying 'in their printedness, their distinctness from any act of speaking or singing whatever': 'Dowson's poems are "perfect song" not because they come so close to the condition of music, but because they are so far from it.'[44] Dowson's poetry might mark a failure of poetry's connection with the world through language and semantic representation,[45] but its silences turn it back in on its own printed form, offering what we might consider a nascent phenomenology of poetic form. By this I mean to recognize an aspect of the life of the lyric poem on the printed page that is in excess of its linguistic meaning, but that is part of our engagement – visually and somatically – with the spatial arrangement of the poem on the page. In relation to Decadent textualities this is intimately connected, I suggest, with desire and the body.

Dowson's 'Villanelle of His Lady's Treasures' makes an explicit connection between the intricate fixed verse forms of aestheticist poetry and the somatic, between the textual and corporeal body.[46] Here he imagines building the fixed verse form from the body parts of the lyric object:

> I took her dainty eyes, as well
>   As silken tendrils of her hair:
> And so I made a Villanelle!
>
> I took her voice, a silver bell,
>   As clear as song, as soft as prayer;
> I took her dainty eyes as well.
>
> It may be, said I, who can tell,
>   These things shall be my less despair?
> And so I made a Villanelle!
>
> I took her whiteness virginal
>   And from her cheek two roses rare:
> I took her dainty eyes as well.
>
> I said: "It may be possible
>   Her image from my heart to tear!"
> And so I made a Villanelle.
>
> I stole her laugh, most musical:
>   I wrought it in with artful care;
> I took her dainty eyes as well;
>   And so I made a Villanelle.

A parody of the medieval 'blason', this is supremely self-reflexive about the process of poem making. The complex form of the villanelle involves two repeating rhymes which end every one of its nineteen lines, and two refrains which are introduced in the first stanza and then alternately form the closing line of each of the four subsequent stanzas. The final quatrain features both refrains as its final two lines. Tied together with the 'silken tendrils of her hair' and the sinuous repetition of the refrains, the poem draws attention to the corporeality, and the physical presence, of the meticulously constructed textual body. A Frankensteinian creature of a poem, it invites us to see something important to a consideration of the late nineteenth-century revival of strict verse forms more generally.

After all, at the time Symons was writing Impressionist poetry, Vernon Lee was theorising not only an embodied vision of the visual arts, but also a similar model of corporeal aesthetic response in relation to the formal features of prose (her essays about the latter were finally, and much later, collected into the book *The Handling of Words* in 1923). Lee's primary interest in literature is, as she states quite explicitly, in the relation between writer and reader, and one of her key themes is the somatic 'impress' of text on reader.[47] In the chapter 'On Style', she makes a clear distinction between content and form, noting how the effect of the text on the body is separable from the content: 'there are words which make the Reader think and feel, in a way make him *live*, slowly; and there are other words which make the Reader think, feel, and live quickly; and quickly and smoothly, or quickly and jerkily, as the case may be'. Success, she goes on to note, is in achieving a harmonious relationship between form and content.[48] Significantly, Lee recognises similar somatic forces at work in relation to much larger-scale formal construction ('Construction is not only a matter of single words or sentences, but of whole large passages and divisions').[49] Writing about the novel, she insists that the 'pattern of words' (like the forms on the canvas of the painting) 'solicits our responsive sensibility and imagination'. According to Lee, we read with the body, and the body responds not just to the 'events and feelings' of the literature's content, but also to the feel of its form.[50] In fact, just as dance represents in Symons's work something of a phenomenological connection with the world, so too with Lee's description of the reader's somatic connection with the shape and rhythms of text: 'Our attention, when we really give it, wants to be made to move briskly, rhythmically, to march, nay, as Nietzsche puts it, *to dance*'.[51]

While Lee writes about literary prose almost exclusively, she claims in the chapter 'On Style' that 'Writing, in the highest artistic sense, tends to the condition of the Lyric'. Most interestingly for my purposes, this claim appears to be founded on the thought that literature of the 'highest artistic sense' aims towards something similar to the phenomenological 'reduction' – something that Lee is here equating with 'lyric'. In this passage, Lee suggests that in the highest-quality literature the author is trying to convey to his or her reader a sense of 'the relations between things': a mood, emotion or frame of mind. Such impressions consist, according to Lee, of 'sights, sounds, words, gestures' and the author's own 'vague conditions of being': mere fragments carried to consciousness.[52] She goes on to say,

> But these fragments contain the active essence, the taste, perfume, *timbre*, the something provocative of the mood. And it is among these fragments that he [the author] selects when he wishes to pass on his mood to others, or to preserve it for himself. Therefore, while Hegel [ahead of Pater, as Lee was well aware] said that all art tends to the condition of music, we might say, more truly, that all Writing, in the highest artistic sense, tends to the condition of the Lyric.[53]

This passage makes strongly the connection between discourses of Impressionism, on the one hand, and, on the other, the phenomenological lyric 'reduction' I have described above. That 'active essence' of the impression, contained in the sensory fragment in order to convey a 'vague condition of being', suggests a desire to distil the essence of immediate somatic experience. And, crucially, it is this process that Lee thinks of as 'the condition of the Lyric'.

So, if for Lee the highest form of literature is 'lyric', and lyric is theorised as something akin to the phenomenological reduction, what happens if we pursue her ideas of the reader's somatic encounter with literary form in relation to poetry? There is, after all, perhaps no more intense awareness of the potential of the 'pattern of words' in the period than in the Parnassian-inspired verse forms of the aestheticist lyric. Following Dowson's equation of the villanelle with the corporeal body, and Lee's somatic reading of literary form, I will take seriously the possibility of poetic form as itself a potential site of phenomenological lyric encounter. In the rest of this chapter and the next I suggest that discourses of the period bring together skin and paper, the textual and the corporeal body, in ways that are focused particularly by the strong physical presence on the page of the strict verse forms characteristic of aestheticist lyric.

*   *   *

The vocabulary of Decadent lyric phenomenology outlined in this chapter so far has demonstrated how we might find in Arthur Symons's Impressionist poetry something that speaks not so much of a disembodied eye as of a phenomenologically embodied mode of vision. It has also shown how one might find in his poetry something that might be described not (or not just) as a failed Symbolism but as an interrogation of Symbolism that resolves into a phenomenological epistemology. The previous section found in aestheticist lyric compression the possibility not just for the poem to *represent* a phenomenological connection with the world, but to offer such a connection to its reader through its printed presence on the page. To end this chapter, these issues are brought together in a reading of a particularly significant poem by Arthur Symons – 'Pastel' – a poem that, I will argue, functions as a type of lyric 'reduction'.

A work that has long featured in criticism of Decadent poetry and is perceived as emblematic of it, 'Pastel' (from Symons's 1896 volume *Silhouettes*) is grounded solidly in a pictorial engagement with the impression or image:[54]

> The light of our cigarettes
>   Went and came in the gloom:
>   It was dark in the little room.
>
> Dark, and then, in the dark,
>   Sudden, a flash, a glow,
>   And a hand and a ring I know.
>
> And then, through the dark, a flush
>   Ruddy and vague, the grace –
>   A rose – of her lyric face.[55]

The poem deals with an intimate encounter between the poetic 'I' and a female companion. The brief sketch intimates, within the context of the book as a whole, an erotic encounter, possibly (given the location in a dark little room) a post-coital cigarette, but certainly a shared moment of Decadent pleasure in the nicotine. Like a Caravaggio painting, the scene described is one briefly and partially illuminated, with sensuous hues appearing out of the dark as a match is struck to light new cigarettes. Notably, the light of the cigarettes 'went and came' rather than the more usual 'came and went'. Rather than a gradual fading of the light, it is a moment of re-ignition within the gloom that surrounds the couple through the four repetitions of the word 'dark'. What is illuminated in the sudden flash of the match is a suitably Decadent combination of skin and jewellery. In the final stanza of the poem the face of the woman appears, or almost appears, in an echo of the light of the match, bringing a 'flush' of colour, both vital and mysterious ('ruddy and vague'): the rose-like image of 'her lyric face'. Yet what is the significance of the word 'lyric' here, and what does it mean? This is a question surely central to our reading of the poem, and I want to spend some time reading its discourse on lyric.

The title, referring to the tradition of drawing in pastels, anchors the poem in the representational visual arts; with its simple, pared-down form one might most naturally see this poem as Impressionist. As Symons himself writes in 'The Decadent Movement in Literature': 'The Impressionist, in literature as in painting, would flash upon you in a new, sudden way so exact an image of what you have just seen, just as you have seen it.'[56] The play of light within the dark – the 'flash', the 'glow', the flame, the reflection of light in the jewel – all speak an Impressionist language. Impressionist painting is nothing if not a representation of light and shadow, of the way light falls. In the final stanza a 'flush' of the face – another glow of colour, this time pink ('ruddy') – is perhaps the colour of a rose, but maybe rose-like also in the sense that the Impressionist painter's depiction of a face was often nothing more than a swirl of pink (a 'vague' marking on the canvas), the impasto giving a formation similar to the swirl of petals in a flower. The image of female beauty as rose-like is in many ways a cliché of femininity, but it is also I think conjuring up a more specific painterly style. Yet the final shift to describing her face as 'lyric' starts to unhinge the image from its painterly depiction. The face is erased in terms of visual depiction by the term 'lyric', which acts as a representational blank at the centre of this visual, pastel-drawn 'portrait'. The page 'decomposes', as Bourget has it, into the single, autonomous word, and here the poem folds in upon itself, taking attention away from its promised visual presence and directing us elsewhere. But where?

One might at first think that the word 'lyric', at this point in the poem, is intended to convey an encounter indescribable in terms of the image and closest perhaps to what can be expressed in non-representational music; the old association of lyric with song certainly suggests that this would be a natural way to read the poem. In this way, one might want to read the significance of this word as Symbolist. To quote from Symons's 'The Decadent Movement in Literature' again: 'The Symbolist, in this new, sudden way, would flash upon you the "soul" of that which can be apprehended only by the soul – the finer sense of things unseen, the deeper meaning of things evident.'[57] This pattern would fit with the way other poems by Symons operate. In 'Javanese Dancers' we can see a progression from impression to symbol as the dancers are abstracted from the physical world into a spectral echo. Here, the word 'lyric' perhaps similarly abstracts and renders the woman's beauty a signifier of something beyond representation, something beyond the material. Perhaps she becomes a symbol of the spiritual? Yet the context of the dark room and the shared pleasure of the nicotine is one that emphasises more the tactile and the erotic than the musical and transcendent. The poem appears to be posing the question of whether woman's beauty can, in this 'modern' context of 'modern' loves, still be a symbol of spirituality. Perhaps what we see here is a failed symbol, or an inter-rogation of the possibility of such Symbolism in modern life – but perhaps also we see the implication of a phenomenological mode of encounter more fitting for the modern lyric. One might see the poem directing our attention to experiences of immediate embodiment as a consequence of its interrogation of lyric Symbolism and lyric transcendence.

After all, the common pairing of hands with lips and/or kisses in Symons's poetry almost by implication (following on from the hands highlighted earlier in the poem) invites us to meet lips as much as 'lyric' in this final line: 'A rose – of her lyric face'. Moreover, there is a powerful intertextual association in Symons's work of 'rose' with lips that strongly reinforces this reading. Poem five of the sequence 'Lilian' ('Caprice'), for example, begins 'Her mouth is all of roses'. The poem 'Kisses' also associates lips with 'rose' in a way that is highly suggestive for 'Pastel': 'That my lips may find their way to the heart/ Of the rose or the world, your lips my rose'. Further relevant examples include the 'flower-soft lips' in 'At the Stage Door' and the 'roses of her mouth' in 'At Glan-y-Wern'.[58] 'Rose', then, in that final line connotes 'lips' where Symons gives us 'lyric'. Indeed, the Decadent erotic kiss signified by the rose is so prevalent a mode of encounter or transaction in Symons's poetry that it becomes associ-ated with the operations of the 'lyric' itself. So when the face appears in the sudden glow of the struck match, the denial of the expected visual image might focus our attention back, I suggest, on a sensuous tactility more associated with the experience of immediate embodi-ment. Indeed, perhaps lips and 'lyric' lock as the sensuality of the silent woman is associated with the concept of 'lyric' itself. We might consider, here, 'lyric' as a point of erotic contact between self and other, becoming, one might say, the focus for an exploration of the meeting point of self and world rather than that between the earthly and the spiritual. The kiss implied here is part of a Decadent erotics, not one of liturgical ritual. This does not resonate with the elevated spiritual engagement Symons himself proposes for the symbol: here, I suggest, we are directed towards contact not so much with the soul as with the skin.

The term 'lyric' here, then, represents a phenomenological connection between lyric subject and object in the poem's 'internal' transaction: the association with lips turns the poem not so much away to the symbolic realm but back to a point of erotic contact with the lyric object. The lyric transaction here is aligned with the incorporating erotics of the Decadent kiss. However, in the age of the print-totalised lyric the self-reflexivity of the word 'lyric' in the final line cannot help but also turn attention back to the poem's own formal presence on the page. Just as Dowson's poem directed its eroticism to a phenomenology of poetic form, so, too, 'lyric' here seems to invoke both the corporeal body and the textual body. I propose that through this duality the poem offers both the skin and its own paper surface as twinned sites of encounter between lyric subject and object. In this poem no 'you' is addressed or invoked directly, but it represents an 'internal' transaction between the lyric subject and a third-person object that might nonetheless function also as a model for what in Chapter 5 I called the 'external' transaction between the reader and the text – and that phenomenological connection is projected through the page itself.

In fact, the significance of the page or the paper of the printed lyric poem as itself a site of phenomenological encounter is a recurring trope in Decadent poetry. In her parody of contemporary Decadent poetry, Ada Leverson imagines a volume consisting entirely of margin, full of 'beautiful unwritten thoughts', with an elaborate cover of 'Nile-green skin powdered with gilt . . . and smoothed with hard ivory, decorated with gold . . . and printed on Japanese paper'.[59] Here Leverson might seem to present the *reductio ad absurdum* of Decadent lyric solipsism. The opulence she parodies is clearly a protest against the newly dominant cheap editions of literature that flooded the market in the nineteenth century. Yet although Leverson's hand-crafted Japanese paper is deliberately different from John Stuart Mill's commercial 'hot-pressed' paper (discussed earlier), what interests me is that for *both* the physicality of the paper (textured or smooth) might be crucial to the idea of lyric in the nineteenth century. The wide white margins of Decadent poetry allow the form of the poem to be dominant, a work of sculpture as much as literature, which embodies its meaning as a somatic encounter as much as a semantic one. This is the aestheticist art that in Swinburne is 'felt on the pulses', which 'makes itself felt in the same ways in which a radical and unpredictable sexuality makes itself felt': for many of those writing in this period, 'the ideal aesthetic experience is the experience of being seduced, being made to feel oneself a body'.[60]

The Victorians were used to a strong association between the book and the body, not only through leather and other skin bindings, but also through the tradition of albums containing nail clippings and locks of hair, and even the use of human skin to bind certain editions.[61] Moreover, to find a haptic awareness of the lyric 'other' discovered through the very page of the text at the end of the century is to think about the connections between paper and skin that Decadent imitations of the decorated vellum medieval page invite more or less consciously in their echo of the calf-skin page. Indeed, skin is a ghost perhaps as powerfully present as that of orality in the Decadent lyric text of the *fin de siècle*. We might, then, consider the potential for paper, like skin, to be a site of transmission in Decadent poetry between the lyric subject and object; the meeting point of inside and outside, of lyric subject and the world; the point at which the self is enmeshed into a system of exchanges with the world.[62]

To read in this way is to recognise the significance of Decadent sensuality to the very operation of the 'internal' lyric transaction, as well as the significance of tactility to the 'external' transaction of the late Victorian book object with the reader. After all, in her cultural history of touch, Constance Classen briefly comments that the late Victorian commodified text (with the visual beauty of the lavish gilt and illuminated text, but also the specifically tactile luxury of embossed decoration, smooth leathers, weighty covers and textured papers) was part of a newly tactile environment of beautiful objects available to satisfy a 'tactile hunger' no longer sated by religious or communal life.[63] To read in this way is to recognise that the Decadent lyric might be less an aesthetic 'dead-end' than a search for a new aesthetic. Read as I suggest, this is a poetry whose focus on the surface materiality of language, rather than creating a 'cynical deadlock' between 'self and other',[64] might ultimately turn attention away from a hermeneutics of language and towards a phenomenological poetics. In the next chapter I explore further the idea that there might be a phenomenology of the printed page operative in late Victorian lyric, but extend beyond the erotics of Decadence to examine two writers whose careers spanned the whole of my period of study, and who reflected deeply and poetically on these issues.

Notes

1. Bourget, *Essais de psychologie contempraine*, pp. 24–5 (from the essay on 'Charles Baudelaire').
2. Symons, 'The Decadent Movement in Literature', p. 861.
3. Ibid., p. 860.
4. Crary, *Techniques of the Observer*, p. 19.
5. See Morgan, 'Critical Empathy', pp. 47–52.
6. Lee and Anstruther-Thomson, *Beauty and Ugliness*, pp. 45–76 ('Aesthetic Empathy and its Organic Accompaniments').
7. Dufrenne, 'The Phenomenological Approach to Poetry', p. 17.
8. See, for example, Berenson, *The Central Italian Painters of the Renaissance*, p. 101.
9. Symons, 'The Decadent Movement in Literature', p. 867.
10. The more developed accounts of Impressionism often discuss its relationship with phenomenology, but tend to find the latter of limited use for reading literary texts (see, for example, Matz, *Literary Impressionism and Modernist Aesthetics*, pp. 12–52). However, I suggest that phenomenological thought can help recognise something crucial within Decadent poetry through its emphasis on a broadly conceived sense of the tactile.
11. Symons, *Silhouettes*, p. 13.
12. Merleau-Ponty, 'The Intertwining – The Chiasm', p. 166.
13. Symons, *London Nights*, p. 47. The poem is dedicated 'To Marcelle', who I believe to be Marcelle Lender, the French singer and dancer who featured in paintings by Toulouse-Lautrec.
14. Merleau-Ponty, 'The Body, Motility and Spatiality', p. 354.
15. Symons, *London Nights*, p. 93.
16. Symons, 'The World as Ballet', p. 246.
17. Ibid., pp. 246, 245.
18. Dowling, *Language and Decadence*, p. 241.
19. Snodgrass, 'Decadent Mythmaking', pp. 85–6.
20. 'Symons [. . .] had been acquainted with Mallarmé since 1890': Morris, 'Mallarmé's Letters to Arthur Symons', p. 346.
21. Gordon, 'The Danse Macabre', pp. 429, 434.
22. Ibid., p. 432.
23. Ibid., p. 441.
24. Quoted in Vadillo, 'Immaterial Poetics: A. Mary F. Robinson and the Fin-de-Siècle Poem', p. 252.
25. Robinson, *Collected Poems*, p. 153
26. Symons, 'The World as Ballet', p. 244.
27. Symons, *Silhouettes*, p. 33. The discourse of race, in particular, in Symons's poetry is, of course, deeply problematic, but it is worth noting, as Barry Faulk has pointed out, that 'Symons translates foreign culture without tact or regard for history, the better to free the dance and the body from the mundane order of signification' ('Camp Expertise', p. 177).

28. Kermode, *Romantic Image*, p. 87; writing about the 'Journal of Henry Luxulyan' (in *Spiritual Adventures*, 1905).
29. Symons, *Silhouettes*, p. 33.
30. Symons, *London Nights*, p. 5.
31. Ibid., pp. 7–8.
32. Symons, 'The Decadent Movement in Literature', p. 859.
33. 'Stella Maris' was published in *London Nights*, pp. 40–1.
34. Merleau-Ponty, *Phenomenology of Perception*, p. ix.
35. Symons, *London Nights*, p. 50; Wilde, *Poems* (1892), frontispiece; Custance, *Rainbows*, p. 42.
36. Shelley, 'Defence', pp. 27, 30.
37. Ibid., pp. 55, 53.
38. Ibid., p. 56.
39. Ibid., pp. 54–5.
40. See Thornton, *The Decadent Dilemma*, p. 130.
41. Dowson, *Collected Poems*, p. 197.
42. Thornton, *The Decadent Dilemma*, p. 105.
43. Weiner, 'Sight and Sound in the Poetic World of Ernest Dowson', pp. 483–4.
44. Ibid., p. 507.
45. Ibid., pp. 504, 509; Weiner writes of the work 'stumbl[ing] under the weight of its own principles'.
46. Dowson, *Collected Poems*, pp. 69–70, 101. See also essays by Alkalay-Gut, 'Overcoming Time and Despair', p. 106, and Benvenuto, 'The Function of Language in the Poetry of Ernest Dowson', p. 161.
47. Lee, *The Handling of Words*, p. 35.
48. Ibid., pp. 58–9.
49. Ibid., p. 1.
50. Lee, 'Vital Tempo', p. 8.
51. Lee, *The Handling of Words*, p. 231.
52. Ibid., p. 36.
53. Ibid., p. 37.
54. See, for example, Kenner, *The Pound Era*, pp. 182–4.
55. Symons, *Silhouettes*, p. 11.
56. Symons, 'The Decadent Movement in Literature', p. 859.
57. Ibid., p. 859.
58. Symons, *London Nights*, pp. 13, 19, 16, 33.
59. See Leverson, 'Reminiscences', p. 105.
60. Psomiades, *Beauty's Body*, p. 90.
61. The latter was discussed interestingly by Deborah Lutz in her paper at the 2013 MLA conference in Boston.
62. This is deliberately to echo Merleau-Ponty's description of the 'chiasm': the point of 'crisscrossing . . . of the touching and the tangible' ('The Intertwining – The Chiasm', p. 166).
63. Classen, *The Deepest Sense*, p. 197 (see pp. 187–97).
64. Peter Nicholls summarises those criticisms of Decadence in *Modernisms*, pp. 65–6.

Chapter 7

'Space, the Bound of a Solid': Alice Meynell and Thomas Hardy

The 1861 reduction in paper taxes, as well as the rise of technological advances in the use of rag substitutes to make paper in the later decades of the nineteenth century, combined to reduce the cost of paper significantly.[1] In her study of the history of the Victorian book, Leah Price suggests that the massive reduction in the price of paper over the century was as dramatic as the reduction in the cost of digital storage 'in our lifetime'.[2] This eye-opening detail gives some indication of the significance of the revolution in print that Price outlines – one that had rapidly altered the texture of daily experience by the late nineteenth century. What resulted, Price argues, was the 'dematerialization of the text and the disembodiment of the reader'.[3] Although poetry had long been circulated in print by this point in history (and its spatial presence on the page had been long exploited even in early manuscript cultures), the specifically Victorian revolution in print that Price charts might be seen to bring new challenges for a genre based around an 'I/you' transaction, contributing to the 'print totalisation' of lyric described at length in Chapter 1. In this chapter I explore the work of two poets whose long writing careers stretched over the later decades of the nineteenth century and the early decades of the twentieth.[4] By bringing together Meynell and Hardy I aim both to motivate a new way of reading the canonical writer, and to integrate the voice of a more recently recovered writer into the poetic lineage to which she rightfully belongs. In so doing, this pairing brings to light similarities in the work of two writers not usually considered together. Both were professional writers who were well aware of the qualities and potential of text in mass-print circulation, and both exploited the possibilities that the textuality of print poetry offered for the rethinking of lyric in relation to the challenges of modernity. Both also share a deep engagement with and mastery of complex prosody. What interests me here, particularly, is the way their interest in poetic form leads, in both cases, to an engagement with the prosodic potential of the materiality of the printed page – and particularly with the play between blank space on the page and prosodic caesura. Ultimately I argue that both poets find within the modern printed page not the 'dematerialization of the text and the disembodiment of the reader' – although what I trace is perhaps a response to this threat – but an attention to paper itself as the site of a new lyric transaction.

I will start with a writer who insists that there is a poetics of the blank white spaces of paper around the printed poem – and who shows us how to read them. Publishing her poetry between 1875 and 1923, Alice Meynell is a poet both central to my period of study and significant for the poetic response I trace in Part II. She was an influential aesthete, presiding over a London 'salon' that was the hub of literary and intellectual activity in the 1880s, as well as a prolific cultural commentator and journalist.[5] Her work provides a theory of poetic space, silence and absence central to the focus of this part of my study, showing how a phenomenological theory might connect with poetry of the period both historically and in terms of literary practice. Moreover, I will devote much of this chapter to showing how Meynell's analysis might be used to provide a reinterpretation of the poetry of Thomas Hardy, unsettling current critical characterisations of his work.

Meynell is particularly interested in the poetic possibilities of the space associated with the silent 'you' beloved addressed within the Petrarchan-style binary of the love lyric. Like Dowson (considered in the previous chapter), she finds the lyric 'other' somehow enmeshed with poetic form, yet, across her oeuvre, Meynell provides a much fuller theorisation. In poems such as 'To the Beloved', for example, she writes: 'Thou art like silence unperplexed,/ A secret and a mystery/ Between one footfall and the next'.[6] Positioned between one metrical foot and the next, the lyric 'you' is to be found in the silences within and around the poetic text. In her essay 'Rhythm of Life' Meynell makes it clear that she, apparently paradoxically, also associates this feminine pause with metre. The piece begins with the claim 'If life is not always poetical, it is at least metrical', and asserts that metre is ingrained in the experience of everyday life: 'Periodicity rules over the mental experience of man'.[7] Yet much as she insists that the 'authenticity' of metrical pulse lies in the everyday experience of the *mind*, the *body* will not quite be silenced: early on in the piece she gives the example of 'Disease' as a form of metrical measure, 'closing in at shorter and shorter periods towards death, sweeping abroad at longer and longer intervals towards recovery'.[8]

Most striking of all is her very final linking of metre to 'the law that commands all things – a sun's revolutions and the rhythmic pangs of maternity'.[9] This link between femininity, silence and poetic metre is one that I want to pursue further.

Meynell's interest in the metrical value of pauses has been explored by Yopie Prins in relation to Coventry Patmore's theorisation of silences (such as catalexis and caesura) as a crucial part of metrical scansion.[10] Reading 'To the Beloved', Prins comments that the poem presents the Beloved of the Petrarchan-style love lyric as a form of 'silent music';[11] one that we might see measured in stanza two by the 'pauses' of breath and the 'hush' of melody:

> My silence, life returns to thee
>   In all the pauses of her breath.
> Hush back to rest the melody
>   That out of thee awakeneth;
> And thou, wake ever, wake for me![12]

The pauses in the poem that represent the drawing of breath breathe life into the silent 'you', the beloved lady, so that she takes shape in those gaps 'Between one footfall and the next'. I suggest that Meynell's essay, 'The Lady of the Lyrics', explains more fully what she is trying to do in this poem, showing her interest to be in the generic role of the female beloved as the absent, silent muse of the love lyric: 'the object of song'. In this piece Meynell pre-empts late twentieth-century feminist literary criticism through her analysis of the gendered 'I/you' dialectic in a Western love lyric tradition.[13] Ultimately, here, she finds the voice of the silent beloved female in the very metre of the poem, asserting that the lady of the lyric 'might be called the lady of the stanzas, so strictly does she go by measure': 'When she is quarrelsome it is but fuguishness; when she dances she does it by a canon. She could not but be perverse, merrily sung to such grave notes.'[14] The essay ends with the assertion that the lady of the lyrics is now outmoded and 'the lovely Elizabethan has slipped away'.[15] Yet, although direct address to the female beloved might, by the late nineteenth century, seem nostalgic, 'To the Beloved' (published in *Preludes* of 1875) recognised the persistent gendering of the lyric 'I/you' binary that still underpinned the tradition and that located the silent, shaping, feminine 'you' in the poetic interstices. Exploring further Meynell's essays, I suggest that while the links Prins traces to Patmore are well taken, Christina Rossetti was also a significant inspiration for Meynell's poetics of the pause. Meynell herself writes that Rossetti distinguishes herself poetically, doing 'a very serious service to English versification' by her musical use of the 'rest'.[16] In Chapter 3 I argued that Dante Gabriel Rossetti suspended every other gesture in his poem so that we could hear the movement of his iambic syllables; here Meynell is interested in how, for Christina, even the silences, blanks or pauses between the syllables of a poem continue that metrical momentum and pattern.

I want to think about Meynell's poetics of the pause in a different way from Prins, suggesting that it offers not only the development of a theory of the relation between music and language, but also a method for reading the phenomenology of poetic form on the page. For Meynell, I argue, these silent beats in and around the poem have not just the sonic presence of a moment of 'hush', but a spatial presence in the blank space on the printed page. This is something that Meynell explores in another poem eventually published in a much later collection, but which continues to think about some of the same themes posed in 'To the Beloved' and 'Lady of the Lyrics'. 'To Silence' begins with an epigraph:

> *'Space, the bound of a solid': Silence, then, the form of a melody*

> Not, Silence, for thine idleness I raise
> My silence-bounded singing in thy praise,
> But for thy moulding of my Mozart's tune,
> Thy hold upon the bird that sings the moon,
>   Thy magisterial ways.
>
> Man's lovely definite melody-shapes are thine,
> Outlined, controlled, compressed, complete, divine.
> Also thy fine intrusions do I trace,
> Thy afterthoughts, thy wandering, thy grace,
>   Within the poet's line.
>
> Thy secret is the song that is to be.
> Music had never stature but for thee,
> Sculptor! Strong as the sculptor Space whose hand
> Urged the Discobolus and bade him stand.
>   *   *   *   *   *   *
> Man, on his way to Silence, stops to hear and see.[17]

It is ultimately the liberation of the space around the figure that creates the sculpture, just as silence and pause is necessary to determining the outline shape and melody of a poem. This play with inverted relationships is typical of Meynell's vision. For Meynell, the one is always threatening to become its opposite in a way that is one of her poetically most arresting and productive strategies. In this poem, a substantial silent pause is dramatised and given a typographic representation through the series of six asterisks in the penultimate line. In this way, the silent line almost becomes an additional line in the stanza, forcing the reader to notice a particular example of the silence that Meynell argues structures around and within each stanza of poetry. Of course, what is so interesting in this poem is the way space and sound intersect in print on the page. In print culture, 'space, the bound of a solid' becomes very literally the representation of 'silence [. . .] the form of a melody': the poem is sculpted out of the white space on the page as it takes a physical shape in black ink. In giving her poetic silence that typographical representation through the asterisks, Meynell marks the white space, the void, in a way that stops it being invisible and invites us to 'read' it – and perhaps even to read it metrically (the six asterisks mirror the six stresses of the last line, and prepare us for that line's breaking of the pattern of the previous two stanzas). Silence here is certainly given tangible form through the spatial pattern of those blank bits of paper that, as Leverson noticed, were so important to aestheticist poetry.

As we can see in 'To the Beloved', for Meynell it is in this tangible body of silence that the feminine is located, as a shaping poetic force. For Meynell, the crisis of the apostrophised 'other' of the Romantic lyric (which Jonathan Culler has written about so interestingly)[18] is a gendered loss – it is an effacing of the 'lady of the lyrics'. From the publication of *Preludes* in 1875 onwards Meynell rediscovers this figure, central to the 'original' transaction of lyric, through the white shapes of the 'hot-pressed paper' that sculpt poetry. It is no accident that Meynell, like the other poets I explore, was wedded to strict forms that give pauses definite shape and meaning. These are strategies available to lyric poets since the birth of poetry as a textual form, but, as Meynell's theorisation in her essays demonstrates, at this moment the potential they offer is particularly significant in an attempt to rediscover the relevance of and possibilities for the lyric poem. Meynell's poetics draws attention to that tangible white space on the page as something seen, but, more than a visual space, it is for her a 'sculptural', 'moulded' space in which the presence of the lyric 'you' can be felt. What I am proposing here then is a phenomenology of the printed lyric in the late nineteenth century that is as much concerned with recording the touch or impress of the world as its appearance; as much about the tactile as the visual.

Reviews of the period usefully unsettle the presumed dialectic in late nineteenth-century lyric poetry between music and image, and support Meynell's sculptural discourse on lyric. Swinburne, for example, describes verse that revels not just in the 'colour', 'sound' and 'flavour' of poetry but also the 'form' and 'shapeliness' of poetic thought: 'it has weight and heat, gravity and intensity'.[19] This sense of the heft of verse works in opposition to connotations of ethereal strains that tend to characterise lyric's association with music, and in opposition to any idea of a disembodied vision. A review of the work of Dante Gabriel Rossetti from 1879 similarly writes of the aestheticist sonnet that it 'should be solid, not spectral, concrete, not ideal in theme'. Written by Thomas Henry Hall Caine (a popular novelist and playwright of the late nineteenth and early twentieth centuries who eventually became Rossetti's secretary and companion in the last year or so of his life),[20] the piece continues:

> Mr. Rossetti's sonnets are solid rather than spectral, but of a solidity nearer akin to that of Michaelangelo [*sic*] than to that of Wordsworth. His is the reality of vision, not the solidity of fact. His sonnets embody at once the spirit of the sensuous and the sensuousness of spirit.[21]

The comparison is primarily with the sonnets of Michelangelo, not his sculpture, but here Caine invokes the physical presence of a sculptural text in the work of both artists. In addition to the investment in the fusion of poetry with music and painting, lyric poetry, specifically, appears to have an important resonance with sculpture at this time. Indeed, it is no coincidence that John Addington Symonds had produced the first rhymed translation of Michelangelo's sonnets in 1878, a publication that both responded to and prompted such comparisons.[22] In spite of mid-nineteenth-century claims for the death of sculpture, which, in parallel with lyric I suggest, underwent a crisis of 'relevance' to the modern world,[23] sculpture was in 1880 (again, I would argue, in parallel to the lyric) noted to have undergone a recent reconsideration. In an essay on how best this revival might be presented engagingly to the general public, the anonymous writer asserts that painting is 'the prose of art' while 'sculpture is the poetry'.[24] In fact, he or she concludes the essay with the thought that 'the study of the best poetry' is 'essential' to the sculptor of the day.[25]

Meynell's connection between lyric and a sculptural presence, then, is not idiosyncratic, and this is a discourse whose significance to late nineteenth-century poetry must be recognised. Crucially, for my purposes, Meynell's theorisation of the physical presence of poetry on the page connects intimately with the theory of phenomenological incorporation introduced in Chapter 5 and read through Decadent poetry in Chapter 6. Merleau-Ponty writes of our knowing things, and other people, by inhabiting them as extensions of our own physical being. In 'The Body, Motility and Spatiality', Merleau-Ponty gives the example of the typist who knows how to type without being able to say exactly where any given letter could be found on the keyboard. Asking how this might be, Merleau-Ponty claims that 'It is knowledge in the hands, which is forthcoming only when bodily effort is made, and cannot be formulated in detachment from that effort': 'It is literally true that the subject who learns to type incorporates the key-blank space into his bodily space.'[26] For Merleau-Ponty, the world is accessed through the body and (in a manner very reminiscent of the nineteenth-century sources cited in Chapter 5) touch is the privileged sense; indeed, an awareness of the body in space – the capacity of touch – is posited as underpinning sight.[27] Phenomenology suggests we find others through our own experience of ourselves as subjects (and crucially as bodies) and through a sense of physical contiguity with the world. In this way, as we saw with Pater's subjectivity, 'Solitude and communication' must be, to quote Merleau-Ponty, 'two "moments" of one phenomenon'.[28] What this suggests, crucially, for poetry is that the lyric 'you' might be rediscovered not as a separate character, as in the dramatic monologue, but as a necessary part of the poetic 'I'. This relationship relies in key part on a sense of 'feeling' the presence of the other; 'you' can be present in the poem as something felt as an extension of the self – just as Meynell's lyric 'you' is manifest in the white spaces sculpted out of the page by the poem. The lyric transaction between 'I' and 'you' that interests me here, then, is more akin to touching than to an objectivist knowing.

This response to the increasing threat of solipsism is apparent in poetry before 1860 (as poems such as Keats's 'This Living Hand' demonstrate),[29] yet I suggest that from the late eighteenth century onwards, and particularly in the late nineteenth century, such gestures acquire a changing significance and increased urgency in tandem with the modernisation of print circulation. This is the poetics of touch that I want to posit in this chapter and that I will now use to explore in Thomas Hardy's work a deft play around the boundaries of the lyric subject. Hardy's lyric space is one in which, like Meynell's, the lyric 'you' is simultaneously understood in relation to the lyric 'I' *and* acknowledged as other and independent and essentially unknown to it.

*   *   *

However much Hardy was invested in the musicality of verse, even his metrical notation of his poetry was, as Stephen Arata has recently put it, 'a perpetual reminder that his poetic "song" was necessarily and multiply mediated by print'.[30] Reading Hardy in relation to the work of Meynell will enable me to suggest new lines of enquiry within his poetry. Hardy is, of all the poets examined in this study, the one least obviously an 'aesthete', yet his is an important voice of the period and, as I noted in Chapter 1, his turn from prose to lyric poetry in the 1860s is an important marker of the new lyric energy I explore in this study. That Hardy's work must be placed in the context of the Parnassian revival is evident from the textual echoes found between the two, however little these are recognised in recent critical discussions of his poetry. Take, for example, the resonances of Hardy's 'Old Furniture' with Mortimer Wheeler's 'Ballade of Old Instruments' (included in Gleeson White's anthology of Parnassian poetry).[31] Likewise, 'The Minute Before Meeting' is similar in basic scenario to Arthur Symons's 'The Broken Tryst' (published in the first Rhymers' Club anthology of 1892).[32] Although Hardy's poetic voice is often identified by scholars as a strikingly modernist one, and included in studies of twentieth-century poetry, his work is also importantly porous to a nineteenth-century context. Not only do we find, if we look, explicit connections with Parnassian poetry, but I suggest that Hardy's work also needs to be read in the context of contemporaries including Alice Meynell, who as a prolific essayist and cultural commentator was a formative influence in the period. Moreover, through placing Hardy's poetry within the context of aestheticism, it is possible to better recognise its sensuality. In what follows I will first (through a reading of 'Old Furniture') establish a basis for thinking about the phenomenological in Hardy's poetry, and then I will draw on Meynell's theorisation of the phenomenology of the poetic page to reconsider the poetic potential of 'The Minute Before Meeting'.

Hardy, in fact, was a man who hated to be touched (as the *Life* records).[33] To offer a poetics of touch through which to read Hardy's work, then, may seem contrary. To read his poetry in this way is to read against the grain, but to do so in a way that this deceptively simple poetry encourages. Indeed, I follow Ralph Pite's biographical reinterpretation of Hardy which has revealed a man whose coldness was a result of acute sensitivity and anxiety – a shield against rejection and hurt. The vulnerable Hardy Pite offers us is a man warmer and more engaged than his defensive exterior might suggest, and one very relevant to my interpretation.[34] In a recent issue of *The Review of English Studies*, Tim Dolin wrote that 'Although a constitution-ally backward-looking man, Hardy's mood was so intensely intro-spective in 1915 that the idea of publishing his own memoirs must have seemed a trivial distraction.'[35] Hardy's poetry, particularly, is still defined through these concepts of introspection and retrospec-tion, and it has become a critical truism that 'so often with Hardy, solipsism is not far away'.[36] Yet this delineation does not recognise the outward-reaching quality of his verse that I want to explore here.

Elaine Scarry's chapter in *Resisting Representation* drew attention to what one might call the phenomenology of work in Hardy's novels, which acknowledges his interest in the contiguity between bodies and objects. To quote Scarry: 'The human creature is for him not now and then but habitually embodied: it has at every moment a physical cir-cumference and boundary'; 'He so persistently calls attention to the visible record of the exchange between the human creature and the world immediately beyond the boundary of the human body that at times it seems an unselfconscious reflex of his style.'[37] Yet for all her assertions about the importance to Hardy's prose works of this kind of hapticity, Scarry does not explore it in relation to the poetry. More-over, there appears to be a generic issue at stake here, a sense that the lyric, as an introspective form, could not reflect these concerns. Indeed, more recent work has articulated this view, arguing that in contrast to the embodied Hardy of the novels, his poetry provides an alternative canon 'concerned with absence, not presence'.[38] But I am interested precisely in reading Hardy's poetry in this way, and to do so is to integrate this work into a trajectory of lyric over the turn of the century that might provide a fresh context for it.

Hardy's 'Old Furniture' is a backward-looking poem about knowing things through history, but it is also about knowing things through touch: furniture is encountered here through the touch of previous generations of hands.

> I know not how it may be with others
>   Who sit amid relics of householdry
> That date from the days of their mothers' mothers,
>   But well I know how it is with me
>   Continually.
>
> I see the hands of the generations
>   That owned each shiny familiar thing
> In play on its knobs and indentations,
>   And with its ancient fashioning
>   Still dallying:

Hands behind hands, growing paler and paler,
    As in a mirror a candle-flame
Shows images of itself, each frailer
    As it recedes, though the eye may frame
        Its shape the same.

On the clock's dull dial a foggy finger,
    Moving to set the minutes right
With tentative touches that lift and linger
    In the wont of a moth on a summer night,
        Creeps to my sight.

On this old viol, too, fingers are dancing –
    As whilom – just over the strings by the nut,
The tip of a bow receding, advancing
    In airy quivers, as if it would cut
        The plaintive gut.

And I see a face by that box for tinder,
    Glowing forth in fits from the dark,
And fading again, as the linten cinder
    Kindles to red at the flinty spark,
        Or goes out stark.

Well, well. It is best to be up and doing,
    The world has no use for one to-day
Who eyes things thus – no aim pursuing!
    He should not continue in this stay,
        But sink away.[39]

Hands and fingers lead the investigation: in the first line of stanza two we are introduced to 'the hands of generations'; at the start of stanza three this is elaborated as a series of 'Hands behind hands'; stanza four traces the touch of 'a foggy finger'; and stanza five works into a now silent, but once musical, image through the play of hands on the fingerboard of an old instrument. Of this last image it is noticeable that touch is the preferred method of access to a history that is there to be felt, but not heard. The fingers and hands that frame each of these stanzas are involved in a variety of types of touch: 'tentative touches that lift and linger'; 'dallying'; fingers 'dancing' and 'play[ing]' over objects. This in turn gives rise to a vocabulary of tactile sensations in this poem. 'Familiar' things are 'shiny', worn smooth with much handling. '[K]nobs and indentations' speak of the rise and fall of the surface to the touch. Yet it is clear that 'seeing' also plays an important role in this tactile apprehension. Stanza two declares 'I see the hands'; stanza three reports a visual experience of seeing hands 'growing paler and paler'; and stanza four sees the visually indistinct 'foggy' finger move the clock's hands.

So, the poetic 'I' here *sees* the hands, but then *feels* the furniture through the hands. This idea of vision as a reaching out to the world in a tactile way is one that, again, resonates strongly with the phenomenological modes of thinking introduced in Chapter 5. In 'Eye and Mind', Merleau-Ponty sets out the intentionality of vision in the following terms: 'Everything I see is in principle within my reach, at least within reach of my sight, and is marked upon the map of the "I can."'[40] This central notion of knowing the world through the possibility of touch and action is worked through by Merleau-Ponty once again in a theory of incorporation:

> Visible and mobile, my body is a thing among things; it is caught in the fabric of the world, and its cohesion is that of a thing. But because it moves itself and sees, it holds things in a circle around itself. Things are an annex or prolongation of itself; they are incrusted into its flesh, they are part of its full definition; the world is made of the same stuff as the body.[41]

In other words, 'vision happens among, or is caught in, things' in a quasi-tactile manner.[42] While the classic empiricists of the seventeenth to nineteenth centuries associated vision and touch in so far as the experience of vision requires the content of tactile experience to make sense of it, phenomenology (in the late nineteenth and early twentieth century) posed a different, more intimate understanding of the relationship. When Merleau-Ponty writes that 'my body is a thing among things', he is asserting that something obviously true of touch is also true of vision: that the experience of the self as a body among other bodies is as central to visual experience as to tactile experience. What we see in Hardy's poem looks like a similar form of epistemology through physical incorporation: knowing things as an extension of body (knowing through touch), and finding the privileged sense of sight dependent on, and inseparable from, the reach of the tactile. The double meaning of the term 'impression' – both visual and tactile – is as relevant to Hardy's work as to Symons's phenomenological Impressionism.

The touch explored in this poem acts as a method of contact not just with the objects observed, but with other people (dead or alive) whose presence is still carried by the objects worn shiny with their touch. Ultimately this poem meets the hands of others in a poetics of touch and touched that both acknowledges and finds a response to the threat of isolation that underpinned *fin-de-siècle* lyric modernity. Indeed, the central image of stanza four – with its pun of hands on [clock-]hands – foregrounds, in an ironic conceit, the possibility of reciprocal touch.[43] In a similar way, the never-ending regression of 'Hands behind hands, growing paler and paler' invokes a notion of mutual formation (in this case between present and past) that is central to phenomenology. In the final stanza of the poem Hardy muses how 'the world has no use for one to-day who eyes things thus'. Yet, typically, what engages us as readers is the modernity of his vision: a very modern way of dealing with familiar problems of subjectivity and scepticism. To think about Hardy's poetry in this context is not to deny the importance of the impressive work done on the significance of vision,[44] but it does aim to recognise another layer in his work that finds new forms of contact with the world even when the poetic 'I' marks his position as a separated visual spectator.

'Old Furniture' shows Hardy's susceptibility to a phenomenological mode of engagement in poetic content, but in the rest of this chapter I want to make a case for that more meta-textual idea that I theorised through Meynell: a phenomenology of poetic form. In an essay from 2006, Marjorie Levinson writes about the difficulty of reading Hardy's poetry critically: of knowing what to do with this deceptively simple work (because, as she says, 'there is so little content to distract us from the forms of writing'). Levinson writes: 'Hardy's lyrics [. . .] somehow avoid turning sensation into perception, perception into experience, and experience into thought, memory, and meaning.'[45] It is precisely the importance of form and sensation that I want to read here, not as a barrier to establishing meaning but *as* the meaning of Hardy's poetry. Hardy's poetry is, as we know, typified by the absence of a person. Much of it seems to be about a failure to connect with other people in the world, a solipsism perhaps typical, generically, of the totalised print lyric. This is true not just of the 'Emma poems', haunted in a very personal way by the ghost of his dead wife; the theme had been apparent in Hardy's poetry long before that.[46] Heidegger writes of Humboldt's studies that 'alluded to certain languages which express the "I" by "here", the "thou" by "there", the "he" by "yonder", thus rendering the personal pronouns by locative adverbs, to put it grammatically'.[47] This passage offers ideas about the inherent spatiality of the terms 'I' and 'you' that I want to take over into my reading of lyric. Thinking about the frame of the lyric transaction within these spatial terms helps us understand it as one motivated by the overcoming of a gap between addresser and addressee. For Hardy, 'you' appears always 'there' and not here; always out of the frame – and the absence so striking in Hardy's poetry might itself be read as a statement of the problem of knowing others, of making those connections when we are only too aware of what separates us.[48]

'The Minute Before Meeting' might appear a classic example[49] – and this is the second poem by Hardy I want to focus on. (This is a poem identified by Hardy as a 'lyric' poem by its placing in a section of *Time's Laughingstocks and Other Verses* called 'love lyrics'.) The poem is dated perhaps to indicate his first meeting Emma Gifford, but clearly is not operating primarily in biographical mode. The poetic 'I' bemoans both the bleakness of the days that must be endured before the longed-for meeting, and the despair anticipated to follow after the meeting is over:

> The grey gaunt days dividing us in twain
> Seemed hopeless hills my strength must faint to climb,
> But they are gone; and now I would detain
> The few clock-beats that part us; rein back Time,
>
> And live in close expectance never closed
> In change for far expectance closed at last,
> So harshly has expectance been imposed
> On my long need while these slow blank months passed.
>
> And knowing that what is now about to be
> Will all *have been* in O, so short a space!
> I read beyond it my despondency
> When more dividing months shall take its place,
> Thereby denying to this hour of grace
> A full-up measure of felicity.[50]

In this moment of anticipation, the person to be met seems entirely absent from the poem's content. '[U]s' is referred to once, but apart from that the 'you' to be met is not mentioned at all. The focus is on '*my* long need' and how 'I' would rein back time, on '*my* despondency' and how '*my* strength must faint to climb'. Never has a moment before a meeting been less filled with thoughts of the one to be met. On the face of it this looks like an example of the modern lyric's failure to connect with 'you'. This conclusion seems reinforced by the diction of loss: 'dividing' (twice), 'hopeless', 'gone', 'part', 'blank', 'denying'. As indicated by the title, the poem appears to operate primarily in a temporal mode, and to meditate on themes of time and loss that are so common within Hardy's work.

Yet to read only in this way is to ignore another discursive layer within the poem. Our language of time generally appropriates the language of space, and in this poem it is striking how the temporal measure becomes spatialised. In line 10 the minute is identified as 'O, so short a *space*', and even the terminology in line 1 of being 'divided' by time surely draws on an intrinsically spatial dead metaphor. Certainly 'rein[ing] back' time is a metaphor that draws an analogy with progress through space. It is a spatial reading of the poem that I will pursue here, in line with Meynell's instruction that we must read the silences, which, in the totalised print lyric, she shows to have become the spatial gaps on the page in poetry of the period. In this way, I suggest, even in a poem like this where 'you' seems so utterly outside the solipsistic frame of the poetic 'I', there is a space created that seems to offer us a glimpse of the very thing the poem denies. This reading is based centrally on the thought that vision is an experience of spatial separation (Heidegger's here and there), but touch one of spatial contiguity: 'Vision presents us with things as *over there*, touch presents us with things as *in the same place* as parts of ourselves.'[51] In 'The Minute Before Meeting', I will argue, 'you' is experienced through a process of touching the world and being touched by it; this poem gives us a sense of the presence of the other as 'here', rather than seeing them as 'over there'. In short, 'you' is delineated phenomenologically and becomes present formally, even while being absent from the poem's content.

The most striking textual feature of the poem on the page in the first, 1909, edition as well as in subsequent editions is the 'O' – that large hole in line 10 of the sonnet: 'in O, so short a space'. 'O' stands out not just typographically but rhetorically as one of only two elements of poetic diction in the poem (the other is 'twain', to which I will return). This figure is a graphic representation of the 'so short a space' – the whole minute itself that precedes the meeting. Yet given the investment of spatial dead metaphors in our language of time (so prominent in this particular line of the poem), that 'O' represents a spatial gap as well as a temporal one. Typographically, in an age of print poetry, it is a circumscribed blank space on the page, perhaps a graphic representation of the space around the person who is bodily missing from the poem – that which is currently absent, and soon will '*have been*' – as well as a temporal caesura. This exclamatory poetic 'O' draws attention to itself at the centre of this bleakly unexclamatory poem, and opens up a space for something else to appear.

In so far as this 'O' is an outline drawn around the absence of 'you', it is also a way of enabling 'you' to become present at the heart of the poem.

To read Hardy in this way is to read as Meynell instructed: to find in the empty spaces on the page shapes as significant as the black type. 'O' is, in Meynell's words, 'the bound of a solid'. If in 'To Silence' Meynell draws our attention to the signifying white space on the page through a line of asterisks, then Hardy does it through this striking rhetorical gesture which circles the poem's object of attention. This 'O' in the middle of the poem becomes, I suggest, a form of incorporation of 'you' into 'I'. To put it in phenomenological terms, it is the mode of tactile bodily incorporation that Merleau-Ponty suggests we know the world by. To return to a passage quoted earlier, if the body is 'a thing among things', 'caught in the fabric of the world' that 'holds things in a circle around itself', then isn't this exclamatory circle a holding on to something? If 'Things are an annex or prolongation of itself' (if 'they are incrusted into its flesh . . . are part of its full definition') then isn't this 'O' not a hole but a making whole: an incrusting into the body of the poem the space of the other in order to make the poetic body complete and full? To be sure, 'you' is not clearly sighted in this poem, but the presence of the other is, I argue, 'felt' – as spatially sited – by the body of the poem.

For Meynell, of course, that white space is, sonically, silence ('the form of the melody') and the lyric 'you' appears in the pauses between the poem's metrical measures. Hardy's 'O' itself creates such a pregnant pause, and one might read his absent poetic presence more generally in terms of the poem's metre. Throughout the poem there is a strong pattern of three against four, or three against five. This syncopation primarily acts as a brake on metrical momentum. For example, the repeated pattern of three stressed syllables (a molossus) brakes the forward flow of the iambic pentameter – see 'grey gaunt days', 'few clock-beats' and 'rein back Time'. Similarly, the repetition of 'expectance' in three lines of a four-line stanza again brakes the forward momentum and slows the sonnet down. This ungainly word, slow to pronounce (and containing an internal aural echo between 'ex' and 'pec' in addition to its three repetitions), occurs in roughly the same place in all three lines and acts as a weight, dragging the poem back. All this is a way of extending the minute, of preventing its conclusion. This sonnet really is (to steal, and misquote, a cue from Dante Gabriel Rossetti) a 'minute's monument' – a stilling of time. This metrically and formally delineated gap clears a space that signifies the absence of the lyric 'you', their unknowability, but also their circumference and their incorporation. In this poem, 'you' is constructed through a process of touching the world and being touched by it; of feeling around the edges of person rather than addressing them directly. Just as Meynell suggested, 'you' is delineated formally, and becomes present phenomenologically even as she appears absent in content.

At the very end, the poetic 'I' describes how the pleasure of the forthcoming meeting is spoilt by his further anticipation of the separation that will follow after it is over: 'Thereby denying to this hour of grace/ A full-up measure of felicity'. The wording here cannot help but highlight that this sonnet is itself very much a 'full-up measure': a perfect sonnet, formally present and spatially complete. In this way the poem invites us to see a formal poetics of presence within and around its proclamation of absence. Of course, Hardy himself, in what Michael Millgate identifies as a note written early in his career, described his 'Lyrical Method' in a manner that suggests not so much a productive tension between content and form but a profound disinterest:

> *Lyrical Meth* Find a situn from expce. Turn to Lycs for a form of expressn that has been used for a quite difft situn. Use it (Same sitn from experience may be sung in sevl forms.)[52]

In marked contrast to T. E. Hulme's description of free verse as 'clothes made to order, rather than ready-made clothes', Hardy refers to mapping out blank 'verse skeletons' (rhythmical outlines) which were later fitted out with content.[53] This marked disjunction between content and form in Hardy's poetry has been noticed by readers from the time of its first publication, and has been a major theme within criticism since, as scholars have debated its meaning.[54] Peter Howarth has entered the debate with a substantial analysis of the 'indifference' of Hardy's predetermined, and apparently unsympathetic, formal patterns (indifferent, that is, to the tales of human suffering they contain). Howarth goes on to interpret the disjunction as a critique of a Romantic ideal of unity between treatment and subject, and of a Symbolist 'union of thing and word'. This reading is coherent with my suggestion that we see Hardy finding a connection with the world more phenomenological than Symbolist.[55]

So, 'The Minute Before Meeting' might be a strict sonnet, an 'indifferent' form, but it is precisely this disjunction that enables the poem to represent, or enact, simultaneously two different ways of knowing. The verse 'skeletons' set up an awareness of the poem's 'body', which Hardy fleshes out in this particular instance with a discourse on time, as so often. Yet this meditation on the temporal itself becomes a form of embodiment – in key part through the spatialised nature of the temporal discourse. This gives the poem a double-sided nature, which through its reflections on the temporal 'gap' before the meeting (the absence of 'you'), opens up a 'space' that simultaneously figures the bodily form of 'you'. To invoke 'you' within the poem in this way is to reawaken the lyric as a 'transaction' between 'I' and 'you', albeit in what I have called a phenomenological manner rather than through lyric's more traditional form of direct address. Read in light of Meynell's more explicit theorisation in 'To the Beloved', this might be seen to revitalise that notion of transaction in a manner appropriate to a lyric aware of itself as a printed form.

Indeed, there is plenty of evidence in Hardy's work that he was as consciously aware as Meynell of the potential of the printed textual space to host an interplay of bodies. For example, in the short story 'An Imaginative Woman', two poems published in a journal on the same topic but in different sections of the same page constitute for Hardy a near-miss encounter of the two authors; something equivalent to the many times they almost, but don't quite, meet in person.[56] If the space of the printed page can accommodate the physical proximity of bodies of lover and beloved within the poem, then it might also, by extension, have the potential to host a point of connection between poet and reader. The kind of connection with a lyric 'you', I have suggested above, might indicate the awareness of a newly phenomenological connection with the reader through the printed page – that textured or smooth surface invoked by Leverson and Mill.

To read in this way is to recognise the potential for individual experience to be something necessarily formed from involvement with the world (for subjectivity to be constituted by its relations with others), and to see lyric as the point of synaptic contact. Crucially, this prompts us to see the potential for lyric introspection to be a route into an apprehension of others.[57] Husserl is interested in the 'intention to communicate something, albeit prelinguistically' which leads him to speak of 'immediate communications – or better, a *touching*, establishing *an original connection between I and You* in originally experiencing empathy'.[58] This is the haptic poetics I find in Hardy's solitude. As Ralph Pite describes in his biography of Hardy:

> Writing became for [Hardy] a precious medium between human beings who were divided from each other by the accidents of circumstance and separated at a deeper level just by the condition of being an individual [. . .] Through writing and reading [. . .] you spoke to others; you reached them.[59]

So, it is, I think, no accident that in this print-culture sonnet the final word of the first line – 'dividing us in *twain*' – is pulled off course, through the prompt of the rhyme in lines 2 and 4 ('climb' and 'time') to veer towards the word 'twine': entwined, twined together. (Indeed the twain/twine echo is one Hardy plays with in other poems such as 'A Duettist at her Pianoforte'.) 'The Minute Before Meeting' is a poem about absence – but one that offers a phenomenology of presence.

Phenomenology focuses attention on individual experience as something necessarily formed from involvement with the world: not something purely internal, but a point of connection with a thing that exists independent of our experience of it. This idea has very interesting implications for what Mill and others characterised as lyric introspection. Nineteenth-century interest in the 'origins' of lyric as an 'I/you' transaction, combined with Paterian worries about our ability to engage with the world outside our own consciousness, ensured that lyric of the period is concerned with the problem of its interaction with the world. The readings I have offered find in lyric poetry the potential to represent that point of connection between the world and the perceiver, where both are relevant, both are engaged, even if not in a relationship of straightforward correspondence. The lyric poem can in this sense be likened to Merleau-Ponty's conception of skin: something experienced as a surface where inside and outside meet, where the experiences of both touching and being touched reside. It is through the 'crisscrossing' of experiences of touching and being touched that the body's 'own movements incorporate themselves into the universe they interrogate, are recorded on the same map as it'.[60] In this way, Merleau-Ponty escapes the traditional binaries of subject and object, inside and outside, by positing the surface of the body as the point at which we are enmeshed into a system of exchanges between self and world.

Ultimately one might argue that a connection between the lyric 'I' and the lyric 'you' might at times be re-found in poetry of the period through a recognition of something like the intentionality of consciousness. Rather like an 'inquiry' or an 'inquest', intentionality is a directing oneself towards, tending towards, or striving towards.[61] Phenomenologically, to be conscious is necessarily to move outside oneself; our own subjectivity is dependent on our awareness of what is outside of ourselves, and is constituted by its relations with the other.[62] In other words, a sense of self might be achieved through our dealings with other subjects; subjectivity is perhaps necessarily embodied and active, and inseparable from a notion of others in the world. Reading poetry of the period in light of such responses to the experience of modernity enables us to consider something of crucial importance to the lyric genre: that a focus on individual experience might, if pursued intently enough, itself hold the potential to offer a route out of the cul-de-sac of lyric introspection.

Notes

1. Price, *How to Do Things with Books in Victorian Britain*, p. 249.
2. Ibid., p. 141.
3. Ibid., p. 220.
4. To read Meynell and Hardy alongside one another is not to assert a direct biographical connection, although there are brief letters from Hardy to Alice's husband, Wilfred Meynell, showing he had some, limited contact with the family, and there is no doubt he would have had an awareness of her work. See Hardy, *Collected Letters* 1, pp. 115–16 (2 March 1883); *Collected Letters* 4, p. 47 (17 September 1909).
5. See Vadillo, *Women Poets and Urban Aestheticism*, pp. 78–116.
6. Meynell, *Poems*, p. 120, stanza 4.
7. Meynell, 'The Rhythm of Life', p. 216.
8. Ibid., p. 216.
9. Ibid., p. 219.
10. See particularly his 'Essay on English Metrical Law' of 1878.
11. Prins, 'Patmore's Law', p. 268.
12. Meynell, *Poems*, p. 120.
13. See, for example, Montefiore's *Feminism and Poetry*; Homans's *Bearing the Word*; DeShazer's *Inspiring Women*.
14. Meynell, 'The Lady of the Lyrics', p. 50.
15. Ibid., p. 51.
16. Meynell, 'Christina Rossetti', p. 205.
17. *Poems*, p. 102. Published in *Last Poems* of 1923.
18. See his chapter on 'apostrophe' in *The Pursuit of Signs*.
19. Swinburne, 'The Poems of Dante Gabriel Rossetti', pp. 576–9.
20. Allen, *Hall Caine: Portrait of a Victorian Romancer*, p. 123.
21. Ibid., p. 809 (the spelling of Michelangelo's name vacillates between several variants at this time).
22. Symonds, *The Sonnets of Michael Angelo Buonarroti and Tommaso Campanella*; here Symonds gives a prefatory note on his reason for choosing the old English spelling of Michael Angelo's name. In the preface he too writes about the sonnets in tactile terms claiming their affinity with the 'rough' rather than the 'smooth' (p. 14).
23. Lene Ostermark-Johansen traces the proclamations of sculpture's death, and Baudelaire's objections to it as an art form too primitive for the modern world ('Caught between Gautier and Baudelaire', pp. 180–5).

24. Anonymous, 'English Sculpture in 1880', p. 179.
25. Ibid., p. 186. Interestingly, Baudelaire too, as his views on sculpture developed, drew connections between it and lyric poetry: 'Just as lyric poetry makes everything noble – even passion; so sculpture, true sculpture, makes everything solemn – even movement' ('Salon of 1859', p. 205).
26. Merleau-Ponty, 'The Body, Motility and Spatiality', pp. 382, 384.
27. Ibid., p. 386.
28. Merleau-Ponty, 'Other People and the Human World,' p. 359.
29. Keats, *The Complete Poems*, p. 459.
30. Arata, 'Rhyme, Rhythm, and the Materiality of Poetry', p. 519.
31. White, *Ballades and Rondeaus*, p. 73.
32. Rhymers' Club, *The Book of the Rhymers' Club* (1892), pp. 19–20.
33. Florence Hardy, *The Life*, p. 25.
34. Pite, *Thomas Hardy: The Guarded Life*, passim.
35. Dolin, 'The *Early Life* and *Later Years of Thomas Hardy*', p. 705.
36. Page, 'Art and Aesthetics', p. 38. His solitary voice seems to signal a scepticism, what Hardy himself acknowledges might be called a 'pessimism' (Hardy, 'Apology', p. 1441).
37. Scarry, *Resisting Representation*, pp. 50, 51.
38. Freedman, *Death, Men and Modernism*, p. 29.
39. Hardy, *The Complete Poems*, pp. 485–6. Published in *Moments of Vision*, 1917.
40. Merleau-Ponty, 'Eye and Mind', p. 283.
41. Ibid., p. 284.
42. Ibid., p. 284.
43. This pre-empts an image later to become central to Merleau-Ponty's work in the celebrated 'reversibility thesis': the image of the thinker's two hands touching one another, used to explore the relationship between touch and touching in the previous chapter (Merleau-Ponty, 'The Intertwining – The Chiasm', p. 166 onwards).
44. Tom Paulin's *Thomas Hardy: The Poetry of Perception* is a case to point: this important study focuses primarily on sight, although also includes a chapter on 'Sounds and Voices'.
45. Levinson, 'Object-loss and Object-bondage', pp. 569, 552.
46. See, for example, 'The Whitewashed Wall', 'In The Street', 'Nobody Comes'.
47. Heidegger, 'The Dasein-With of Others and Everyday Being-With', pp. 437–8.
48. Harold Bloom has claimed that while modern poetry may be able to help us understand ourselves, it cannot overcome the problems of the perceived gap between self and other (*Kabbalah and Criticism*, pp. 24–49).
49. In his iconic study, *Distance and Desire*, Hillis Miller writes of Hardy's obsession with 'obstructed relationships' ('unfulfilled hope') – mainly

in the novels – but points briefly to 'The Minute Before Meeting' as a poetic example of this (pp. 156–7).

50. Hardy, *The Complete Poems*, p. 236; dated 1871, although the poem was not published until *Time's Laughingstocks and Other Verses* in 1909.

51. Hopkins, 'Painting, Sculpture, Sight and Touch', p. 155.

52. Find a situ[atio]n from exp[erien]ce. Turn to Ly[ri]cs for a form of express[io]n that has been used for a quite diff[eren]t situ[atio]n. Use it (Same sit[uatio]n from experience may be sung in sev[era]l forms.) This is Michael Millgate's transcription of a manuscript source; see *Thomas Hardy: A Biography*, p. 89.

53. Millgate (ed.), *The Life and Work of Thomas Hardy*, p. 324; Hulme, 'A Lecture on Modern Poetry', p. 62.

54. See, for example, Alfred Noyes, writing in the *North American Review* in 1911 (Noyes, 'The Poetry of Thomas Hardy', p. 102); Jean R. Brooks, writing in 1971 (Brooks, *Thomas Hardy: The Poetic Structure*, p. 32); and later, James Richardson (Richardson, *Thomas Hardy: The Poetry of Necessity*, p. 90).

55. Howarth, *British Poetry in the Age of Modernism*, pp. 181, 169.

56. Hardy, *Wessex Tales*, p. 10.

57. Merleau-Ponty, *The Prose of the World*, p. 135.

58. Husserl, *Zur Phänomenologie der Intersubjecktivität*, p. 167; translation given by A. D. Smith, *Husserl and the Cartesian Meditations*, p. 246.

59. Pite, *Thomas Hardy: The Guarded Life*, p. 474.

60. Merleau-Ponty, 'The Intertwining – The Chiasm', p. 166.

61. Connor, 'How to Get Out of Your Head', pp. 4–6.

62. Matthews, *The Philosophy of Merleau-Ponty*, p. 89.

Part III: Subjectivity

Chapter 8

Desire Lines: Subjectivity and Collectivity

[The poem's] content is not the object but the subject, the inner world, the mind that considers and feels, that instead of proceeding to action, remains alone with itself as inwardness, and that therefore can take as its sole form and final aim that self-expression of the subjective life.

Hegel, *Aesthetics*, p. 1038

Today, when individual expression, which is the precondition for the conception of lyric poetry that is my point of departure, seems shaken to its very core in the crisis of the individual, the collective undercurrent in the lyric surfaces in the most diverse places [. . .]

Adorno, 'On Lyric Poetry and Society', p. 46

While Part II ended with an analysis of the significance of lyric as a transaction between 'I' and 'you', Part III considers the construction of the lyric subject itself. Both topics require an engagement with that central dilemma of modernity: the accompaniment of the 'inward turn' (the idea that all we can ever really know, we must know through our own subjective impressions) with a questioning of the relevance of 'inner worlds' and a drive towards a more objectivist or depersonalised ideal. Yet my focus on the lyric subject in this part enables me to draw out some different issues within the poetry I study, and to reveal the importance of some very different responses to modernity within an aestheticist lyric trajectory. In this initial short framing chapter I will set up a nexus of ideas to contextualise, conceptually, my exploration of lyric subjectivity in the following two case studies. In order to respond to the problems of a Romantic legacy in which the lyric voice is simultaneously personal, introspective *and* universal, the poetry I explore looks back to pre-Romantic models. In Part III, then, the focus falls particularly on the significance of an engagement with lyric history to devising fresh models of lyric subjectivity. This chapter introduces the idea of 'desire lines' to provide a conceptual frame for the poetic negotiation between the personal and the collective that is at the heart of the renegotiation of lyric subjectivity that I trace in my focal poems.

Susanne Langer describes the lyric subject as an 'impersonal subjectivity', and captures the characteristic territory of the lyric as introspection, but an introspection that attains an impersonal universality.[1] This was certainly an idea of lyric subjectivity current at the start of the nineteenth century, as can be seen in the quotation from Hegel that supplies my first epigraph above. In his more detailed account of the lyric, Hegel returns to this theme, arguing that the key purpose of the lyric poem is not to represent material externality but to reflect on the experiences to which it gives rise within the poet's '*subjective* disposition'. It is the movement of the heart and the imagination that are the territory of lyric for Hegel: 'the contents and activity of the inner life itself'.[2] Yet, crucially, in the lyric this introspection must also be a route outwards, towards the universal. Hegel continues:

> But in order that this expression may not remain a merely casual expression of an individual's own immediate feelings and ideas, it becomes the language of the *poetic* inner life, and therefore however intimately the insights and feelings which the poet describes as his own belong to him as a single individual, they must nevertheless possess a universal validity [. . .][3]

It is the universalising impulse in lyric that, in the early nineteenth century, enables a subjectivity that both is and is not personal; a lyric poet that 'both is and is not himself'.[4] Hegel assures us that we have no real interest in the poet's 'particular fancies', but in 'something universally human' with which we can feel in sympathy.[5] Yet this idea that the lyric subject could be simultaneously individual and 'universal' became increasingly untenable as the nineteenth century progressed. If the lyric's claims to 'universality' became increasingly suspect, then its claims to a 'personal' voice also became embarrassing. From Wordsworth's 'spontaneous overflow of powerful feelings' to T. S. Eliot's 'escape from personality', the nineteenth-century lyric can be defined as an arena for exploring the tension between individuality and universality.[6] It is in this arena that, in the following two chapters, I situate two further poetic case studies. But first, in the remainder of this chapter, I will sketch the broader historical and theoretical context a little more.

The 'dramatic monologue' of the mid-nineteenth century has typically been seen to mark a notable point of concern with a Romantic transcendent formulation of lyric subjectivity, such as that articulated by Hegel. Victorian poets, so the story goes, introduced more objective (narrative or dramatic) elements as a reaction against the Romantic emphasis on lyric subjectivity. Recent challenges to this narrative have pointed out that 'persona poems' were common currency around the start of the century and not a new poetic mode of the mid-century.[7] However, it would be a mistake to see every poem that speaks through a persona clearly differentiated from the poet as a 'dramatic monologue' – at least in the sense in which the term is applied to a mid-nineteenth-century poetic innovation. The claims made for the dramatic monologue are more specific than this, as I will try to show. Langer's sense of lyric's 'impersonal subjectivity' suggests a poetic voice that, as Hegel explains, is never spoken by the poet *as* the poet. For this reason, adopting a persona is not in itself a breaking of the conventions of lyric's claim to being a 'personal' utterance, so long as the poet speaks through the persona sincerely, if performatively, and therefore credibly.[8] If mid-century dramatic monologues (or 'dramatic lyrics' as we might more rightly call them) present a challenge to lyric, it is not through their use of a persona who is clearly not the poet *per se*. Rather, as discussed in Chapter 5, it is through the creation of a clear distance between the poet and the speaker, and/or the incorporation of a listener into the frame of the poem, so that the poem becomes a meta-lyric, played out at one remove from the poet.[9] This breaks the bond of the lyric's 'impersonal subjectivity', identifying the subject with a specific character in a specific transaction. This mimetic particularity represents a point of crisis for lyric subjectivity because it suggests an anxiety about the relevance of both introspection and universalisation.[10] Indeed, such self-consciousness around the distance created between poet and persona in the mid-nineteenth-century dramatic monologue appears to reflect that increasing sense, discussed in my first chapter, of 'lyric' as an isolatable poetic genre that demands a degree of introspection and personal expression. As E. Warwick Slinn writes:

> the fact remains that something happened to Victorian poetry that the poets themselves named as 'dramatic'. The massive Victorian production of poems where the speaker is not the poet, or where personal expressiveness is placed in a context which objectifies its process [. . .], or where a speaker objectifies herself for self-scrutiny [. . .], marks a literary phenomenon that amounts to a virtual paradigm shift.[11]

If this is true for the mid-Victorian dramatic monologue, then something similar is also true for early twentieth-century modernist poetry that defined itself through a reaction against a Romantic conceptualisation of the transcendent lyric subject. (In his study of early twentieth-century poetic subjectivity, Bernard Duffey comments that while Romantic lyric asserted an 'essential selfhood over and above all accidence', modern poetry 'has been troubled by the loss of that voice'.)[12] More specifically, and as I noted in earlier chapters, free verse seemed to signify, for writers including T. E. Hulme, a rejection of any claim to a universalising voice (itself associated with the conventions of regular rhyme and metre).[13] As Peter Howarth has pointed out, early modernism turned to free verse because 'free verse allows the poet to be natural, at one with himself, his individuality never compromised by convention'.[14] This desire for the poet to be 'himself' marks the difficulty in seeing the poet any longer as something bigger than him- or herself.[15] This is all part of what Paul de Man describes as a gradual process of 'the crisis of the self and of representation in lyric poetry of the nineteenth and twentieth centuries'.[16]

To ask again the question I pose repeatedly in this study: where does this leave us with the largely strict-verse-form aestheticist lyric poetry of the late nineteenth century that shares neither the dramatic experiments of the mid-century nor the free verse challenge of the early twentieth century? In order to understand it as not simply a regressive or nostalgic retreat from the problems of modernity, it is important to recognise how this poetry fostered different responses – very different responses to those of modernism, but responses that reacted to the same problems of lyric subjectivity. In these next chapters I argue that one significant strategy to be seen in poetry of the period is the search for a subject that is part of a collectivity: a lyric subject that is both personal and social. The rest of this chapter will be devoted to introducing this idea, starting with one of the most important analyses of modern lyric subjectivity.

*   *   *

Theodor Adorno's 1957 essay (originally a radio broadcast) 'On Lyric Poetry and Society' deals with what happens to lyric at a time when, to return to my second epigraph for this chapter, 'individual expression, which is the precondition for the conception of lyric poetry [. . .], seems shaken to its very core in the crisis of the individual'.[17] In the following two chapters I will be asking, in key part, what effect this had on the construction of the subject through lyric *form*. In this essay, Adorno recognises that the concept of lyric risks bypassing the social realm altogether: in seeking to 'attain universality through unrestrained individuation', it appears to have no contact whatsoever with society or commerce.[18] Through Hegel, Adorno identifies the 'paradox specific to the lyric work' as 'a subjectivity that turns into objectivity' – a paradox that was difficult to sustain as the nineteenth century progressed.[19] Lyric's apparent detachment from society was exaggerated in the later nineteenth century by the 'art for art's sake' agenda of aestheticism, and it is no coincidence that in addition to the influence of Hegel, Adorno's inspiration in this essay comes in key part from the aestheticism of Baudelaire. Although a piece from the mid-twentieth century, this essay reflects on a poetic trajectory that began with aestheticism, and for this reason it is a crucial part of my theoretical frame.

Adorno begins by pointing out that his title must, to his audience, seem perverse; his insistence on linking literature with society will seem 'especially distressing to you in the case of lyric poetry':

> The most delicate, the most fragile thing that exists is to be encroached upon and brought into conjunction with bustle and commotion, when part of the ideal of lyric poetry, at least in its traditional sense, is to remain unaffected by bustle and commotion. A sphere of expression whose very essence lies in either not acknowledging the power of socialisation or overcoming it through the pathos of detachment.[20]

We might think here of poems such as Michael Field's 'Penetration', which imagines, and enacts, the perfect aestheticist lyric by aspiring towards an art so rarefied, so divorced from the contaminations of society – the 'havoc and harsh hum/ Of the arraigning world' – that it is untarnished by commerce and almost unsullied by communication.[21] Yet, in spite of, and because of, lyric's eschewal of society, Adorno's essay insists on asking what relation the lyric has with the social realm. He makes three main claims here. First, he states that the studied separation of the genre from society is itself a way of rebelling against a corrupt consumerist modern society, and so is a form of engagement with society. Next, he points to the medium of language, which 'establishes an inescapable relationship to the universal and to society'.[22] Language mediates between the lyric and society (and between subjectivity and objectivity) at the most fundamental level: 'This is why the lyric reveals itself to be most deeply grounded in society when it does not chime in with society, when it communicates nothing, when, instead, the subject whose expression is successful reaches an accord with language itself.'[23] For Adorno, the mere fact that the lyric subject is expressed through language is enough, in one sense, to negate its opposition to society.[24]

The third claim for the social within the lyric is the one that I want to pursue in the rest of this part of this book, however, and relies on the notion of a 'collective undercurrent' in the lyric that

> provides the foundation for all individual lyric poetry [. . .] participation in this undercurrent is an essential part of the substantiality of the individual lyric as well [. . .] Romanticism's link to the folksong is only the most obvious, certainly not the most compelling example of this.[25]

This idea that the lyric subject 'always stands in for a far more general collective subject' is one that I will suggest resonates very interestingly with the operations of lyric in the later nineteenth century.[26] Adorno does not say very much about what this notion of collectivity might be, except that it originates from 'the linguistic and psychic residues of a condition that is not yet fully individuated, a state of affairs that is prebourgeois in the broadest sense'.[27] This notion of a pre-bourgeois 'dialect' that signifies community rather than individuality provides the basis for my exploration of ways in which the modern lyric subject finds a sense of the collective at a time when the risks of alienation of the individual from society were increasing, and when the transcendent, universal voice is out-dated. In the following two chapters I will be asking how, in my period of study, writers confronted the problems of lyric subjectivity in modernity through appeal to models from a pre-Romantic lyric history.

Interest in the Elizabethan lyric in the later nineteenth century resulted in new editions, such as A. H. Bullen's *Lyrics from the Song-Books of the Elizabethan Age* (1887), which seemed to provide a particularly relevant model of lyric for the period.[28] Returning to John Addington Symonds's comparison of Victorian and Elizabethan lyric poetry, one can read that 'The Elizabethans seem to sing with one voice', while 'The Victorians have each a voice of his own [. . .] Each has been born something separate, and made something still more separate by education.'[29] Victorian poetry, Symonds says, is dominated by 'individualities' and 'particular natures':

> This intimate and pungent personality, settling the poet's attitude toward things, moulding his moral sympathies, flavouring his philosophy of life and conduct, colouring his style, separating him from fellow-workers,

is the leading characteristic of Victorian literature – that which distinguishes it most markedly from the Elizabethan.[30]

This sense of the loss of such a communal voice, among other keenly felt losses, ensured that earlier models of the lyric subject were particularly important to his own period. The fascination with this pre-bourgeois history resulted in a new wave of historical and philological scholarship that rediscovered the 'origins' of the modern lyric in ancient Greece and medieval France as well as in Elizabethan England. What was sought through these pre-bourgeois models was frequently not only the echo of a direct address or verbal communication with an audience (an answer to the solipsism and felt lack of connection that was the topic of Part II) but, more pertinently for the issues discussed here, a model of the lyric subject that finds through lyric introspection not a universal, transcendent voice, but rather a sense of community. As I will go on to show in the following chapter, this might be the case even with the new interest in Sappho, in spite of the Victorian construction of her – discussed in Chapter 7 – as in many ways the very image of modern, alienated and fragmented lyric subjectivity.[31]

Indeed, contemporary scholarship on the 'origins' of what we now think of as 'lyric' poetry has suggested that Sappho's songs were not in fact primarily a vehicle for emotional introspection, but a way of integrating personal experiences into communal paradigms.[32] Recent scholarship suggests that the social and public function of lyric songs pulls the oral lyric away from complex personal interiority and aligns it much more with ritual and conventionalised conceit. Paul Allen Miller argues, in fact, that Sappho's seemingly personal lyrical effusions turn out to be 'in many ways closer to choral song than to what we normally think of as lyric'.[33] Indeed, he suggests that the commonly given characterisation of the lyric ('a short poem of personal revelation, confession or complaint, which projects the image of an individual and highly self-reflexive subject consciousness') is only possible within the sustained patterning of written collections.[34] It is for this reason that Miller situates the rise of the genre within the formation of a culture of writing, with Catullus in the first century BC, rather than with the earlier Greek lyricists such as Sappho, Alcaeus and Pindar. Rather than a medium that impedes the spontaneous oral song definitive of the genre, a culture of writing actually imposes the remit that gives birth to the genre as we now understand it.[35] The nineteenth-century understanding of the history of lyric was rather different, but the connection made by recent scholars between

Sappho's lyrics and choral song is one that I will argue is highly relevant to the poetry I study.

While the excavation and incorporation of lyric history is strongly apparent in the last third of the nineteenth century, it is currently better recognised within the more canonical work of the early twentieth-century modernists. T. S. Eliot's essay 'Tradition and the Individual Talent', first published in 1919, is one of the best-known statements about how the modern lyric subject might find a collective voice through its relationship with the past. This essay argues that the poet must recognise not only 'the pastness of the past', but 'its presence':

> the historical sense compels a man to write not merely with his own generation in his bones, but with a feeling that the whole of the literature of Europe from Homer and within it the whole of the literature of his own country has a simultaneous existence and composes a simultaneous order.[36]

This writing in chorus with a literary past ensures that the poetic subject finds an escape from isolating subjectivity through joining a lyric community. Eliot's essay famously describes how the community to which the lyric subject belongs is a mutually influencing one, with voices that might, presumably, be heard in a different way once the new poet speaks with them. It is in this essay, too, that Eliot writes about poetry as 'an escape from personality'.[37] Eliot's theory of the impersonality of the emotion of art is based on the importance of the poet living 'in what is not merely the present, but the present moment of the past'.[38]

I will be looking at similar impulses, but from the decades before 1919, and this requires a different model to Eliot's, one that can encompass not the 'impersonality' of the high modernists but the effusion of Swinburne and the experiments with identity of Ezra Pound's early work. The model I propose for recognising the impetus towards a collective lyric subject in my period is one of 'desire lines'.[39] To use this term (taken from urban planning and cultural geography) to suggest a theory of the modern lyric subject is deliberately to invite a *double entendre*. The phrase, decontextualised and in connection with the lyric poem, might seem to allude to the most simplistic and clichéd of notions of what lyric poetry might be: lines written freely and spontaneously as an expression of personal desire. Yet as a concept borrowed from the social sciences, it brings quite a different conceit to our understanding of the lyric, and one that illuminates much more profoundly the relationship between individual desire and the structures of a highly conventional lyric tradition. In well-populated urban spaces, there are often signs of human desire that do not tally with the prescribed architectural planning of the space: those foot-worn paths that cut through municipal flower-beds or lawns, cutting a corner or tripping down a steep slope instead of taking the long, more gradually contoured path. These deviations from the prescribed and designated pathways, cut out by general consensus rather than planners, are called 'desire paths' or 'desire lines'.[40]

Lyric subjectivity functions, I suggest, in a similar way, in that the conventions of the lyric are both individually and freely inhab-ited (chosen afresh each time by an individual subject) while at the same time following along well-worn routes that express a collec-tive, although not prescribed, need. Crucially, transposing this con-cept to a poetic context emphasises that the conventions of the lyric genre are not the tarmacked paths laid down by urban planners, but the well-worn routes carved out over generations, and chosen repeatedly because they suit personal desires. They are not the cold, arbitrary structures they often appear to students struggling with poetic discourse, but the lines of the heart; they are the anarchic, not formulaic, traces of the erosion of exuberant or ecstatic metrical feet. I use this term poetically, to signify the power of poetic conven-tions that are established not through edict but through consensus: an interlocking of desire and community. The negotiation between the personal and the collective is intrinsic to the operations of lyric, and provides a particularly interesting point of confrontation with the experience of late nineteenth-century industrialised modernity. If the paradox of simultaneous individuality and universality was definitive of the conceptualisation of lyric subjectivity formulated by Hegel at the start of the century, then 'poetical Decadence' was being characterised by one influential critic in 1897 through the loss of the 'perfect balance between the universal and individual elements'.[41] Yet if the poetic subject cannot, by the end of the nine-teenth century, hope to speak for all humanity through a transcen-dent introspection, she or he can speak from a historically collective position that acknowledges a lyric community with which the poet inevitably writes. Through the idea of 'desire lines', then, I want to recognise that a lyric subject might be conceived as highly individual while not necessarily being at odds with certain ideas of collectiv-ity. The individuality of the lyric subject is not necessarily aligned with solitariness, and might feel the community of tradition, of a worn pathway. This idea is particularly relevant, I suggest, to both a nineteenth-century fascination with history and the greater avail-ability of the work of previous traditions of lyric poets.

I suggest that the nineteenth-century lyric subject provided an experimental space in which relationships of identity and difference could be productively negotiated, enabling the lyric poem to both recognise and respond to the rifts newly opening up between the subject and her or his world. This is expressed in the poetry examined in the following two chapters by various means, but particularly through a heightened awareness of lyric polyphony: sometimes through a very self-conscious handling of intertextuality that makes explicit what Rowlinson describes as the totalised print-lyric's incorporation of 'models it has itself superseded'.[42] If the genre is, in the later decades of the nineteenth century, influenced by the developing technologies and experiences of mass print in the way Rowlinson suggests, it is also defined by a self-conscious location in a web of half-heard echoes and half-remembered resonances that confirm even the mass-produced printed surface as a culturally palimpsestic medium. I returned in Chapter 6 to Rowlinson's claim that 'By the 1860s, British lyric poetry displays a new sense of confronting the prior history of lyric as a totality.'[43] Perhaps no figure better exemplifies this than Swinburne, whose engagement with a wide variety of models from a long poetic tradition – ancient, medieval and modern – results in highly individual but simultaneously highly communal poems. It is to Swinburne that I turn next, the poet who, more than any of the others, marks the beginning of the phase of lyric reconceptualisation that I explore in this study.

Notes

1. Langer, *Feeling and Form*, p. 260.
2. Hegel, *Aesthetics*, p. 1111.
3. Ibid., p. 1111.
4. Ibid., pp. 1121–2.
5. Ibid., p. 1121.
6. Wordsworth, 'Preface', p. 246; Eliot, 'Tradition and the Individual Talent', p. 43.
7. Morgan, *Narrative Means, Lyric Ends*, p. 3.
8. Mutlu Konuk Blasing writes of the lyric 'entirely depending on the [. . .] credibility of the speaker' (*Lyric Poetry*, p. 34); and in his chapter on 'Truth, Sincerity and Tragedy in Poetry', Malcolm Budd also discusses the importance of 'concurrence' between the beliefs of the imagined speaker and those of the implied author (*Values of Art*, pp. 87–8).

9. See Howe, *The Dramatic Monologue*, pp. 6–7; and E. Warwick Slinn's 'Dramatic Monologue', which stresses the importance of the framing devices to distinguishing dramatic monologue from lyrics spoken through personas (p. 81).

10. Peter Childs outlines the Marxist perspective of an 'erosion' of 'the vision of an organic society' over the 'second half of the nineteenth century', which results in a 'European loss of communal identity, out of alienating capitalism and constant industrial acceleration' (*Modernism*, p. 29).

11. Slinn, 'Dramatic Monologue', p. 85.

12. Duffey, 'The Experimental Lyric in Modern Poetry', p. 1086.

13. Hulme, 'A Lecture on Modern Poetry', p. 63.

14. Howarth, *British Poetry in the Age of Modernism*, p. 30.

15. Ibid., p. 8.

16. de Man, 'Lyric and Modernity', p. 182.

17. Adorno, 'On Lyric Poetry and Society', p. 46.

18. Ibid., p. 38.

19. Ibid., p. 43.

20. Ibid., p. 37.

21. Field, *Wild Honey from Various Thyme*, p. 13.

22. Adorno, 'On Lyric Poetry and Society', p. 43.

23. Ibid., p. 43.

24. Ibid., p. 44.

25. Ibid., p. 45.

26. Ibid., p. 46.

27. Ibid., p. 46.

28. See Bristow, 'Michael Field's Lyric Aestheticism'.

29. Symonds, 'A Comparison of Elizabethan with Victorian Poetry', p. 79.

30. Ibid., p. 79.

31. In *Victorian Sappho*, Yopie Prins describes how 'The interest in Sappho as an increasingly fragmentary text of many parts is a distinctly Victorian phenomenon' (p. 4).

32. Miller, *Lyric Texts and Lyric Consciousness*, p. 80.

33. Ibid., p. 85. Judith Hallet has also argued that Sappho's lyrics functioned much more as public rather than personal statements ('Sappho and her Social Context: Sense and Sensuality', pp. 447–64).

34. Miller, *Lyric Texts and Lyric Consciousness*, p. 1 and passim.

35. Ibid., p. 171: it is the 'highly interiorized and temporally complex poetry first illustrated by the *Carmina* of Catullus that inaugurates the genre as we know it'.

36. Eliot, 'Tradition and the Individual Talent', p. 38.

37. Ibid., p. 43.

38. Ibid., p. 44.

39. See Blunden, *The Land-Use/Transport System: Analysis and Synthesis*, Chapter 8, 'Desire Lines'.

40. See Catherine Dee's *Form and Fabric in Landscape Architecture*: ' "Desire Lines" are tracks worn across unsurfaced ground that indicate frequent pedestrian use. If a surfaced route has been made but does not provide (or appear to provide) the easiest way, desire lines occur. Desire lines can also indicate where paths are needed' (p. 84).
41. Courthope, 'Life in Poetry: Poetical Decadence', p. 140.
42. Rowlinson, 'Lyric', p. 60.
43. Ibid., p. 70.

Chapter 9

A. C. Swinburne in the Round: Drama, Personae and Lyric Subjectivity

The lines of Swinburne's poetry delineate the poetically perverse, the metrically masochistic and the sensuously sadistic. Yet to bring the concept of 'desire lines' to his poetry is to tease from it a perversely chaste account of lyric community. To give his own account of what in my previous chapter was delineated as the power of poetic norms that are established not through edict but through consensus: Swinburne writes that 'Law, not lawlessness is the natural condition of poetic life; but the law must itself be poetic and not pedantic, natural and not conventional.'[1] I begin this chapter by reading Swinburne's discourse on lyric contained within one of his best-known poems (from the 1866 *Poems and Ballads*),[2] but then focus on a later and little-known collection, *A Century of Roundels* (first published in 1883), to argue that what Swinburne develops here is a 'desire lines' of lyric community. In this way, the chapter reconsiders work from a critically neglected volume in its own right but also suggests that it can be used to better illuminate the nature and effect of some of the complexities of genre experimentation found in Swinburne's earlier work.

Swinburne represents clearly a turning point, poetically, from the mid-nineteenth century to the late that marks the start of the (broadly aestheticist) period of lyric that I trace in this study. He is best known for what are often now called his long 'dramatic monologues' (a category retrospectively applied to Swinburne's poetry), but he was also credited with the beginnings of English Parnassianism. It is the 'dramatic' rather than the 'lyric' that has received most attention in Swinburne's poetry in recent years, but his engagement with the fixed French forms that typified aestheticism might repay further study. After all, *Poems and Ballads* is, as the author himself writes in his 'Dedicatory Epistle' to the *Collected Works*, a volume of many poetic types and forms: 'lyrical and dramatic and elegiac and generally heterogeneous'.[3] Swinburne is particularly interested, in fact, in classifying poetry in terms of poetic type, admitting to liking the idea of seeing a poet's 'lyric and elegiac works ranged and registered apart, each kind in a class of its own, such as is usually reserved [. . .] for sonnets only'.[4] Swinburne was clearly, then, a poet highly aware of the implications of genre categories. In the 'Dedicatory Epistle', his use of the term 'lyric' is interesting. He sometimes uses it to denote a particular poetic mode, linked to the 'song' forms which he considers the essence of 'lyric' poetry.[5] Yet he also uses it to identify his poetry as of the 'lyric' genre as opposed to the 'narrative' or 'epic'; and he also uses it to signify all his poetic work as distinct from his verse drama.[6] In this way, Swinburne's use of the term reflects the shifting nature of the concept as its remit grew larger and larger, while not entirely leaving behind its connections with particular poetic song forms.

Given Swinburne's concern with poetic categorisation, it is interesting that the major issue of reception of *Poems and Ballads*, both now and at the time of its publication, has resided precisely in a problem of classification, a problem of understanding what type of poetry we are reading. As Nicholas Shrimpton says, 'Swinburne writes dramatic lyrics, monodrama, mask lyrics, and dramatic monologues, and mixes them without warning'.[7] My purpose here is not a survey of the lyric impulses throughout the book (Shrimpton has already done a thorough job of that), but to think about his best-known 'dramatic' poem as to some extent a meditation on the nature of lyric subjectivity. Camille Paglia called 'Anactoria' 'the most sensuously finished and intellectually developed of Swinburne's poems';[8] there is no doubt that it appeals to us in key part as a poem that speaks about poetry. Indeed, Swinburne's preoccupation with Sappho marks something of that nineteenth-century interest in the origins and history of lyric that raises particular questions about its role in the modern world.

What type of a poem is 'Anactoria'? Scholars currently tend to call it a dramatic monologue because its poetic 'I' is named as Sappho and, furthermore, it incorporates quotations from her work; but this categorisation raises crucial problems of subjectivity that have continuously troubled interpretations of the poem. Indeed, as has often been noted, the balance of the personal voice and the dramatic creation became a contested issue even within Swinburne's own claims about the book.[9] Catherine Maxwell devoted a few pages of her 2006 study of Swinburne to a useful summation of the problems involved in thinking about Swinburne's use of 'dramatic' speakers, noting the 'lack of actual dramatic action' in some of the monologues and the attendant lack of distance between Swinburne and his personae. While the dramatic is apparently more personal in these poems, it is also the case, she argues, that the personal is more dramatised in that it is less 'individual' and more 'generic'.[10] Yet most scholars still now tend to identify these poems as 'dramatic monologues'. Perhaps we should let those questions about exactly who is speaking loom a little larger. By unsettling preconceptions and attending more closely to questions of poetic genre in *Poems and Ballads* it is possible to reflect on the discourse on lyric subjectivity in 'Anactoria'.

To be sure, 'Anactoria' is a long poem, narrated by the persona of Sappho and written in couplets – a form rarely associated with concentrated lyrical effusion and, particularly at this time, more usually found with the controlled language of longer narrative and dramatic works. Yet sitting oddly within these bounds, the content of the poem is entirely about lyric song, and is couched within lyric's condensed and highly wrought style. For example, the poem begins with the very tight patterning more usually found in the short lyric form; here we see how the linking of each couplet through the end-rhyme is supplemented by a lexical patterning within each line:

> My life is bitter with thy love; thine eyes
> Blind me, thy tresses burn me, thy sharp sighs
> Divide my flesh and spirit with soft sound,
> And my blood strengthens, and my veins abound.
> I pray thee sigh not, speak not, draw not breath;
> Let life burn down, and dream it is not death.[11]

In these few lines, for example, one can see a repeated balancing of 'my', 'thy', 'me' and 'thee', and the use of that repeated negative in line 5 in a structural pattern. Such density of formal patterning might serve within a short lyric form to foster meaning, but within a long form such as this it easily comes to seem excessive. We see here a linguistic intensity that threatens to override the forward momentum needed to sustain the long form, offering instead a circular motion that keeps directing the movement of the poem inwards, towards its own echoes and its own internal linguistic point of reference. This is the effect also of the Petrarchan rhymes that abound within the first page or so of the poem: 'eyes'/'sighs', 'breath'/'death', 'fire'/'desire', 'cleaves'/'leaves', 'pain'/'vein', 'flower'/'hour', 'thine'/'mine', 'dove'/'love'. Over a fairly short space, such rhymes foreground a highly conventional language of love that marks the intensity of feeling and the close allegiance of strong desire with destructive forces (fire, pain, death) and with transience (flower, hour).

Indeed, one might argue that the transience of a short poetic form itself became necessarily allied to such a language of love, and crucial to the depiction of intensity, because it provides tight formal control of the emotion. Yet when sustained over a longer form, the focus placed on the Petrarchan language through these end-rhymes causes the sentiment to seem not just powerful but potentially excessive: a piling-up of weighted signifiers that risks intoxication. The end-rhyme hour[s]/flower[s] is repeated three times in fairly quick succession,[12] with the result of not only exacerbating this sense of content overspilling the form, but also, ironically, stressing the brevity to which great passion is usually, and perhaps necessarily, allied. In spite of the repeated stress on images of impermanence, Swinburne's form here does not provide the short formal structure that would enable the contrast of intensity and brevity, excess and control, to interplay. Lines 47–58 mirror exactly the end-rhymes of lines 35–46, but, again, this tight formal patterning rather highlights the expanse of the poem.[13] It is as if Swinburne wants to draw attention to the free rein he gives to passion in this poem. The result, I suggest, is that the reader is made to experience the overflow of Sappho's desire through the poem's affective form; the couplets of the poem, rather than being given narrative momentum and direction, break repeatedly over the reader in incessant waves.

Within *Poems and Ballads*, I suggest, this generic hybridity played a role in the volume's construction of an erotics of excess. Indeed, we might consider whether the obscenity of 'Anactoria' comes as much from genre perversion as sexual perversion. If the indeterminacy of the sexual content has played a large role in the offence caused by this poem, as Richard Sieburth has argued,[14] then its indeterminacy in relation to genre might also contribute. There is surely something transgressive in the non-narrative sensuality of lyrical effusion frothing at length within the orderly couplet form. It is this genre 'problem' that must be seen lurking behind the charge most often levelled against Swinburne by critics, both contemporary and contemporaneous: that he prizes language more for its musical qualities than its communicative ones. It is well known that Oscar Wilde's 1889 review accused Swinburne of a surrendering 'of his own personality' to the mastery of language over him ('words seem to dominate him'),[15] and that T. S. Eliot charged him with 'uproot[ing]' language and offering 'merely the hallucination of meaning', but the issues of genre embedded within these criticisms might be usefully explored.[16] The renewed interest in lyric form within aestheticism was in some sense, I suggest, a claim for an erotics of poetic style, and to make this claim from within the less intimate dramatic forms of the mid-century was particularly provocative.

Of course, the dramatic monologue or 'dramatic lyric' was itself a 'hybrid' poetic form. What is interesting about 'Anactoria' is that in its generic disjunction between narrative or dramatic form and lyric content, it offers a different kind of hybridity to that usually seen in the dramatic monologue of the 1840s and 1850s, and that, I suggest, should prevent us from reading this poem as a dramatic monologue – albeit an odd one. What I posit in this chapter is not the mid-century turn to the dramatic monologue,[17] but rather a subsequent reconsideration of lyric subjectivity from within those more 'objective' narrative or dramatic poetic forms. In other words, the hybridity that we witness in 'Anactoria' might best be read as a further supervention on the questions of genre raised by the dramatic monologue. This is certainly how some nineteenth-century reviews saw it. I will focus here on a long piece in *Fraser's Magazine for Town and Country* (1866), but many of the concerns raised here reflect what was written by others.[18] This piece starts from the consideration of similarity between Swinburne's poetry and Browning's hybrid dramatic lyrics, but moves gradually away from this comparison to identify Swinburne as primarily a 'lyric' poet. For this reviewer, the volume's hybridity is clearly identified as one between content and form: 'lyrical faculty' is wedded to 'dramatic form'. Indeed, it is the substantial length of Swinburne's poetic form that he or she finds particularly inimical to the compression of lyric, remarking on Swinburne's characteristic seizing of 'bright, sudden, characteristic moments', which are 'the moments which lyric poetry should seize', but noting that 'Mr. Swinburne neglects this rule', allowing his poems the range usually denied to the short lyric, so that his lyric moments run and run. While identifying this poetry as not wholly lyric, the reviewer also questions whether it is dramatic in the manner by now familiar to scholars from the dramatic monologues of Browning and others:

> Mr. Longfellow's is the conscientious work of a mimic who wears his mask very cleverly; whereas Mr. Swinburne enters into the humour and spirit of the representation; he becomes for the nonce the old monk; and his scriptural familiarities and chronological confusions cannot properly be said to be *borrowed*.

The review refers here to Swinburne taking on the persona of the 'old monk' in 'The Leper', but argues that this is not a dramatic persona, but rather the inhabitation of a body outside of his own. This review comes to the conclusion that Swinburne knows how to achieve an intriguing union between the lyric and the dramatic, but urges us to think of him as a writer of lyric poetry first and foremost.[19]

Significantly, and interestingly, the identification of *Poems and Ballads* as primarily a lyric, rather than a dramatic, work is the basis of the author's defence of Swinburne against the charge of profanity: 'We believe that Mr. Swinburne is a true lyric singer, and so believing, we should think it madness and worse to gag him':

> He does not *compose* poetic sentiment and painfully adapt it to appro-
> priate metres; the song *wells* from him, if one may so speak, as water
> from a perennial spring; the strong light of true passion, however disas-
> trously clouded at times, shines upon it; in all its movements it keeps the
> harmony and the rhythm of life.[20]

It seems that Swinburne's defence is his spontaneous outburst of lyric song. Lyric should, it is suggested, be accepted purely on the criterion of whether it '*ring[s] true*' – whether it is genuine, and from the heart. The responsibility of the lyric poet is only to him or herself and cannot be judged in social terms.[21] The dramatic mono-logue is usually defended with the claim that the views expressed are not necessarily those of the author. Following the precedent of Baudelaire,[22] Swinburne argued, rather formulaically, in 'Notes on Poems and Reviews' that much of the obscenity found in his verse could be traced back to the ancient poets whose texts he drew on so profoundly in his own work.[23] Yet the fact that the reviewer defends the poems as lyrics, not as dramatic monologues, gives an important indication of how they were actually read.

While distinguishing the hybridity of *Poems and Ballads* from that of the 'dramatic lyric' form, the review cited above might pro-vide evidence for Nicholas Shrimpton's reading of 'Anactoria' which (following Adena Rosmarin's 1985 work on dramatic monologue)[24] understands 'Anactoria' as 'mask lyric'. This is a type that R. W. Rader defines as a form in which 'the poet speaks through an actor who is registered almost overtly as an artificial self', and Shrimp-ton sees Swinburne here as speaking as a woman and inhabiting a female sexuality.[25] Yet in this chapter I suggest that there is perhaps something less personal and more conceptual at stake in Swinburne's inhabitation of Sappho: the poem's central conceit of Sappho as metaphor ('metaphors of me') might alert us not only to Sappho as metrical rhythm or Sappho as lesbian, but, more centrally, Sappho as lyric.[26] Anactoria herself becomes, as Yopie Prins has discussed at length,[27] an emblem of lyric song: she is not a woman in her own right, but Sappho's song, the lyre Sappho fashions out of her body ('Take thy limbs living, and new-mould with these/ A lyre of many faultless agonies').[28] Yet this might surely point up another allegory: that Sappho in this poem is not primarily operating as a dramatic persona, nor a female mask, but as lyric itself, placing the genre as the central object of the poem. I suggest that what we see in *Poems and Ballads* is something of an aestheticist reconsideration of lyric following the mid-century turn to hybrid forms.

The poem's concern with identity and difference – the very basis of metaphor – is worked out through a long, and much critically studied, tussle between the separateness and commingling of Sappho and Anactoria. Lexical repetition in and between many of the early lines of the poem speaks of an identity within difference or separation:

> I feel thy blood against my blood: my pain
> Pains thee, and lips bruise lips, and vein stings vein.
> Let fruit be crushed on fruit, let flower on flower,
> Breast kindle breast, and either burn one hour.[29]

Further, the poem imagines the absorption of 'you' into 'I':

> That I could drink thy veins as wine, and eat
> Thy breasts like honey! that from face to feet
> Thy body were abolished and consumed,
> And in my flesh thy very flesh entombed![30]

In this melding of 'I' into 'you', the poetic voice desires to be 'Mixed with thy blood and molten into thee!'[31] This merging between Sappho and Anactoria has been read as metaphorical of the poetic relationship between Swinburne and Sappho. Jennifer Wagner-Lawlor writes that this enables Swinburne to speak not only as Sappho, but also as himself: 'This double-voicing, which maintains simultaneously the figures of Sappho and Swinburne, allows the two poets to become, each to the other, "metaphors of me" – Sappho as Swinburne, and Swinburne as Sappho.'[32] Paglia later read the poem as enacting a different merging, seeing Swinburne's identification with Anactoria, not Sappho; for Paglia, Anactoria's absence in the poem is Swinburne's imaginative projection of himself as the lyric body abused by Sappho's mastery.[33] Both of these must surely be true; as Maxwell argues, this is 'a contradictory poem' of constantly shifting and merging identities between Anactoria, Sappho and Swinburne.[34] Maxwell goes on to offer a scenario in which 'Anactoria is Swinburne, but by virtue of being Anactoria he is also Sappho'.[35] That all of these different critical analyses of the poem seem valid should perhaps lead us to see the importance of the poem as ultimately not in any narratable drama of egos on the stage of a dramatic monologue, or an inhabitation of particular masks as such, but in a dramatisation of the very process of formation of poetic voice itself. Crucially, the poem's own tussle with identity and difference enacts and explores the core paradox of lyric subjectivity that I discussed in the previous chapter: what Langer called the 'impersonal subjectivity' – the paradox that the poet can inhabit a speaking voice which is and is not him- or herself. What all of these different critical readings of poetic voice in 'Anactoria' emphasise is the lack of distance between poet and speaker needed to provide the frame characteristic of the dramatic-poetic mode. Moreover, 'Anactoria' takes this as its own subject matter: it is a poem in some sense about the construction of the lyric (rather than dramatic) poetic subject. In other words, I suggest that when Swinburne speaks through Sappho, we might see him as speaking in key part through lyric, through a genre, rather than through a personal mask or a persona.

Making this distinction has some important consequences, and I will devote the rest of this chapter to exploring what is for my purposes the most significant: the possibility of reading the poetic voice in this poem as one that speaks not as a dramatic persona or, as Shrimpton more persuasively argues, through the mask of another, but as a voice in *chorus* with other voices. To think about the poem as a dramatisation of a lyric polyphony (of a multitude of voices resonating simultaneously), rather than the adoption by one voice of another mask or persona, is to suggest that Swinburne recognised lyric as inherently multi-vocal. For Swinburne, the lyric subject did not need to be rescued from isolating subjectivity by the 'dramatic lyric' or other dramatic hybrids that became popular in the mid-century because it was already constitutively a communal subjectivity. In other words, in 'Anactoria' Swinburne demonstrates how lyric is itself always multiply voiced (even without invoking an explicitly and identifiably 'other' persona) by virtue of its conventional nature and its repetition of the tropes of a long historical tradition. To read in this way is to find in Swinburne something similar to what Adorno finds in Baudelaire, but within the English tradition: a confrontation within lyric of its relation to modernity, and one that self-consciously raises crucial questions as to what the lyric subject is, and can be, at this time. Swinburne's work of the 1860s was centrally a response to what he found in Baudelaire.

Having reviewed *Les Fleurs du mal* in 1862, *Poems and Ballads* is in many ways a reflection on this volume, both through the figure of Sappho and otherwise. According to Adorno, what Baudelaire confronts is the role of language in anchoring the lyric in society while simultaneously marking its distance from 'mere functioning within a wholly socialized society' – in other words, from mere communicative language.[36] The same might be said of Swinburne, although in a rather different way. In 'Anactoria', Swinburne couches his lyric in forms that embrace and embed a lyric 'collective', ensuring a generic balance of, to echo Adorno's terms, the poetic and communicative.

*   *   *

The communitarian impulses to which I allude can be linked to the Republican politics developed in various ways throughout Swinburne's work of the 1870s, in volumes such as *Songs Before Sunrise* (1871) and *Songs of Two Nations* (1875). Working consciously with echoes of the French Revolution and addressing key issues and topics in the Italian struggle, these volumes contain much that supports my positioning of poetic collectivity as a concern in his earlier work. Yet ultimately it is not to these volumes that I turn to develop the hypothesis outlined in the previous paragraph, but to a later work which, although critically neglected, provides a reflection on many of Swinburne's earlier concerns: *A Century of Roundels*. This is a volume whose concern with form renders it particularly significant within the remit of my study. Here, I suggest, Swinburne explores what I am calling the 'desire lines' of lyric community more self-consciously, and certainly more formally than in his earlier work. If 'Anactoria' takes as a fundamental trope the exploration of sameness and difference between bodies that mix and merge, then *A Century of Roundels* meditates on this same theme in many different ways. The 'roundel' is Swinburne's English variation on the French 'rondeau'; in addition to a tight rhyme-scheme, it has a refrain which is set at the start of the first line and repeats in lines 4 and 11 of the 11-line form. Fundamental, then, is a pattern of lexical repetition that teasingly poses the question of aesthetic, and possibly semantic, difference within linguistic reiteration.[37] Here I explore that iteration as indicative of a broader investment in a communal lyric subject: a merging of multiple voices, in a manner similar to the merging of subjects seen in 'Anactoria'.

The layering of the refrain in the roundel seems to suggest the form of the sung 'round' in which different voices sing the same words at overlapping intervals in a 'follow the leader' pattern. It is a form, then, whose very essence draws attention to the subject as a multi-layered, multi-vocal one whose repetition gives the echo of different voices singing the same song – not in unison, but in (harmonious) turn. The collection is dedicated to Christina Rossetti (who followed Swinburne in composing roundels),[38] setting up from the outset the sense of a chain 'song' that is passed from one poetic voice to another: a repetition that is both identical and multi-vocal. The roundel form inscribes, through its central refrain, the image of the poet re-treading the paths of previous poetic feet. Swinburne's poem called simply 'The Roundel' sets the parameters for this self-reflexive form and its commentary on poetic voice. Here the roundel is likened to a 'ring', 'a starbright sphere', 'round as a pearl or tear'. The refrain, 'A roundel is wrought', sets up the making of the poem as its own subject matter – the assonance between 'round' and 'wrought' further spiralling the refrain in on itself. Identifying the roundel here as a 'jewel of music', 'carven of all or of aught', speaks to the Parnassian influence which, again, pushes the poem in on itself and its own multiple refractions. Most significantly for my purposes, the refrain of the roundel is imagined in this poem 'As a bird's quick song runs round, and the hearts in us hear/ Pause answer to pause, and again the same strain caught'. Here the image is of the repeated 'round' of a bird's song, but the echoes within that single voice are described in terms of a dialogue – 'pause answer to pause' – as if the bird is singing in response to some unheard and unseen audience. This encapsulates the fascination of the roundel, in which repetition creates its own dialectic.[39]

It is with this in mind that I turn to the two roundels that appear under the title 'On an Old Roundel (Translated by D. G. Rossetti from the French of Villon)':

I

Death, from thy rigour a voice appealed,
And men still hear what the sweet cry saith,
Crying aloud in thine ears fast sealed,
   Death.

As a voice in a vision that vanisheth,
Through the grave's gate barred and the portal steeled
The sound of the wail of it travelleth.

Wailing aloud from a heart unhealed,
It woke response of melodious breath
From lips now too by thy kiss congealed,
  Death.

II

Ages ago, from the lips of a sad glad poet
Whose soul was a wild dove lost in the whirling snow,
The soft keen plaint of his pain took voice to show it
  Ages ago.

So clear, so deep, the divine drear accents flow,
No soul that listens may choose but thrill to know it,
Pierced and wrung by the passionate music's throe.

For us there murmurs a nearer voice below it,
Known once of ears that never again shall know,
Now mute as the mouth which felt death's wave o'erflow it
  Ages ago.[40]

This poem plays with all the elements identified above as central to the purpose and meaning of Swinburne's new form. The first roundel is a response to Rossetti's 'To Death, of His Lady (François Villon)', which is in turn a close translation of Villon's 'Le Testament', lines 978–89, in French rondeau form.[41] The translation was made in 1869 and published in Rossetti's 1870 *Poems*. Rossetti's poem, like Villon's, is a complaint to Death about the recent demise of his beloved lady – a grief which, he claims, saps his own life:

Death, of thee do I make my moan,
  Who hadst my lady away from me,
  Nor wilt assuage thine enmity
Till with her life thou hast mine own;
For since that hour my strength has flown.
  Lo! what wrong was her life to thee,
    Death?

Two we were, and the heart was one;
  Which now being dead, dead I must be,
  Or seem alive as lifelessly
As in the choir the painted stone,
    Death![42]

The love that united the pair in life must now unite them in death.

Yet Swinburne's poem is rather a meta-commentary on the process of Rossetti's translation than another straight repetition of the poem. His verse makes no mention of the beloved lady, but takes as its subject matter Villon's appeal to Death and its continuing echo through Rossetti's translation. Like Rossetti, Swinburne uses the one word 'Death' as his thrice-repeated refrain, but in Swinburne's poem it takes on a special significance because of the three voices he is aware of representing in his poem. This refrain should represent the three different, but layered, invocations to the dead beloved 'lady' (Villon's, Rossetti's and Swinburne's), yet it comes instead, in its meta-poetical manner, to direct attention away from the supposed female object of the poem and towards what is for Swinburne's poetics a more important threesome: the three male poets who write in community. In this way, the three 'deaths' in Swinburne's poem are Villon's death, Rossetti's very recent death in 1882 ('lips now too by thy kiss congealed,/ Death) and a reflection on Swinburne's own mortality. This poem is about the significance of the lover's complaint, rather than the dead beloved; the beloved lady's death simply cements the bonds between the three male poets, and Swinburne writes about the immortality of poetic voice as it is passed and shared between them. He is able to gesture towards his own death in that repetition of three refrains because his connection with these other poets means they live through his poem, and he dies a living death in sympathy with their voices. Their poetic voices are bound, living and dead, through this form whose repetition makes both dead return to life and what is living find community in death. This community of lyric voices encompasses the living death that Rossetti writes of in his poem, but also a bringing back to life of the voices of the dead so that 'men still hear what the sweet cry saith'. Swinburne is writing here about Villon's voice being preserved through Rossetti's, and his own voice preserving both those others by writing in community with them. The poem is, then, an elegiac cry to Death to imagine the speaker's own living death upon that of his beloved, but it is also an ode to the immortality of the poetic voice.

Terms signifying vocalisation occur in nearly every line: 'voice', 'what the sweet cry saith', 'crying aloud', 'voice', 'wail', 'wailing aloud', melodious breath', 'lips'. Villon's cry evoked 'response of melodious breath' from Rossetti (who now too is dead), which in turn has been joined by Swinburne's own voice. The process of mourning is a sung 'round' started by Villon, with the burden taken up by Rossetti, and then repeated by Swinburne, in an overlapping sequence of voices that, crucially, awake answering 'response[s]' in each other. Such vocal layering is depicted in the poem not only by the repetition of the refrain but also by the layering of language in other ways that invite us to find voices within voices. For example, the first line – 'Death, from thy rigour a voice appealed' – plays on the nesting of 'peal', yet another term for vocalisation, or the ringing out of the voice, within 'appeal': a voice that pleads with Death to take him as he has taken his beloved, but whose plea for a living death is simultaneously a more positive act – like a peal of celebratory bells – that precisely ensures the immortality of his voice.

The second roundel in the poem reflects at a further level of remove on this round of lyric voices, answering the first with a distancing refrain of 'ages ago' – a term imprecise and casual enough to both acknowledge the huge temporal gap between the voices while also being quite dismissive of it. In this roundel Swinburne traces the mediation from Villon, the 'sad glad poet', to Rossetti:

> For us there murmurs a nearer voice below it
> Known once of ears that never again shall know,
> Now mute as the mouth which felt death's wave o'erflow it
>   Ages ago.

Although a much 'nearer' voice, Rossetti is somehow already encompassed within the same imprecise historical plane as Villon: 'ages ago'. Both are merged within an immortal collective lyric consciousness that is a part of every lyric subject. It is no coincidence that both Villon's and Rossetti's deaths are imagined in terms of drowning. Just as 'Anactoria' ended with Sappho merging into the sea – 'around and over and under me/ Thick darkness and the insuperable sea'[43] – these later poets merge with the collective lyric consciousness that Sappho symbolises for Swinburne. Indeed, Sappho's watery demise resonates powerfully with imagery of the sea as a figure for a collective voice that is significant for both Swinburne and Rossetti. Rossetti's 'The Sea-Limits' invites the reader to 'Hark where the murmurs of thronged men/ Surge and sink back and surge again', imagining the voice of 'all mankind' echoing in the 'whole sea's speech'.[44] In turn, Swinburne comments on Rossetti's poetic imagery of the sea, remarking on its use to express 'a living thing with an echo beyond reach of the sense, its chord of sound one part of the multiform unity of mutual inclusion in which all things rest and mix'.[45] As much Swinburne's own sense of the sea as Rossetti's, this is the collective lyric chorus that overtakes Sappho, Villon, Rossetti and, in some strange projection throughout Swinburne's poetry, eventually himself too. It is in this 'multiform unity of mutual inclusion' where the souls of lyric poets merge that Swinburne finds his lyric community – the lines of desire that he too will follow – and it is, ironically, through this process of mourning that he avoids the isolation that threatens the modern lyric subject.

Yet interestingly, although Swinburne writes *with* many other poets, his contribution is distinctly marked as neither a straight translation nor imitation of his sources. I referred earlier in this chapter to Wilde's review of Swinburne's work. Wilde goes on to say that Swinburne 'is the first lyric poet who has tried to make an absolute surrender of his own personality, and he has succeeded': 'We hear the song, but we never know the singer. We never even get near him.'[46] For Wilde, as Yopie Prins has noted, 'Swinburne's claim to lyricism can only be the surrendering of that lyric persona'.[47] Yet, ironically, a comparison of the lyric voices of Swinburne and Wilde, and particularly their relationship to previous poets and poetic models, might turn this criticism more properly towards Wilde himself. Indeed, such a comparison is one that might actually help to clarify the distinction I draw in this chapter between the communal lyric subject, on the one hand, and, on the other, the strategies of the mask or persona. Swinburne constructs a subjectivity that works in a collective but without sacrificing individuality. By contrast, the reception of Wilde's own *Poems* (first published in 1881) can be characterised through accusations that his voice is barely discernible behind the lines of the others he imitates.[48] The Oxford Union declared that his poems 'are for the most part not by their putative father at all, but by a number of better-known and more deservedly reputed authors'.[49] The *Athenaeum* similarly failed to find any 'distinct message' from this new poet.[50] Indeed, *The Spectator* criticised the volume for being too much a study of poetry than an original poetic text.[51] *Poems* was received as a composite text, what Harold Bloom called an anthology of 'the whole of English High Romanticism'.[52]

Wilde's *Poems* has been of interest to scholars in recent years particularly as a complex and beautiful material object.[53] Nicholas Frankel's *Oscar Wilde's Decorated Books* (2000) represents an important study of this phenomenon but he also offers something of an explanation of Wilde's pastiche-subjectivity by reading it as a way for an Irishman to 'pass' within an English literary tradition (by 'simulat[ing] the Englishman' and displaying the signs of 'English culture, civilization, and power').[54] Indeed, what is perhaps most striking about Wilde's poems is their performativity, and this is true not solely of the 'dramatic' poems (such as those in the section titled 'Impressions de Théatre', where we see engagement with 'Portia',

'Queen Henrietta Maria' and other 'characters'). The poem entitled 'My Voice' near the end of the volume is interesting given how little many felt they had heard of Wilde's own voice, and indeed what is presented here is a cliché:

> Wherefore my cheeks before their time are wan,
> For very weeping is my gladness fled,
> Sorrow has paled my young mouth's vermillion,
> And Ruin draws the curtains of my bed.[55]

Ultimately, many have thought that Wilde found his poetic voice not in lyric but in the more narrative and dramatic form of 'The Ballad of Reading Gaol' – of which Arthur Symons wrote: 'We see a great spectacular intellect, to which, at last, pity and terror have come in their own person, and no longer as puppets in a play.'[56] Although Swinburne's *Poems and Ballads* is much more explicitly invested in ostensibly dramatic devices such as masks, models and personae than is Wilde's apparently more lyrical *Poems*, it is Swinburne who manages to register a more distinctive personal voice. While contemporaneous responses to Wilde's *Poems* suggested that he lost individuality in the 'mimic echo' (to quote again 'My Voice'), I argue that Swinburne joined a lyric chorus in which the personal was strengthened by the collective.

Of course, if Wilde's *Poems* were accused of imitation, then the dominant modernist criticism of Swinburne's poetry was that it managed, in a very original manner, to say nothing at all.[57] Yet, as Herbert Tucker has argued in relation to *A Century of Roundels*, one needs to read Swinburne's meaning through his form;[58] to isolate meaning in content may indeed prove frustrating. The 'meaning' I propose from the *Roundels*, then, is one expressed formally, but it is one that connects directly with the better-known work from *Poems and Ballads* and offers a new way to think about the earlier volume's discourse on lyric.

*   *   *

To return, then, finally to 'Anactoria'. An essay in the *Edinburgh Review* from 1890 notes just how many verses in *Poems and Ballads* write 'in celebration or derogation of persons, dead or living', peopling Swinburne's poetry with a sociable hum of voices.[59] 'Anactoria' is clearly a multi-layered composition written through the dramatised metaphors of both Sappho and Anactoria. Yet Swinburne writes too in community with Catullus, who had produced a poetic translation of the same Sapphic fragment that Swinburne refers to as 'The Ode to Anactoria' (also commonly known as 'To a Beloved Girl', the 'Second Ode' or 'Phanetai moi'). When Swinburne incorporates Sappho's words into his poem he cannot help but also write in light of Catullus's translation. Indeed, in his roundel 'To Catullus' we find the refrain 'my brother', clearly asserting a lyrical kinship with the poet whose voice is such an important part of his multi-layered subject in 'Anactoria'. In this roundel Catullus's voice lives through Swinburne: 'How should I living fear to call thee dead,/ My brother?'[60] In 'Notes on Poems and Reviews' (1866), Swinburne is critical of Catullus's translation of the 'Second Ode' and distances himself from it.[61] He claims to turn from Catullus's attempt to capture the body of the text to a desire to go more directly to the spirit of Sappho (although, ironically, he reaches the spirit by playing the body, or corpus, of Sappho like a lyre, just as Sappho does with Anactoria). Yet even in marking his distance from Catullus's translation, Swinburne writes with him, recognising him as another voice in the train of voices around the fragment of 'Anactoria', a train in which he consciously takes his place – just as he writes with Villon in 'On an Old Roundel'. Swinburne situates himself similarly in both poems, writing in relation to two other poets: one ancient and the other a translator of the ancient verse. And he follows in each case not with another translation but with a meta-commentary, aiming – as he said of 'Anactoria', but this is equally true of 'On an Old Roundel' – to 'represent not the poem but the poet'.[62] In turning to the poet rather than the poem, Swinburne chooses to comment first and foremost on the operation of the lyric subject, figuring a collective subjectivity that projects both backwards and forwards in time.

Swinburne's personification of lyric in 'Anactoria' enables a double-faced poem that is both a love song and an exploration of poetic genre; it also enables him to turn the lyric subject from a marginalised, interiorised voice into a lyric polyphony. In other words, the personification of lyric enables him to make explicit a belief that writing lyrics inevitably involves the author's entering into a community. It is no accident that his personification of lyric is Sappho, who was, for the Victorians, the archetypal lyric subject.[63] I discussed in my previous chapter the distance between an enduring construction of Sappho as the most personal and subjective of poets, and what has been described by scholars such as Miller as the social role of Sapphic lyric. The Victorians may have constructed Sappho as an alienated and fragmented 'modern' figure, but she also represented a lyric community in which she sang with her maids. Swinburne embraced this quintessentially marginalised lyric voice to find through it a mode of poetry that emphasises the commonality of lyric subjectivity that is the twin to its individuality. Indeed, Sappho symbolises for Swinburne not a lone individual voice but an immortal chorus that will not die with her death:

> [. . .] but thou – thy body is the song,
> Thy mouth the music; thou art more than I,
> Though my voice die not till the whole world die[64]

This notion of singing in timeless chorus is reiterated throughout the poem:

> Violently singing till the whole world sings –
> I Sappho shall be one with all these things[65]
> [. . .]
> Yea, though thou diest, I say I shall not die[66]

The fragments of Sappho laid down a track on which others walked their own walk, but in her company. In this way, Swinburne resolves a contemporary crisis in lyric subjectivity into an exploration of the paradox inherent in a nineteenth-century lyric subject that is both highly individual and yet expressed within long-established paradigms. It is in this sense that I read the poem not as a dramatic monologue voiced by Sappho, nor exactly as a poem that takes Sappho as a mask through which the poet becomes another, but as Swinburne's orchestration of a polyphonic lyric chorus showing the lyric subject as one which, far from isolated, actually occupies a unique position for holding together the individual and a collective voice. While this might be a response to the same concerns that motivated the turn to forms such as the dramatic monologue in the mid-nineteenth century, it is a rather different response: one that turns back to lyric in order to reconceptualise and reimagine it rather than rejecting it in favour of hybrid forms.

If the 'totalisation' of lyric in print over the century means that it becomes a palimpsest through which lyric history – aural and textual – both appears and is incorporated, then it is perhaps through this summation that Swinburne finds the means to theorise the lyric subject as a community rather than an isolated visionary. When the anonymous reviewer in *Fraser's Magazine for Town and Country* writes how, in sustaining the lyric mode over a whole volume, Swinburne strenuously resists 'the temptation to fall into the beaten track, which has grown easy, pleasant, and habitual', he or she presents the 'beaten track' of familiar poetic idiom as inimical to the individual subjective genius of lyric invention. Yet it is precisely to a 'beaten track' of lyric – that worn by Sappho, Catullus, Villon and Rossetti, among others – that Swinburne turns in 'Anactoria'; not to give up on a distinctive lyric subjectivity but to recognise the necessity of community to the modern incarnation of that subject. The 'desire lines' concept I elaborated through a reading of the *Roundels* aimed to alert us to the possibility that Swinburne finds in his earlier articulations of sexual desire a trope for the community of the lyric subject. This might alter our understanding of the workings of desire in 'Anactoria'. In addition to Swinburne's metrical masochism (another kind of 'beaten track'), we might think about the importance of sexual desire as a way of dramatising a lyric subject that is simultaneously individual and blended into a generic voice. In 'Anactoria' the imagery of merging bodies that are 'mixed', 'molten' and mutually consuming speaks not just of a masochistic dyad of pain and pleasure, but also of a lyric collective: Anactoria, Sappho, Catullus, Swinburne. This is the process of sublimation of the self into a lyric society that is hidden within the tropes of masochistic submission; and Swinburne plays relentlessly on the fine line between the disintegration of self and the finding of community that is attendant on the interplay of bodies he depicts in Anactoria.

Notes

1. Swinburne, *Collected Poetical Works*, I, p. xvi.
2. Throughout this chapter, *Poems and Ballads* refers to the 1866 volume and not the later volume, *Poems and Ballads Second Series* of 1878.
3. Ibid., p. vi.
4. Ibid., p. xiv.
5. Ibid., pp. xiv–xv.
6. Ibid., pp. xvii, ix–x.
7. Shrimpton, 'Swinburne and the Dramatic Monologue', p. 61.
8. Paglia, *Sexual Personae*, p. 477.
9. First, in 'Notes on Poems and Reviews' (1866), he insists that his collections are 'dramatic, many-faced, multifarious; and no utterance of enjoyment or despair, belief or unbelief, can properly be assumed as the assertion of its author's personal feeling or faith' (p. 6). Later, in the 'Dedicatory Epistle' that prefaced the 1904 edition of the *Collected*

Poetical Works, Swinburne hedged rather differently, commenting that 'There are photographs from life in the book; and there are sketches from imagination' (*Collected Poetical Works*, I, p. vii).

10. Maxwell, *Swinburne*, pp. 17, 18.
11. Swinburne, *Collected Poetical Works*, I, p. 57 (all references to the poem are made to this edition, pp. 57–66).
12. Ibid., p. 57, lines 13–14, 39–40, 51–2.
13. This is what McGann writes about as 'poetry aspiring to the condition of music': 'even the poem's semantic features – the idea of being sickened with love, for instance – get subordinated to the logic of musical and sensuous transformation' (McGann, 'Wagner, Baudelaire, Swinburne', p. 628).
14. Sieburth, 'Poetry and Obscenity: Baudelaire and Swinburne', pp. 343–53.
15. Wilde, 'Mr Swinburne's Last Volume', pp. 148, 146.
16. Eliot, 'Swinburne', p. 149.
17. Herbert Tucker describes Tennyson and Browning turning away from lyric as a rejection of a form 'heard overmuch, overdone, and thus in need of being done over in fresh forms' ('Dramatic Monologue and the Overhearing of Lyric', p. 227).
18. See, for example, another long and significant review entitled 'Mr Swinburne's Lyrics', which appeared anonymously in the *Edinburgh Review* in 1890, and which also takes issues of genre as central to its response.
19. Anonymous, 'Mr Swinburne and His Critics', pp. 643–4.
20. Ibid., p. 644.
21. Ibid., p. 644.
22. In court, Baudelaire's lawyer famously blamed the blasphemy of *Les Fleurs du mal* on his dramatic persona, claiming that in acting a role, the poet was not speaking for himself (see Sieburth, 'Poetry and Obscenity: Baudelaire and Swinburne', p. 347).
23. Swinburne, 'Notes on Poems and Reviews', p. 9.
24. Rosmarin, *The Power of Genre*. Her key task in this study is to explore dramatic monologue with reference to, but separate from, the mask lyric (see p. ix).
25. Shrimpton, 'Swinburne and the Dramatic Monologue', pp. 63, 64; Rader, 'The Dramatic Monologue and Related Lyric Forms', p. 150.
26. Swinburne, *Collected Poetical Works*, I, p. 64, line 214.
27. Prins, *Victorian Sappho*, pp. 126–31.
28. Swinburne, *Collected Poetical Works*, I, p. 61, lines 139–40.
29. Ibid., p. 57, lines 11–14.
30. Ibid., p. 60, lines 111–14.
31. Ibid., p. 61, line 132.
32. Wagner-Lawlor, 'Metaphorical "Indiscretion" and Literary Survival in Swinburne's "Anactoria"', p. 930.
33. Paglia, *Sexual Personae*, p. 478.

34. Maxwell, *The Female Sublime*, pp. 39–40.
35. Ibid., p. 40.
36. Adorno, 'On Lyric Poetry and Society', p. 44.
37. Herbert Tucker has recently explored this 'harboured difference maturing within the iteration of the same' in his essay on the volume ('What Goes Around', p. 132).
38. For an overview of the relationship of mutual poetic admiration between Swinburne and C. Rossetti, see Dinah Roe, ' "Good Satan": the Unlikely Poetic Affinity of Swinburne and Christina Rossetti'.
39. Swinburne, *Collected Poetical Works*, V, p. 161.
40. Ibid., pp. 174–5.
41. See Paull F. Baum's analysis, which notes that this is a close translation, although he 'introduces a different image in the last line' (see Rossetti, *Poems, Ballads, and Sonnets*, ed. Baum, p. 177).
42. Rossetti, *Poems* (1870), p. 179.
43. Swinburne, *Collected Poetical Works*, I, p. 66, lines 303–4.
44. Rossetti *Poems* (1870), p. 254.
45. Swinburne, 'The Poems of Dante Gabriel Rossetti', p. 557.
46. Wilde, 'Mr Swinburne's Last Volume', p. 148.
47. Prins, *Victorian Sappho*, p. 156.
48. Echoes of Swinburne himself, D. G. Rossetti, Theophile Gautier, as well as the major Romantic poets have been traced by critics in detail in Wilde's volume (Beckson and Fong, 'Wilde as Poet', pp. 61–5).
49. Ellmann, *Oscar Wilde*, p. 146.
50. Beckson, *Oscar Wilde: The Critical Heritage*, p. 34 (*Athenaeum*, 23 July 1881, pp. 103–4).
51. Ibid., p. 45 (*Spectator*, 15 August 1881, pp. 1048–9).
52. Bloom's assessment of the volume is that Wilde 'knew he had failed as a poet because he lacked strength to overcome his anxiety of influence' (*The Anxiety of Influence*, p. 6).
53. For example, Lorraine Janzen Kooistra has read Ricketts's illustration of Wilde's poetic works as 'at least as esoteric, self-conscious, and inter-textual as Wilde's poem', while in Joseph Bristow's *The Fin-de-Siècle Poem*, Wilde's lyrics feature most prominently as 'one of the most sig-nificant innovations in modern publishing' (Kooistra, *The Artist as Critic*, p. 99; Bristow, 'Introduction' to *The Fin-de-Siècle Poem*, p. 14).
54. Frankel, *Oscar Wilde's Decorated Books*, pp. 38–9.
55. Wilde, *Poems*, p. 199.
56. Beckson, *Oscar Wilde: The Critical Heritage*, pp. 218–21 (*Saturday Review*, 12 March 1898); see also Nathan, 'The Ballad of Reading Gaol: At the Limits of the Lyric', passim.
57. T. S. Eliot accused Swinburne of 'literally saying next to nothing' ('Isolated Superiority', p. 6).
58. Tucker, 'What Goes Around', p. 131.
59. Anonymous, 'Mr Swinburne's Lyrics', p. 447.

60. Swinburne, *Collected Poetical Works*, V, p. 185.
61. Swinburne, 'Notes on Poems and Reviews', p. 9: 'Where Catullus failed I could not hope to succeed; I tried instead to reproduce in a diluted and dilated form the spirit of a poem which could not be reproduced in the body.'
62. Swinburne, 'Notes on Poems and Reviews', p. 10.
63. See Prins, *Victorian Sappho*, p. 5.
64. Swinburne, *Collected Poetical Works*, I, p 59, lines 74–6.
65. Ibid., p. 65, lines 275–6.
66. Ibid., p. 66, line 290.

Chapter 10

Ezra Pound's Troubadour Subject: Community, Form and 'Lyric' in Early Modernism

This final chapter focuses on the early work of Ezra Pound to offer a brief poetic study extending my analysis of lyric subjectivity and lyric chorus; but it also fulfils a rather different function from the other poetic case studies by offering a historical 'coda' to the aestheticist poetic trajectory that I trace across this book. Much of this chapter will be concerned with sketching out some connections with a modernist idea of poetry in the twentieth century. I take Pound as my subject because he is a modernist whose early work is deeply formed by aestheticism, but also because (particularly in his pre-*Mauberley* work) he shows a profound engagement with the concept of lyric specifically. His early poetry and essays grapple with the idea of lyric, directly in relation to the experience of modernity, in ways that are particularly relevant to my core concerns. It has been more common in recent years for scholars to look to T. S. Eliot than Pound to provide a link from aestheticism through to modernism. Thaïs E. Morgan, for example, has argued for Eliot's desire to reinstate Swinburne into the English canon, and more recently Cassandra Laity has argued for 'Prufrock' 'drawing directly on Swinburne's "A Leave-Taking"', noting 'Prufrock's shift from the irony and paralyzing self-consciousness of the urban sections toward childlike wonder and longing for self-dissolution in Swinburnian seas'.[1] (And indeed, 'The Love Song of J. Alfred Prufrock' is one of the great meditations on lyric introspection.) Yet I am more interested here in the less discussed but equally visceral connections between Swinburne and Pound that take them both back to an idea of lyric based around a multiple and communal subject.

Pound's rediscovery of Swinburne in 1910 speaks of his excitement in encountering one who embraces life so completely: 'I have gone back to my Swinburne with new eyes – at least to the poems in the "*Laus Veneris*" edition'. Poems such as 'The Ballad of Life', Pound claims, 'give us the *great* Swinburne, the high priest, the lifter of the hearts of men. His vision of our marvellous vitality, of our power for survival!' He writes of Swinburne seeing humanity 'divided not according to "good" and "evil" but into those who have accepted & those who have rejected life. The first are the conquerors. [. . .] The unhappy are only those who refuse to live.'[2] It may not be too fanciful to see a continuum between these qualities that Pound admires in Swinburne and the idea of lyric community that I will suggest we see in the work of both poets. The influence of Swinburne might best be seen in Pound's *A Lume Spento* (1908) – particularly through the presence of Villon in this volume. The two imitations of Villon ('Villonaud for this Yule' and 'A Villonaud: Ballad of the Gibbet')[3] are of Swinburne's Villon. Moreover, David Moody has suggested we read the poet of 'Anima Sola' as Swinburne, seeing in the second half of Pound's volume the 'gloom' of Decadence overpowered by a positive affirmation of the power of art which sees Swinburne 'hailed as the high priest of the life-principle in "Salve O Pontifex! – an hemichaunt"'.[4]

Indeed, Pound follows Swinburne in his search for the origins of a lyric tradition in both classical and medieval sources. While suspicious of the term 'lyric' (an issue to which I will return later in this chapter), Pound's interest in what Palgrave's *Golden Treasury* had identified as a 'lyric' tradition can be seen in his essay 'The Tradition' (1913). The absence of the word 'lyric' from the title says much about the awkwardness of his eschewal of the term which hovers around, and sometimes within, the piece. The essay begins:

> The tradition is a beauty which we preserve and not a set of fetters to bind us. This tradition did not begin in A.D. 1870, nor in 1776, nor in 1632, nor in 1564. It did not begin even with Chaucer.
> The two great lyric traditions which most concern us are that of the Melic poets and that of Provence. From the first arose practically all the poetry of the 'ancient world', from the second practically all that of the modern.[5]

The purpose of Pound's essay is clearly to situate himself within an ongoing tradition of poetry. Pound identifies various possible key moments of formation and transformation in the genre that might be considered the 'start' of something new, but rejects each in favour of an ever earlier point of genesis. The dates he identifies go without commentary, but the list itself presents its own quirky history of lyric. Regressing rapidly back through many different ages of poetry, Pound ties it all to two great originating traditions:

the classical melic lyrics, and the troubadour lyricists of medieval Provence who brought the ancient form into the modern world. Turning to the troubadours rather than Sappho as the 'root' of a modern literary 'civilization'⁶ brings a politics of gender and sexuality very different to that which we saw in Swinburne, one perhaps easier for Pound to negotiate.

Pound's doctoral thesis investigating troubadour poetry built on a trajectory of scholarship that had been gaining momentum since the date Pound implicitly gives for the rise of the contemporary lyric, 1870 – see, for example, Francis Hueffer's *The Troubadours: A History of Provençal Life and Literature in the Middle Ages* (1878), Ida Farnell's *The Lives of the Troubadours* (1896) and H. J. Chaytor's *The Troubadours of Dante* (1902). Pound was certainly familiar with these studies as well as some of those being written at a similar time in Europe, although he also undertook considerable original work with the troubadour manuscripts.⁷ Much of the scholarship on Pound's engagement with the troubadours focuses on the spiritual idea that Pound discovered in their lyrics. Stuart Y. McDougal, for example, argues that Pound was attracted to a vision of 'radiant virtue' through which he could find 'divine illumination' and 'contrast between the barren present and the radiant medieval world'.⁸ McDougal's analysis draws closely on Pound's essay 'Psychology and Troubadours' (1910), with its claim that the troubadours' literary learning in the cloisters led them to seek the divine within the earthly: not to 'grasp[] at the union with the absolute', but to discover a reflection of it in earthly love.⁹ Pound certainly engages with the problem of lyric transcendence through his discourse on the troubadours, but what interests me here particularly is the different set of concerns he articulates in another essay: 'Troubadours – Their Sorts and Conditions'. Here Pound engages much less metaphysically with the type of lyric subjectivity embodied by the troubadours. One can see from this essay that in addition to prompting thoughts about the relationship between the earthly and the divine, the troubadour minstrelsy brought into focus the idea of direct connection with a physically present audience; a rethinking of the importance of aural and musical qualities to the genre; and, perhaps most prominently, a reconceptualisation of the lyric subject and his or her relationship with society.¹⁰

Such issues clearly inflect Pound's early work, and his political engagement was apparent long before he began writing for the socialist journal *The New Age*. In poems such as 'Famam Librosque Cano' (Virgil: 'I sing of fame and books'), from *A Lume Spento*, he compares the songs of ancient poets with his own poems in order to invoke a time when lyric had social currency: 'Your songs' will be sung by 'little mothers . . . in the twilights'; 'Mine' will be at best picked up by a scholar at a second-hand bookshop.[11] Indeed, a string of personae in the early work represent an interest in the relationship of the poet with his or her community. In representing a form of lyric that was both a social art as well as an aesthetically valuable form of 'high art', the troubadours signified a meaningful interchange that placed poetry, and the aesthetic, at the heart of social interaction. Pound's troubadour poems also, I suggest, raise separate but related issues of communal lyric subjectivity that resonate strongly with Swinburne's vocal experiments traced in my previous chapter, and this is what I want to pursue here. W. R. Johnson's seminal study of lyric argued for the 'choral' having made a comeback in nineteenth- and twentieth-century poetry. He suggests that such work attempted to counteract feelings of isolation within the mechanised world – in which introspection had become less a source of inspiration than one of alienation – by reaffirming social kinship.[12] Johnson's study takes Walt Whitman as its focus, but he comments very briefly that Pound had the choral poetic gift more fully than any other poet after Whitman, (even though 'middle and late Pound attempted to escape his choral vocation; or rather, he tried to legitimate his choral poems with bogus history and fertile cant').[13] The choral is, I suggest, used by Pound to imagine a lyric connected both with a community of poets and with society more generally.

I will focus here on 'Cino' (again from *A Lume Spento*), a poem narrated by an itinerant troubadour on the open road in 1309 in the Italian countryside, presumably walking to a different court to ply his lyric trade to a new audience. His song reflects on his role singing love lyrics to many different women:

> I have sung women in three cities,
> But it is all the same;
> And I will sing of the sun.[14]

In this way, the poem meditates on the pre-conditioned convention-ality of the love lyric. Moreover, the final line seems a great leveller in two directions, conflating all women with the light of the sun, but also the singer with everything else that exists under the sun. Indeed, within the poem the women wooed ('eh? . . . they mostly had grey eyes') and the songs sung may merge into one, but Cino also merges within a tradition of singers as even his name is a generic shortened form for any of the common Italian personal names ending with 'cino': Baroncino, Leoncino, Pacino, Simoncino and others.[15] The poem appears to meditate on genre and the generic, and the communal 'origins' of lyric:

> 'A saucy fellow, but . . .
> (Oh they are all one these vagabonds),
> Peste! 'tis his own songs?
> Or some other's that he sings?
> But *you*, My Lord, how with your city?'

Embedded within a social setting of court interaction, this dialogue between two gentlemen speculates on the shared nature of lyric song, which might be the singer's own or something passed around between minstrels. In Michael Coyle's exploration of the importance of popular genres to Pound's work he comments that Pound 'pursued his attack on exclusive views of poetry both in his critical and poetic writing, but his broadest ambition was to create a work more inclusive than anything since Homer': 'He wanted a poetry of the agora, a poetry that could include the transactions of economic and political power.'[16] In a sense, the troubadour poets provided exactly this: a poetry that not only included, but was itself a transaction of economic and political power, through the social and romantic relations of the court.

About half-way through, 'Cino' returns to the refrain with which it began, and (in quotation marks) to the song of the sun that he promised us in the first refrain. This song calls on the sun as a muse for his 'wander-lied'. The song speaks of 'Seeking e'er the new-laid rast-way', but is followed again by the poem's refrain: 'I have sung women in three cities/ But it is all one'. Walking and singing are closely connected in this poem in a way that makes the 'open road' that Cino follows a kind of 'desire line': a symbol of the collective pathway of lyric song, in which each new singer follows the path worn by previous poets; an emblem of the collective nature of lyric song. His desire for the 'new-laid rast-way', balanced by the generic refrain, suggests the formative tension in lyric between on the one hand the individual subjectivity and search for novelty and, on the other hand, the conventional nature of the genre. The poem constantly returns to the generic merging of women, songs and, at a textual level, Cino with the other troubadours. I suggest that this poem literalises the 'lines of desire' in the troubadour's pathway from court to court, and the theme of the poem might be seen as lyric community and the role of the collective in the construction of the individual lyric subject.

The final three lines of the poem open up a new image:

> I will sing of the white birds
> In the blue waters of heaven,
> The clouds that are spray to its sea.

This new song takes conventional images of birds, clouds, spray and sea (the 'white birds' being an allusion specifically to the eponymous poem by Yeats), but inverts them, putting the blue waters in the sky and the clouds as spray to the sea. This assertion of innovation through convention and the commonality of allusion suggests a genre formed somewhere between the individual and the collective. The figure of the troubadour, then, provides a way of asking questions about lyric subjectivity that are particularly pertinent to Pound's own time. It is no coincidence that in 'Troubadours – Their Sorts and Conditions', Pound stresses more than once how much they are, as people, similar to his contemporaries.[17] As with Swinburne's turn to Sappho, the early poetry of Pound rediscovers pre-Romantic formulations of lyric as a source of inspiration for a renegotiation of the connection between subject and world, inner and outer, subjective and objective, personal and impersonal, that can refit the lyric for a more meaningful relationship with modernity.

As with 'Anactoria', I suggest that 'Cino' might be read as more of a dramatisation of an idea of lyric subjectivity than a dramatisation of a specific subject. Even the often-quoted letter in which Pound refers to 'the short so-called dramatic lyric – at any rate the sort of thing I do' goes on, if we care to read further, to identify his interest in a moment of lyric intensity.[18] In a striking echo of that anonymous critic who wrote in 1866 of Swinburne becoming his personae rather than borrowing from them, Pound writes in the poem 'Histrion': 'Thus am I Dante for a space and am/ One François Villon, ballad-lord and thief'.[19] When Pound writes of *Personae* involving 'the "search for oneself," . . . the search for "sincere self-expression"' through 'casting off, as it were, complete masks of the self in each poem', 'casting off' takes on a double meaning of both moulding likenesses of the self and throwing them away.[20] However dismissive he is of his own earlier enterprise, it is clear that it was the drama of the self he found in his personae, not the drama of others. Indeed, Pound wrote under the pseudonym 'Cino' in some of his earlier work, and identified so personally with Betran de Born that, as McDougal notes, he wonders 'if the troubadour had "a red straggling beard" and green eyes, like himself'.[21]

This is not to say that Pound was not influenced by the dramatic poetics of Browning (a debt he openly proclaimed in 'Canto 2' and which he voiced in his admiration for the troubadour poem 'Sordello'),[22] but it is to draw attention to the very real differences in their poetics. For Browning, Sordello is a way of exploring a psychological dramatic narrative, but for Pound his troubadour personae appear to represent, at least in part, something very different: a model of lyric that is generic, stylised, impersonal and social, yet able to assume a specific personal meaning when performed within a particular context. The troubadour wooed sometimes for himself and sometimes on behalf of others, as Pound was aware.[23] The troubadour song was made up of a conventional thematic repertoire which was eminently transferable from one particular situation and audience to another, while simultaneously holding context-specific meaning and undergoing a spontaneous reinvention within each performance. Such a model of lyric was particularly interesting at this time, perhaps, because it blurred the personal and the collective, the heartfelt and the conventional. Relatively little is still known for certain about the context in which these songs were sung and quite what social 'work' they achieved,[24] but they were clearly an intriguing paradigm for those looking to address the perceived problem of an isolated and introspective lyric subject: one of interest also to D. G. Rossetti (who, like Pound, translated Cavalcanti) as well as to Browning and Swinburne.[25] Of course, Pound drew from both Browning and the aesthetes,[26] but the breadth and importance of his reading of aestheticist poetry is generally underexplored. A letter to William Carlos Williams reveals something of his reading habits:

> If you'll read Yeats and Browning and Francis Thompson and Swinburne and Rossetti you'll learn something about the progress of Eng. poetry in the last century. And if you'll read Margaret Sackville, Rosamund Watson, Ernest Rhys, Jim G. Fairfax, you'll learn what the people of second rank can do, and what damn good work it is. You are out of touch. That's all.[27]

This 'touch' of the work of the previous generation, I suggest, left its mark.

Pound may claim to have returned to Swinburne in order to find a life-force against the gloom of Decadence, but the broader influence of aestheticist and Decadent poetry should not be so easily dismissed. 'Cino' might, for example, be compared to Arthur Symons's 'Wanderers' (to quote just the first stanza):

> I have had enough of women, and enough of love,
> But the land waits, and the sea waits, and day and night is enough;
> Give me a long white road, and the grey wide path of the sea,
> And the wind's will and the bird's will, and the heart-ache still in me.[28]

This is a poem in which Pound was particularly interested during his youth, and 'Cino' seems marked by it.[29] Indeed, for all that Pound's Provençal poets aim to offer a counter-Decadent image of masculinity, they are surprisingly similar to aestheticist bohemian models of masculinity.[30]

In the same vein, one might also look to poems such as Ernest Dowson's 'Villanelle of the Poet's Road', which again invokes the motif of the wandering minstrel whose chosen path is one of 'Wine and woman and song':

> Wine and woman and song,
>   Three things garnish our way:
> Yet is day over long.
>
> Lest we do our youth wrong,
>   Gather them while we may:
> Wine and woman and song.
>
> Three things render us strong,
>   Vine leaves, kisses and bay;
> Yet is day over long.
>
> Unto us they belong,
>   Us the bitter and gay,
> Wine and woman and song.
>
> We, as we pass along,
>   Are sad that they will not stay;
> Yet is day over long.
>
> Fruits and flowers among,
>   What is better than they:
> Wine and woman and song?
>   Yet is day over long.[31]

Pound's own comment on Dowson's use of the villanelle refers to the refrains as containing the 'emotional fact' of the poem,[32] yet here the two refrains seem to pull in rather different directions: the *carpe diem* 'Wine and woman and song' is balanced by the more 'Decadent' refrain of 'Yet is day overlong'. Vincent Sherry has suggested that the latter gives the poem a central rhetorical structure of the 'fade away',[33] yet one might see these two refrains presented as the flip-side of one another (an inevitable counterbalance, with neither taking precedence): the 'now' of modernity will always entail a recognition of belatedness and a moment always passing. Indeed, this is a dialectic matched in Pound's 'Cino', which expresses a world-weary 'but it is all one', at the same time as embracing the 'saucy' role of lover and wanderer. Crucially, Dowson's poem also makes strongly the connections between lyric, desire, travelling and community that we can see echoed in 'Cino' ('*We*, as we pass along' [my emphasis] suggests a path well-travelled poetically, in opposition to a reified solitary transcendent subject). It is this nexus of concerns that invoke community and enable a return to what Symonds identifies, in the quotation given in Chapter 8, as a pre-Romantic idea of lyric that eschews the solitary voice of the Victorians.

As Cassandra Laity notes in her introduction to a 2008 special issue of *Modernism/modernity*, there is still a lack of scholarship extending the issues of study within high modernism back into nineteenth-century English literature, and 'British Decadence and/or Aestheticism is still perceived by many modernists as a "Baudelairean" derivative or dismissed as blandly "effeminate", socially irrelevant, and elitist'.[34] Yet Pound's relationship with Dowson is, I suggest, as interesting as it was conflicted. At the University of Pennsylvania in 1906, Pound took a course on contemporary poetry with Cornelius Weygandt, who, as Helen Carr documents, was perhaps a greater influence on Pound than he later acknowledged. Weygandt's enthusiasm for Lionel Johnson and John Davidson went along with a particular admiration for Dowson that might well have been a major motivation for Pound's desire to find the remaining members of the Rhymers' Club when he first reached London.[35] Later accounts figure Dowson as a strong presence during Pound's early time in London. Visiting Pound in 1910, William Carlos Williams accompanied him to an evening of readings by Yeats at the Abbey Theatre at which 'Cynara' was read in the hush of a séance-like atmosphere.[36] Pound himself recalled reading 'Fiona Macleod, and Dowson and Symons', and feeling 'drunk with "Celticism"'.[37] Such twilight intoxication was generally presented by Pound as a lassitude he had to overcome.

In a prose-poem-type passage from his college notes, Pound writes that 'When I read Dowson':

> I am ashamed to call my
> halt lines verse, ashamed to dream I might be poet.
> Yet comes the answer, 'He hath no strong glad message to give
> to men that be over weary.
> It is only in the power of your optimism
> that you can succeed; in the strength that you
> have or must have. [. . .][38]

Such statements capture well the complicated nexus of feelings (simultaneous awe, threat and the need to disparage) that Dowson aroused in Pound.

Yet Dowson *was* an important interlocutor for Pound, both in his thinking about poetry and in his composition; and he was a figure with whom Pound was frequently engaged in his early work. Victor Plarr remarked later, in a volume of reminiscences, that for the young Pound, 'Dowson [was] a kind of classical myth'.[39] Compositions such as 'Autumnus (To Dowson – Antistave)'[40] and the poem inspired by Dowson's 'In Tempore Senectutis'[41] both express a kinship of surprising passion. These poems have been read as a rejection of Dowson's 'dreary world-weariness', replacing a Decadent despondence with a claim for the possibility of positive renewal.[42] Yet these homages to Dowson are at worst ambivalent, claiming, at least at times, something more like an identity in their role as beacons of light in a gloomy twilight world. 'Autumnus (To Dowson – Antistave)', for example, begins by presenting the 'dreari[ness]' of the world, but the first stanza ends with the claim that 'Yet the Spring of the Soul, the Spring of the Soul/ Claimeth its own in thee and me'. *Personae* – Pound's 1909 volume of selected early work, which replaced his earlier volumes – omits the poems explicitly invoking Dowson, and he distances himself quite comprehensively from his influence. Indeed, Pound's public prescriptions for an Imagist doctrine do not acknowledge the fact that Dowson and his generation had already reacted against much of the 'Victorianism' that the Imagists sought to unseat.[43] Yet Pound's private letters tell a different story. In spite of his quarrel with Dowson, he terms him (in 1911) 'a very sincere man & a very fine craftsman' who 'has epitomized a decade – exquisitely, unaffectedly [. . .] To me he holds a very interesting position, strategically, in the development of the art.' In the same letter Pound goes on to recognise that 'The whole set of "The Rhymers" did valuable work in knocking bombast, & rhetoric & Victorian syrup out of our verse.'[44]

The Rhymers' Club was a short-lived gathering (founded in 1890, the group was still meeting in 1896, although at that point numbers already seem to have been dwindling),[45] but it provided visibility and focus for the work of a group of male poets. Founded by W. B. Yeats, Ernest Rhys and T. W. Rolleston, the club was large and popular, welcoming many 'minor poets' of the period.[46] I referred very briefly in Chapter 6 to the publishing practice of the Rhymers' Club, and it is a topic particularly pertinent to the themes I have been following here. While Dowson writes of a choral community in 'wine and woman and song', the books of the Rhymers' Club to which he contributed enact such a poetic communality typographically. Representing writers such as Dowson, Symons, Lionel Johnson and Richard Le Gallienne, in addition to the founder members and others, *The Book of the Rhymers' Club* (1892) and *The Second Book of the Rhymers' Club* (1894) appear to set out deliberately to create in print a 'desire line' of lyric collectively. The volumes negotiate a communal lyric voice in which individual voices are merged by, for example, their use of a running header ('The Rhymers' Club') that supersedes the titles of individual poems and, as Nicholas Frankel has observed, complicates the attribution of each poem to a particular authorial voice.[47] Frankel's reading of these texts as material objects concludes that 'the Rhymers' interest in seemingly closed linguistic structures masks a deep, collective concern with shifting poetry away from the persona of the author and a corresponding insistence on the textual event of the poem in performance'.[48] It is this articulation of a lyric both social and performative that has such resonance with the issues discussed here, and that I suggest demonstrates a particular type of negotiation between the lyric and modernity in the work of Swinburne, some of the Decadents, and in the early work of Pound. In response to a model of lyric subjectivity perceived as simultaneously introspective and universalising, this communal subjectivity offers a solution very different from the dramatic poetic persona proposed by Browning and others earlier.

While very much an 1890s phenomenon, the Rhymers' Club nonetheless marks the type of intersection of *fin-de-siècle* and modernist literary culture that often gets overlooked. The club was used by a generation of young modernists as a model for their own successor venture: in 1908 – the same year that 'Cino' was published in *A Lume Spento* – T. E. Hulme founded the 'Poets' Club'. Hulme left the club the following year, but it attracted as members some of the former Rhymers, marking that continuation also in its publication of two anthologies based on the model of the Rhymers' volumes: *The Book of the Poets' Club* (1909) and *The Second Book of the Poets' Club* (1911). Yet modernist poetry became increasingly invested in a narrative of rupture with the work of the previous generation. Pound's 'Hugh Selwyn Mauberley', published in 1920, clearly marks this point in his own career – and in this poem Pound satirised Dowson, claiming that he 'found harlots cheaper than hotels'.[49] Here Pound does much to contribute to a myth of the Decadent lyric poet that belittles their work and satirises them personally. His criticism of 'the obscure reveries/ Of the inward gaze' masks the modernity of the communal subject imagined by poets such as Swinburne and the Rhymers.[50] The first part of 'Mauberley' contains twelve lyric sections and an 'envoi' (the French term itself now used parodically because of its association with what had come to be seen as a rather affected Francophilia of Parnassianism) which ends with a satirical declaration of the value of beauty: 'Till change hath broken down/ All things save Beauty alone'.[51] In contrast, the second part, containing just four sections, appears to be written in a modernist style, and declares the death of aestheticist lyric through the epitaph of Mauberley: ' "I was/ And I no more exist; Here drifted/ An hedonist'.[52] In this poem, Pound is often considered to be rejecting his early poetry, and any affiliation with aestheticism or with lyric.[53] Ultimately, though, what I have shown through a comparison of 'Cino' and Dowson's 'Villanelle of the Poet's Road' is the way that Decadent hedonism might – through the paradigm of the troubadour – take a communal function and identity as a way of reconciling a nineteenth-century lyric paradigm with modernity. Far from drifting on a sea of Decadent hedonism, Pound was developing a poetics of modernity inspired by the work of the previous generation. I suggest that Pound's early work was influenced by poets such as Dowson (as well as Swinburne) to use the figure of the troubadour to consider the relationship between self and society, between a poetry at once personal and performative, a rhetoric both individual and traditional, and a genre both introspective and social.

*　*　*

In tracing connections and continuations between the Decadents, Swinburne and Pound's experiments with lyric subjectivity in 'Cino', I have so far not commented on the one area of difference that is particularly important within the remit of my study: poetic form. 'Cino' does not look much like the strict-form, late Victorian lyrics that are my main focus. The previous chapter traced an idea of lyric chorus through both the roundel and the intricate formations of 'Anactoria'. Pound's poem, on the other hand, has a freer form, with dramatic interludes. The poem has no thoroughgoing regular rhyme or metrical structure, but presents itself as a song by way of a ballad-like refrain and through its focus in content on song and the act of singing. It is in this way a marker of a modernist shift away from the strict forms that see a distinctive resurgence in my period of study, but also, I will suggest, from a late Victorian idea of 'lyric' poetry itself. For many early twentieth-century modernist poets, it seems the very term 'lyric' had become an object of suspicion. The 'totalised' lyric genre, which encompassed and subsumed many different forms of poetry, was to them a rather fuzzy concept that clashed with the hard, concrete and 'scientific' values of modernism. T. S. Eliot's dismissal of 'lyric' is known best from his question, posed in *The Three Voices of Poetry*, 'How short does a poem have to be to be called a "lyric"?' He is at this point (in 1954) examining the contemporaneous *OED* definition:

> *Lyric*: Now the name for short poems, usually divided into stanzas or strophes, and directly expressing the poet's own thoughts and sentiments.[54]

In fact, Eliot suggests discarding the term 'lyric poetry' in favour of 'meditative verse'.[55] Yet, although making this substitution, Eliot's 'three voices' of poetry still represent a fairly traditional taxonomy of meditative, epic and dramatic verse.[56] The key for him is the recognition that these are more modes than genres, so, while one 'voice' may be dominant, 'in every poem there is more than one voice to be heard'.[57] Avoiding the term 'lyric' enables Eliot to recognise a particular poetic mode which the greatly expanded remit of the 'lyric' genre can no longer signify.

Pound also largely avoids the term, yet he simultaneously engages deeply with its historical roots. When he does use it, he tends to refer specifically to the song heritage in poetry. Writing to Margaret C. Anderson in 1918, he comments:

> I desire to go on with my long poem [. . .] And I desire to resurrect the art of the lyric, I mean words to be sung, for Yeats' only wail and submit to keening and ch*au*nting (with a *u*) and Swinburne's only rhapsodify. And with a few exceptions (a few in Browning) there is scarcely anything since the time of Waller and Campion. And a mere imitation of them won't do.[58]

Pound's desire to reconnect the category of 'lyric' poetry with song recognises that song had become what I described earlier as a 'dead metaphor' within the genre. More commonly, however, he prefers a different terminology. Introducing a set of terms taken from ancient Greece, he aims to provide a more 'precise' classificatory system for poetry, identifying 'three "kinds of poetry"': melopoeia (a poetry charged with a 'musical' property), logopoeia ('the dance of the intellect among words'; a poetry of language) and phanopoeia (a poetry of images).⁵⁹ Melopoeia is most clearly associated with the song-heritage Pound thinks of as 'lyric' (although logopoeia is also described as 'lyrical' in the 'Cavalcanti' essay).⁶⁰ For Pound, melopoeia is itself subdivided into three types: 'poems made to speak, to chant and to sing'.⁶¹ He goes on to say that the poetry of medieval Provence and Tuscany was 'in general', 'all made to be sung'. Indeed, his return to Provençal minstrels such as 'Cino' appears to be in key part motivated by a desire to return to a more musically motivated verse.⁶² The sonnet (the 'little tune', and a core constituent of 'lyric' for the later nineteenth-century sources quoted in my study) is the form that comes to mark, for Pound, the 'beginning of the divorce of words and music', and by 1290 the sonnet already represents a poetry in which rhetoric is divorced from tune.⁶³ He describes 'lyric' here as a 'cantabile quality' in poetry and laments the points in history at which lyric poetry has turned from its musical basis to a rhetorical basis.⁶⁴

The tendency towards complex 'Parnassian' forms within aestheticism might mark the apotheosis of this rhetorically invested lyric (something that for Pound is a contradiction in terms), and it has provided a central focus for my study. As I have already noted, however, it did not go unchallenged before Pound launched his critique. In Chapter 6 I discussed the different poetic politics of the English ballad and the French *ballade*, suggesting that the association of complex Parnassian rhetoric with a poetry written for the eye brought with it a simultaneous oppositional movement that saw simple song forms as a way of returning lyric to the ear. The conceptualisation of lyric in the final third of the nineteenth century was, however, usually capacious enough to include both. Indeed, through the idea of a textual chorus, these last few chapters have addressed something of the intersection of rhetoric and song in ways that show how complicated the politics of the ballad became over the turn of the century. While invoking an aural tradition in its very title, Swinburne's *Poems and Ballads* are intricately rhetorical poems, as much as are his roundels (which also take a sung 'round' as their basis); and whatever the investment by some writers in the simple English ballad form as a reaction against complex 'rhetoric' and Parnassian jewel forms, it too was, in turn, rejected by many modernists because of its regular form.[65] 'Cino', significantly, uses neither the consistent patterning of the ballad stanza, nor the dense rhetorical patterning of rhyme and metre that Swinburne employs. In his free-verse ballad, Pound is engaged in the task of reclaiming song from the 'rhetorical' forms that many modernists (and many later scholars, who follow their lead) saw as ossifying song in print.

Ultimately, then, poems like 'Cino' reflect Pound's interest in extracting from the capacious late nineteenth-century concept of lyric a musical poetry. This is in many ways an attempt to return to a more authentic 'lyric' poetry, but Pound avoids the word 'lyric' (using 'lyrical' occasionally to describe a mode but rarely writing of the 'lyric' genre) because he wants to separate the musical impulse from what he saw as a genre that had come to be defined in relation to introspection, affect and the rhetoric of regular form. Indeed, later in his career Pound combined this musical impetus with a form more epic in its scope and aspiration when he embarked on *The Cantos*. Readers of Pound's early poetry often, therefore, see in it a desire to reject the nineteenth-century conception of lyric as an enemy to the ethical, the collective and the modern. Particularly interested in defining Pound's work through a rejection of the nineteenth-century lyric, Thomas Grieve writes that 'He had to train his voice to speak for a world outside himself and to transform his art into a medium for other voices, for tradition, and for history.'[66] Yet there can be no doubt as to Pound's investment in the history and conception of lyric, and its generative powers within some of his own early work. I suggest that before Pound moved towards his musical epic, he was quite profoundly engaged with the experiments of the previous generation to find *within* lyric subjectivity the very things that Grieve suggests he ultimately sought through other genres. In Pound's own early engagement with the medieval Provençal poets, as in Swinburne's engagement with Sappho, I suggest that we see a desire to discover in the 'origins' of Western lyric a subject that is both personal and communal; a voice both individual and choral.

In fact, when high modernism turned away from the rhetoric of Parnassian forms and from the aestheticist conception of lyric, it was, I suspect, not simply because the nineteenth-century lyric subject was considered problematically introspective and divorced from society. For many aesthetes and Decadents, lyric subjectivity had become something more like a poetic stage for a 'postmodern' play of the self that dramatised the multiplicity of the self and, at times, its permeable boundaries with others. The rejection of this kind of performative lyricism – and some of the challenging issues it raised – almost certainly stemmed, in part, from the reaction against Decadence that followed the sentencing of Oscar Wilde in 1895.[67] It also seems likely that after the First World War, with its dreadful images of bodies literally atomised and fragmented, this confident play around notions of a multiple, personal, lyric subjectivity became, temporarily, if not impossible then highly problematic. In tandem, certain possibilities for lyric were closed down by a high modernist concern with 'authenticity' – as opposed to that sincerely personal Wildean 'insincerity'[68] – which aimed at 'freeing one's potential Self from the bonds of convention'.[69] Free verse was, as I have discussed throughout this book, a marker of this modernist quest for the authentic poetic subject which ultimately led away from the rhetorical experiments of aestheticist 'lyric' poetry.

Clearly, however, the high modernist turn to more 'authentic' and epic structures (widely identified by scholars as one of the key generic developments of poetic modernism)[70] did not mark the end of the road for the late nineteenth-century conception of lyric and lyric subjectivity that I have been tracing. The multiply performative self and something of the rhetorical investment in lyric (particularly in the form of the sonnet) resurfaced powerfully later in the twentieth century. Writing about the fate of the aesthetic in postmodernity, Simon Malpas takes up the problem of introspective lyric subjectivity in this essay from *The New Aestheticism*, arguing that 'Subjectivity is irreducible and unique, and yet indissociable from relations with the plurality of others (each of whom will also be singular). Community thus obtains in this plurality of singularities each existing on the basis of its relations with others [. . .]'[71] This phenomenological argument has a strong resonance with what I have traced in this part of my study through a set of examples ranging from the 1860s to the late aestheticist work of Ezra Pound. Moreover, Ford Madox Hueffer (as he still called himself at that point) was writing in 1920 of the tenacious survival of nineteenth-century ideas of poetry into the twentieth century. Comparing the 'Parnassian opulence' of the later nineteenth century and the new generation ('Les Jeunes': Pound, D. H. Lawrence, Wyndham Lewis, Flint, H.D., T. S. Eliot and others), he suggests that the modernists 'made a great deal of noise' around 1914, but that the First World War cut short *their* movement:

> they plotted the blowing of Parnassus to the moon. They came near to doing it. They stood for the Non-Representational in the Arts; for *Vers*

Libre; for symbols in Prose, *tapage* in Life, and Death to Impressionism. They were a fine band, and did useful work. The war is said to have extinguished them – as if the Germans' invasion of Belgium saved their Parnassian Allies.[72]

He goes on to imagine the 'war' as one between modernists and Parnassians, in which the modernists were defeated:

> Mr. Pound, I am told, is dead. Mr. Lewis, I think, amongst the Immortals of Burlington House; Futurism is a bye-word; Vers Libristes have all been put into decasyllabic strait-waistcoats; all the Imagistes are in the workhouse [. . .][73]

The Parnassianism and 'Academicism' that triumphed is that of an older generation, one invested in the strict-form revival of the later nineteenth century and in a conceptualisation of lyric that looks back for its models to a history of lyric 'origins'.[74]

We do not now think of literary modernism as such a short-lived literary movement in the public consciousness, but one might still argue that the definition of the 'lyric' genre formed in the nineteenth century did indeed continue to have strong currency throughout the twentieth century. Charles LaPorte notes that the Victorians had a mania for classifying genre equivalent to their desire for categorising nature. It involved not only borrowing and adapting long-standing systems of genre identification but also adding their own additional and idiosyncratic extra distinctions: 'the Victorians propagated quasi-Aristotelian genre theory so successfully that we still apply it to historically unrelated works'.[75] For poetry this is marked spectacularly by the retro-projection through poetic history of a distinctly later nineteenth-century understanding of lyric. Eliot's and Pound's desire to avoid the term in favour of a new taxonomy did not catch on; the very nineteenth-century definition of 'lyric' poetry Eliot rejected in *The Three Voices of Poetry* is the one that came to dominate. Indeed, Pound's own attempt to propose a new anthology of English poetry 'to replace that doddard Palgrave' came to nothing, with the prospective publisher responding in disbelief: 'don't you know [. . .] that the whole fortune of X & Co. is founded on Palgrave's *Golden Treasury*?'[76] The definition of lyric poetry most commonly given in dictionaries of poetic terms across the twentieth century was as a result almost certainly more indebted to Palgrave's conceptualisation than to Pound's.

Notes

1. Morgan, 'Influence, Intertextuality and Tradition', p. 142; Laity, 'T. S. Eliot and A. C. Swinburne', pp. 438, 439.
2. Letter from Ezra Pound to Margaret Cravens (from Swarthmore, 30 June 1910), in Pound and Cravens, *A Tragic Friendship, 1910–1912*, p. 42.
3. *Collected Early Poems of Ezra Pound*, pp. 15, 16–17.
4. Moody, *Ezra Pound: Poet*, Vol. I, pp. 52–3.
5. Pound, *Literary Essays*, p. 91.
6. See 'The Tradition', in *Literary Essays*, p. 91; and 'Troubadours – Their Sorts and Conditions', in *Literary Essays*, p. 102.
7. See McDougal, *Ezra Pound and the Troubadour Tradition*, p. 4; and Paden, 'Pound's Use of Troubadour Manuscripts', passim.
8. McDougal, *Ezra Pound and the Troubadour Tradition*, pp. 99, 89.
9. Pound, *The Spirit of Romance*, p. 99.
10. Sometimes Pound's observations on this last point are surprising, and certainly not much discussed in relation to his own poetry. See, for example, the following comment: 'The chivalric singing was devised to lighten the boredom; and this very singing became itself in due time, in the manner of all things, an ennui' ('Troubadours – Their Sorts and Conditions', in *Literary Essays*, p. 101).
11. Pound, *Collected Early Poems*, pp. 22–3.
12. Johnson, *The Idea of Lyric*, p. 177.
13. Ibid., pp. 178, 193.
14. Pound, *Collected Early Poems*, pp. 10–12. All subsequent references to the poem are from these pages.
15. I offer this explanation to supplement previous suggestions, such as Witemeyer's, that 'Cino Polnesi' is based on the Italian poet 'Cino da Pistoia', who was exiled from his city in 1307; as Witemeyer acknowledges, that parallel 'sheds little light on the poem' (*The Poetry of Ezra Pound*, p. 78).
16. Coyle, *Ezra Pound, Popular Genres and the Discourse of Culture*, p. 5.
17. Pound, 'Troubadours – Their Sorts and Conditions', in *Literary Essays*, pp. 99, 101.
18. *Selected Letters of Ezra Pound, 1907–1941*, pp. 3–4.
19. Anonymous, 'Mr Swinburne and His Critics', pp. 643–4; Pound, *Collected Early Poems*, p. 71.
20. Pound, 'Vorticism', p. 463: 'In the "search for oneself," in the search for "sincere self-expression," one gropes, one finds some seeming verity. One says "I am" this, that, or the other, and with the words scarcely uttered one ceases to be that thing.'
21. McDougal, *Ezra Pound and the Troubadour Tradition*, p. 51.
22. See also Pound's review of 'T. S. Eliot' where he claims 'The most interesting poems in Victorian English are Browning's *Men and Women*' (*Literary Essays of Ezra Pound*, p. 419).

23. See Pound, 'Troubadours – Their Sorts and Conditions' in *Literary Essays*, p. 94.
24. Studies such as Linda M. Paterson's *The World of the Troubadours* show the limits of our knowledge of this world for all the new scholarship it offers.
25. The differences between Pound's and Rossetti's translations of Cavalcanti make for interesting comparison; see Preda, 'D. G. Rossetti and Ezra Pound as Translators of Cavalcanti'.
26. Witemeyer has argued at length that Pound's personae 'stand somewhere between Browning's dramatic monologues and Yeats's masks' (Witemeyer, *The Poetry of Ezra Pound*, p. 60).
27. *Selected Letters of Ezra Pound 1907–1941*, p. 8.
28. Symons, *Images of Good and Evil*, p. 178.
29. See Witemeyer, *The Poetry of Ezra Pound*, p. 78.
30. See Helen Carr's discussion of Pound's troubadour subject (*Verse Revolutionaries*, p. 98).
31. Dowson, *Collected Poems*, p. 182.
32. Pound, *The Poetical Works of Lionel Johnson*, p. xvii.
33. Sherry, *Modernism and the Reinvention of Decadence*, p. 71.
34. Laity, 'Editor's Introduction: Beyond Baudelaire', p. 427.
35. See Carr, *Verse Revolutionaries*, p. 68.
36. Nadel, *Ezra Pound: A Literary Life*, p. 46.
37. Pound, 'Lionel Johnson' (1915), in *Literary Essays*, p. 367.
38. Among 'College Notes' (Yale Collection of American Literature, Beinecke Rare Book and Manuscript Library, Yale University); quoted in Moody, *Ezra Pound: Poet*, Vol. I, p. 43.
39. Plarr, *Ernest Dowson 1888–1987* (1914); quoted in Ruthven, *A Guide to Ezra Pound's Personae: 1926*, p. 136.
40. Pound, *Collected Early Poems*, p. 249 (Poems from the San Trovaso Notebook).
41. Ibid., pp. 21–2, 50–1 (*A Lume Spento*).
42. See Moody's analysis in *Ezra Pound: Poet*, Vol. I, p. 43.
43. This is a point Helen Carr follows up in her study *The Verse Revolutionaries* (see, for example, p. 533).
44. Pound, letter to Floyd Dell (February 1911), in 'Two Early Letters of Ezra Pound', ed. Tanselle, p. 118.
45. Harper and Beckson, 'Victor Plarr on "The Rhymers' Club": An Unpublished Lecture', pp. 379, 383.
46. A letter from Lionel Johnson uses that term when it describes a typical meeting of 'eighteen minor poets': ibid., pp. 380, 379.
47. Frankel, ' "A Wreath for the Brows of Time" ', p. 137.
48. Ibid., p. 150.
49. Pound, *Personae*, pp. 189, 190.
50. Ibid., p. 186.
51. Ibid., p. 195.

52. Ibid., p. 201.
53. Although Michael Coyle has astutely argued that the second part of the poem does not represent a modernist triumph over the aestheticism of the first part, but that the two balance one another, suggesting 'a dilemma': 'As the poem gives form to – and so performs – this conflict, it suggests that the utter rejection of the aesthetic would come at too high a cost' (Coyle, 'Hugh Selwyn Mauberley', p. 436).
54. Eliot, *The Three Voices of Poetry*, p. 16.
55. Ibid., p. 17.
56. Ibid., p. 21.
57. Ibid., p. 21.
58. *Selected Letters of Ezra Pound 1907–1941*, p. 128.
59. Pound, 'How to Read', in *Literary Essays*, p. 25.
60. Pound, 'Cavalcanti', in *Literary Essays*, p. 197.
61. Ibid., p. 167.
62. A desire explored, in more general terms, in an essay by Robert Stark ('Pound Among the Nightingales – From the Troubadours to a Cantabile Modernism').
63. Pound, 'Cavalcanti', in *Literary Essays*, pp. 170, 171.
64. Ibid., p. 167.
65. See, for example, Hulme, 'A Lecture on Modern Poetry', p. 63.
66. Grieve, *Ezra Pound's Early Poetry and Poetics*, p. 23.
67. Most recently, Helen Carr has written a little about how experiments with, and challenges to, gender roles became untenable after the Wilde trials, and I suggest this had an effect on the play of performative lyric subjectivity too (*Verse Revolutionaries*, p. 98).
68. 'What we call insincerity is simply a method by which we multiply personalities' (Wilde, 'The Critic as Artist', p. 393).
69. See Moody's discussion of Pound's affinity with Dora Marsden's philosophy (*Ezra Pound: Poet*, Vol. I, p. 220).
70. See Beasley, *Theorists of Modernist Poetry*, pp. 80–1.
71. Malpas, 'Touching Art: Aesthetics, Fragmentation and Community', p. 91.
72. Hueffer, 'Thus to Revisit. . . (iii)', pp. 209, 211, 212.
73. Ibid., pp. 212–13.
74. Ibid., pp. 212–13.
75. LaPorte, 'Post-Romantic Ideologies and Victorian Poetic Practice', p. 522.
76. Pound, 'How to Read', in *Literary Essays*, p. 18; an episode reflected in Canto XXII.

Afterword

Poetry is not just a commentary on culture or a reflection of it, but a shaping participant within it. The history of genre, particularly, is the story of the changing ways in which we discuss, describe and think. I suggest that poetry of the period under discussion might be read with greater alertness to its formal negotiation with some of the key philosophical questions of modernity even while, and perhaps particularly when, its content may appear conventional and nostalgic. After all, lyric poetry responded to some of the key conceptual shifts of the nineteenth century because it had to: some of its core generic conventions were deeply challenged by changing ways of thinking and being.

Of course, the questioning of what were seen as Romantic formulations of lyric within a rapidly changing cultural context was apparent before the period I study, but what can broadly be termed 'aestheticist' poetry had the potential for different kinds of responses. This is a period both late Victorian and early modernist, but also one that had distinctive modes not recognised through a co-option to either. What we see in aestheticist poetry are possibilities that are different from those that emerge out of, for example, the turn towards dramatic and hybrid generic forms around the middle of the century; possibilities distinct also from the high modernist challenges to lyric poetry, and the turn to free verse. However much the theorists of modernity (Benjamin, Merleau-Ponty and Adorno) have been crucial to my analysis, what I have identified is not high modernism *avant la lettre* but a largely different array of responses to similar concerns.

At the beginning of this study I characterised aestheticist lyric poetry in terms of the revival of compressed, fixed verse forms, and two key impetuses: totalisation and reduction. At the heart of the crisis, and remaking, of lyric in the final decades of the nineteenth century is printed poetry's sense of having lost an intrinsic generic connection with musical and aural forms through its 'totalisation' in print culture. The extent to which 'lyric' poetry has *not* been defined in this study through an appeal to music and aurality reflects the expansion of the remit of the genre over the nineteenth century that had taken it away from a core Romantic association with song that David Duff has described.[1] This should complicate any attempt to project through history an understanding of 'lyric' poetry unified around an originary association with music or song. Aestheticist lyric frequently engages with the intermingling of multiple art forms and multiple senses,[2] in which the aural has ceased to hold a *necessarily* privileged position. While, as I have discussed, the strict verse forms so characteristic of the period were said to be symptomatic of lyric's shift of affiliation from the ear to the eye, close attention to this fashion for intricate formal patterning has unearthed potentialities in poetry of the period that complicate the narrative of a lyric pulled between a nineteenth-century affiliation with music, and a growing dominance of visuality and the image: not least, aestheticist lyric's affinity with the sculptural. The rhetoric of strict verse forms did not, I have argued, leave poetry dead on the page but, rather, had the potential to renegotiate the terms of poetry's engagement with the page.

At the same time as lyric was 'totalised' in print, one might want to say that what had earlier in the century been conceptualised more commonly as a component of poetry – or an ideal, essence or aspiration (in the case of John Stuart Mill's essays) – was envisioned as an isolatable actuality towards the end of the century. Aestheticism attempted to realise a pure lyric reduction, divorced from other elements. It is no accident that this happened when that lyric essence was most in danger of looking irrelevant to modernity: it was a consummate expression of an aestheticist ideal of art's autonomy. Yet my analysis suggests that the compressed, highly patterned poetry distinctive of the later decades of the nineteenth century engaged with the challenges of writing lyric in the modern era not in spite of its 'archaic' forms, but through them – using the very resources of regular and intricately patterned form to think afresh about the operation of lyric within modernity.[3] (Herbert Tucker has written of those who read poetry's content without attention to its form as 'Jiggering away at the lock of conceptual meaning while, just a shift of perspective away, the doors of perception stand open wide';[4] this observation is particularly relevant in relation to a period that saw such a prominent interest in poetic form.) This study has been underpinned by the claim that aestheticist poetry marks a distinctive point of confrontation of lyric's potential irrelevance to the modern world, and a response to those conceptual challenges. What emerges, I suggest, is a self-aware poetics that has much to tell us about the consideration and conceptualisation of lyric at this time – a crucial part of a much longer story of the genre and of a more general narrative of cultural formation.

In Part I, I explored a confrontation between temporalities of the Romantic-transcendent lyric and what might be identified as post-Enlightenment temporalities of the later nineteenth century. Reading these concerns through metre identified the significance of poetic form in theorising the interplay of temporal modes, as well as its ability to echo in provocative ways the rhythms of a newly industrialised and mechanised society. Part II addressed the significance of a phenomenological mode of connection, ultimately tracing it through the spatial presence of those intricately patterned poetic forms on the page. The problems of lyric address in the print-totalised lyric were, I have argued, countered by a somatic connection in the 'internal' lyric transaction that (sometimes explicitly and sometimes implicitly) projected an encounter with the reader through the phenomenology of the poetic page. Part III followed concerns about the relevance of a lyric subjectivity inherited by the Victorians, one characterised by pronouncements simultaneously introspective and universal. Exploring the importance of experiments in choral subjectivity in the period, I have argued that we see a reimagining of romantic lyric subjectivity. What I have uncovered here is a response to the same concerns that motivated the turn to forms such as the dramatic monologue in the mid-nineteenth century, but one that turns back to the resources of lyric in order to reconceptualise it rather than rejecting it in favour of hybrid forms. Central to this reconceptualisation are both the collective subject positions enabled by a print 'totalisation' that absorbed and preserved poetic precedents, and the repetitively patterned forms of aestheticist lyric that enable complex vocal patterns to be imagined.

What has been apparent from my initial reading of 'Grow vocal to me, O my shell divine!' by Michael Field is that the themes dealt with (separately, for the purposes of identification and analysis) in each part might also at times be found intertwined in a single poem; and, of course, they will be relevant to poets other than those central to my analysis in each part. The issues of temporality and historicism explored in Part I are also, for example, relevant to Swinburne's work; the issues of tactility raised in Part II might, as I will briefly indicate below, be seen to connect with a theme of physical encounter that is prominent throughout this book; and the choral lyric subjectivity followed through in Part III resonates, for example, with the experiments of the Rhymers' Club. The purpose of this book is to identify in specific case studies features that might help to understand aestheticist lyric more broadly. While not aiming at an exhaustive characterisation or survey of aestheticist lyric poetry, the threads I have identified will, I hope, be generative for finding new ways forward in our reading of this poetically fascinating and too often overlooked body of work.

In addition to forming the second case study for Part III, my final chapter provides a historical coda to the period I explore. Representing some of the connections with modernism, this chapter marks a continuation of the themes of the study as well as opposing currents. While 'Cino' is a poem that looks back to the same medieval world that inspired the revival of fixed forms characteristic of the poetry explored in this book, there is no doubt as to the importance of the politics motivating Pound's rejection of the visual 'rhetoric' of strict form in favour of a music of free verse. Like the revival of highly patterned fixed forms, free verse might also be seen as a response to the problems of lyric transcendence in the modern world. Yet Pound's desire to return poetry to the ear seeks a musicality that rejects any association with what had become for him an inauthentic idea of 'lyric'. Out of the complicated set of shifts around the turn of the century one might, then, follow various narratives into the twentieth century. For example, one might trace an attempt to redirect a totalised printed lyric poetry back to simple song through the work of poets of the later nineteenth century, and on into Pound's attempts to find the music of poetry within free verse. Or one can follow the interest in visual Impressionism within aestheticist lyric poetry, as it was simultaneously continued and opposed by the visual free-verse experiments of the Imagists. One can witness both a poetics of the image replacing an 'old-fashioned' Romantic idea of musical lyricism (H.D.'s imagistic poems, for example, translate Sapphic song into visual image) *and* a simultaneous reclamation within lyric of a song tradition. Certainly music and image are still the two frames of reference most commonly brought to articulate these shifts in the early twentieth century.

Yet the significance of the totalised print lyric's sculptural and tactile presence that I pursued particularly in Part II pointed towards a different aesthetic frame, and one arguably more characteristic of aestheticist poetry specifically. In Part II (particularly through the work of Alice Meynell and others), I linked the importance of somatic encounter to the haptic potential of the totalised print lyric's physical presence on the page. But it may be that more generally there is a congruence between attention to fashioning the intricate bodies of the fixed-form poems that characterise aestheticist poetry (an investment in the spatial relations and resonances between words in the poem) and an awareness of the capacity for touch between actual bodies. While lyric tactility is not a 'new' mode of poetic operation at this time, to recognise its importance to the period is, I suggest, to recognise something significant to the particular conceptualisation of lyric that emerges out of the sensual erotics characteristic of aestheticism and Decadence. It is striking that within a movement of poetry often castigated for its lack of connection with others – a blip between the socially aware dramatic monologue of the mid-century and the return to social consciousness in modernism – there appears often to be a profound investment in the capacity of touch or contact between bodies. 'Art for art's sake' may appear destined to produce work irredeemably solipsistic and introspective, yet in its awareness of the body there are new possibilities for connection. Whether the felt 'swish' of hair in Rossetti's 'For an Allegorical Dance of Women, by Andrea Mantegna'; the flirtation with the materiality of objects (whether gems or commodities) in Parnassian poetry; the centrality of physical sensuality to a Decadent configuration of lyrical phenomenology; Hardy's formal construction of a tangible presence within his poetics of absence; or the many and varied somatic sensations of mutual encounter in Swinburne's verse: what is 'felt' seems as central as what is heard or seen.

Indeed, this physical touch is significant at a more general level within my investigation for its ability to unsettle the aspirations towards transcendence that I outlined in Chapter 1. Whether through a touch across time, or through the temporality of the commodity (both of which might substitute for a Romantic dialectic with the eternal); through investment in the tactile sensualities of lyric's spatial presence; or through the desire for a somatic construction of the lyric subject in connection with other subjects: aestheticist poetry offers alternative conceptualisations of lyric to those premised on a transcendence of time, space and subjectivity. Yet the difficulty scholars have often had in acknowledging the value and interest of this period of literary history within longer narratives of lyric is undoubtedly due, to some extent, to the difficult reception of such aestheticist somatics after the sentencing of Oscar Wilde in 1895. It is worth thinking a little here, in conclusion, about the conceptualisation of lyric that has emerged from my investigations, and its fate and significance within a broader literary trajectory.

In my final chapter I noted that the events of the First World War were in part responsible for a loss of faith in the performativity and play around subjectivity that characterised aestheticism. Yet more profound even than this was the rejection of much that characterised this period through what can only be characterised as homophobia and sexual panic.[5] Aestheticism and Decadence still exist for many through the parody of the next generation, and the somatic potential within the sensual erotics of the period has perhaps still not been adequately recognised because of the 'taint' of that perceived sexual 'deviancy' and effeminacy. Certainly when that somatic lyric potential resurfaced in modernism it was often given a decidedly masculinist twist as in, for instance, T. E. Hulme's insistence in 'Cinders' that all poetry 'is an affair of the body'.[6] Where there do appear to be important and interesting continuations – such as in the phenomenology of Virginia Woolf and the Bloomsbury group[7] – it has often also been subject to many of the same dismissive attitudes we still see towards aestheticism.

Other factors have meant that the significance of aestheticist poetry to the development of the concept of lyric more generally is less visible than it might be. The trajectory of lyric that I take as my focus might best be seen as ending with the growing importance of epic and dramatic forms within high and late modernism, and the divergence of a popular lyric tradition established in the anthologies of Georgian poetry. The legacy of this period of poetry was split between what became two very separate traditions of poetry through the twentieth century.[8] Both Georgian poetry and modernist poetry presented themselves as making a radical break with what came before in order to offer a new kind of literature, but both were also strongly influenced by the writers I explore here,[9] and one might say that both continued (in different ways) a legacy of this work: modernism in its absorption of aestheticist theory (although it avoided traditional forms), and the Georgian poetry in its celebration of more traditional and regular forms (although by and large it avoided the theorisation of aesthetic critical doctrine). A general interest in 'lyric' poetry was promoted by the anthologies of Georgian poetry that appeared in the second decade of the twentieth century, continuing in the wake of Palgrave's *Golden Treasury* to appeal to a broad middle-class readership.

In the first half of the twentieth century, then, one might say (to put it crudely) that lyric became the mainstay of that more popular poetic lineage, even while high poetry, or the avant-garde, tended to try to distance itself from the genre. Despite modernism's scepticism about the value of 'lyric' poetry, then, the consolidation of all poetry under the banner of 'lyric' (noted by Symonds in 1889) continued through the twentieth century. The aestheticist poetry explored here marks not only a period of intense self-reflexive negotiation of lyric but also an important point in the conceptualisation of a genre that came to assume prominence in the literary landscape of the twentieth century and beyond. Indeed, while New Critical interest in the genre played an important role in cementing its ubiquity and popular appeal in the following century, it might be noted that its formulation of lyric as unmediated, socially unconcerned and worthy of close attention in itself reflects in many ways a profoundly aestheticist ideal.

Notes

1. Duff, 'The Retuning of the Sky: Romanticism and Lyric', passim.
2. See, for example, W. J. Courthope's fairly typical assertion in 1897 that what characterises 'poetical decadence' is the search for novelty through each of the arts borrowing 'some principle' from the others ('Life in Poetry: Poetical Decadence', p. 140). Courthope was Professor of Poetry at Oxford between 1895 and 1901, and a historian of poetry who published the *History of English Poetry* – the first volume appearing in 1895.
3. For all that these highly patterned forms would later be seen to constitute another kind of rhetorical turn that modernism in turn would reject.
4. Tucker, 'What Goes Around', p. 131.
5. The turn against the Decadents after 1895 was swift, and quickly followed by the popularity of the 'counter-Decadent' poets (W. E. Henley and others) and the fashion for the 'masculine' imperialist verse of Rudyard Kipling, William Watson, Henry Newbolt and others (see Carr, *Verse Revolutionaries*, p. 104).
6. Hulme, 'Cinders', p. 34.
7. A case well made, for example, by Perry Meisel in *The Absent Father: Virginia Woolf and Walter Pater*.
8. Peter Howarth summarises this division in his analysis of the 'poetry wars' in *British Poetry in the Age of Modernism* (pp. 1–14).
9. See Reeves (ed.), *Georgian Poetry*, p. xiv; and Keynes (ed.), *The Letters of Rupert Brooke*, p. 11 (where Brooke writes about his engagement with Wilde and Symons).

Bibliography

Abrams, M. H., *The Mirror and the Lamp* (Oxford: Oxford University Press, 1953).

Adorno, Theodor, *Aesthetic Theory* (London: Routledge, 1984).

— 'On Lyric Poetry and Society' (1957), trans. Shierry Weber Nicholsen, in Rolf Tiedemann (ed.), *Notes to Literature*, Vol. 1 (New York: Columbia University Press, 1991), pp. 37–54.

Agosta, Lucien L., 'Animate Images: The Later Poem-Paintings of Dante Gabriel Rossetti', *Texas Studies in Literature and Language* 23.1 (1981), pp. 78–101.

Alkalay-Gut, Karen, 'Overcoming Time and Despair: Ernest Dowson's Villanelle', *Victorian Poetry* 34.1 (1996), pp. 101–7.

Allen, Vivien, *Hall Caine: Portrait of a Victorian Romancer* (Sheffield: Sheffield Academic Press, 1997).

Anonymous, 'A Dreary Anthology' [Review of *English Lyric Poetry, 1500–1700*, ed. Frederic Ives Carpenter], *The Saturday Review* 84.2191 (October 1897), p. 445.

Anonymous, 'Art. VI. – Mr Swinburne's Poetry', *Westminster Review* 31.2 (April 1867), pp. 450–71.

Anonymous, 'Art. VIII. – 1 The Poetical Works of Robert Browning', *Quarterly Review* 170.340 (April 1890), pp. 476–502.

Anonymous, 'Art. VIII – The Poetry and Criticism of Mr Swinburne', *Quarterly Review* 203.405 (October 1905), pp. 525–47.

Anonymous, 'Art. IX. – Characteristics of Mr. Swinburne's Poetry', *Edinburgh Review* 204.418 (October 1906), pp. 468–87.

Anonymous, 'Art. IX. – John Stuart Mill', *National Review* 9.18 (October 1859), pp. 474–508.

Anonymous, 'English Literature in 1892', *Athenaeum* 3402 (7 January 1893), pp. 19–25.

Anonymous, 'English Sculpture in 1880', *Cornhill Magazine* 42.248 (August 1880), pp. 173–86.

Anonymous, 'Mr Hardy as a Poet', *The Academy* 1393 (14 January 1899), pp. 43–4.

Anonymous, 'Mr Swinburne and His Critics', *Fraser's Magazine for Town and Country* 74.443 (November 1866), pp. 635–48.

Anonymous, 'Mr Swinburne's Lyrics', *Edinburgh Review* 171.350 (April 1890), pp. 429–52.

Anonymous, Review of *A Century of Roundels* by A. C. Swinburne, *The New York Times* (15 July 1883).

Anonymous, Review of *Poems Dramatic and Lyrical* by John Leicester Warren, *Athenaeum* 3417 (22 April 1893), pp. 497–8.

Anonymous, 'The Quest of Lyric Poetry', *The Academy* (September 1913), pp. 362–3.

Anonymous, 'The Sublime and Beautiful – Progress of Criticism', *Dublin University Magazine* 62.369 (August 1863), pp. 158–67.

Arac, Jonathan, 'Afterword: Lyric Poetry and the Bounds of New Criticism', in Chaviva Hošek and Patricia Parker (eds), *Lyric Poetry: Beyond New Criticism* (Ithaca, NY: Cornell University Press, 1985), pp. 345–55.

Arata, Stephen, 'Rhyme, Rhythm, and the Materiality of Poetry', *Victorian Studies* 53.3 (2011), pp. 518–26.

Ardis, Ann L., *Modernism and Cultural Conflict: 1880–1922* (Cambridge: Cambridge University Press, 2002).

Armstrong, Isobel, 'D. G. Rossetti and Christina Rossetti as Sonnet Writers', *Victorian Poetry* 48.4 (2010), pp. 461–73.

— *Victorian Glassworlds: Glass Culture and the Imagination 1830–1880* (Oxford: Oxford University Press, 2008).

— *Victorian Poetry: Poetry, Poetics and Politics* (London: Routledge, 1993).

— *Victorian Scrutinies: Reviews of Poetry 1830–1870* (London: The Athlone Press, 1972).

Armstrong, Tim, *Haunted Hardy* (Basingstoke: Palgrave, 2000).

Arnold, Matthew, 'The Study of Poetry', in R. H. Super (ed.), *English Literature and Irish Politics*: Vol. 9 of *The Complete Prose Works of Matthew Arnold* (Ann Arbor: University of Michigan Press, 1973), pp. 161–88.

Attridge, Derek, *Poetic Rhythm* (Cambridge: Cambridge University Press, 1995).

Austin, Carolyn F., 'Mastering the Ineffable: Dante Gabriel Rossetti's "The Vase of Life" and the Kantian Sublime', *Victorian Poetry* 45.2 (2007), pp. 159–73.

Bachelard, Gaston, *The Poetics of Space*, trans. Maria Jolas (Boston: Beacon Press, 1969).

Bain, Alexander, *The Senses and the Intellect* (London: John W. Parker and Son, 1855).

Baker, David, ' "I'm Nobody": Lyric Poetry and the Problem of People', *Virginia Quarterly Review* 83.1 (2007), n.p.

Barclay, John, 'Consuming Artifacts: Dante Gabriel Rossetti's Aesthetic Economy', *Victorian Poetry* 35.1 (1997), pp. 1–21.

Baudelaire, Charles, *Prose and Poetry*, ed. T. R. Smith (New York: Boni and Liveright, 1919).

— 'Salon of 1859', in Jonathan Mayne (ed. and trans.), *Art in Paris, 1845–1862: Salons and Other Exhibitions* (London: Phaidon, 1965), pp. 144–216.

— *Selected Writings on Art and Literature*, trans. P. E. Charvet (Harmondsworth: Penguin, 2006).

Bayne, Thomas, 'The Poetry of Dante Gabriel Rossetti', *Fraser's Magazine* 627 (March 1882), pp. 376–84.

— 'Three Phases of Lyric Poetry', *Fraser's Magazine* 611 (November 1880), pp. 627–39.

Beasley, Rebecca, *Theorists of Modernist Poetry* (London: Routledge, 2007).

Beckson, Karl (ed.), *The Critical Heritage: Oscar Wilde* (London: Routledge, 1974).

Beckson, Karl and Bobby Fong, 'Wilde as Poet', in Peter Raby (ed.), *The Cambridge Companion to Oscar Wilde* (Cambridge: Cambridge University Press, 1997), pp. 57–68.

Beckson, Karl, and Arthur Ganz, *Literary Terms: A Dictionary* (London: André Deutsch, 1990).

Bell, Charles, *The Hand: Its Mechanism and Vital Endowments as Evincing Design* (London: William Pickering, 1833).

Benjamin, Walter, *The Arcades Project*, trans. Howard Eiland and Kevin McLaughlin, prepared on the basis of the German volume ed. Rolf Tiedemann (Cambridge, MA: The Belknap Press of Harvard University Press, 1999).

— *Charles Baudelaire: a Lyric Poet in the Era of High Capitalism*, trans. Harry Zohn (London: Verso, 1983).

— 'On the Concept of History', trans. Edmund Jephcott et al., in Howard Eiland and Michael W. Jennings (eds), *Selected Writings 4: 1938–1940* (Cambridge, MA: The Belknap Press of Harvard University Press, 2003), pp. 389–400.

— *Selected Writings 1: 1913–1926*, ed. Marcus Bullock and Michael W. Jennings (Cambridge, MA: The Belknap Press of Harvard University Press, 1996).

— *Selected Writings 2: 1927–1934*, ed. Michael W. Jennings, Howard Eiland and Gary Smith (Cambridge MA: The Belknap Press of Harvard University Press, 1999).

— 'The Work of Art in the Age of its Technological Reproducibility', trans. Edmund Jephcott, Howard Eiland et al., in Howard Eiland and Michael W. Jennings (eds), *Selected Writings 3: 1935–1938* (Cambridge, MA: The Belknap Press of Harvard University Press, 2002), pp. 101–33.

Benvenuto, Richard, 'The Function of Language in the Poetry of Ernest Dowson', *English Literature in Transition* 21 (1978), pp. 158–67.

Berenson, Bernhard, *The Central Italian Painters of the Renaissance*, 2nd edn (New York and London: G. P. Putnam's Sons, 1909 [1897]).

Bevis, Matthew, *The Art of Eloquence: Byron, Dickens, Tennyson, Joyce* (Oxford: Oxford University Press, 2007).

Blasing, Mutlu Konuk, *Lyric Poetry: The Pain and the Pleasure of Words* (Princeton: Princeton University Press, 2007).

Bloom, Harold, *The Anxiety of Influence*, 2nd edn (Oxford: Oxford University Press, 1997).

— *Kabbalah and Criticism* (New York, Continuum, 1984).

— *The Visionary Company: A Reading of English Romantic Poetry* (London: Faber and Faber, 1961).

Blunden, W. R., *The Land-Use/Transport System: Analysis and Synthesis* (London: Pergamon Press, 1971).

Bourget, Paul, *Essais de psychologie contemporaine* (Paris: Alphonse Lemerre, 1883).

Bowie, Andrew, *Aesthetics and Subjectivity: From Kant to Nietzsche*, 2nd edn (Manchester: Manchester University Press, 2003).

Brewster, Scott, *Lyric* (London: Routledge, 2009).

Brinkman, Bartholomew, 'Making Modern Poetry: Format, Genre and the Invention of Imagism(e)', *Journal of Modern Literature* 32.2 (2009), pp. 20–40.

Bristow, Joseph, 'Michael Field's Lyric Aestheticism: Underneath the Bough', in Margaret Stetz and Cheryl A. Wilson (eds), *Michael Field and Their World* (Aylesham: Rivendale Press, 2007), pp. 49–62.

— (ed.), *The Fin-de-Siècle Poem: English Literary Culture and the 1890s* (Athens: Ohio University Press, 2005).

Brooks, Jean R., *Thomas Hardy: The Poetic Structure* (London: Elek, 1971).

Brooks, Van Tyne, 'The Lyric Origins of Swinburne', *Poet Lore* 18.4 (1907), pp. 468–77.

Browning, Elizabeth Barrett, *Poetical Works* (London: Smith, Elder and Co., 1907).

Browning, Robert, *An Essay on Percy Bysshe Shelley* (London: Reeves and Turner, 1888).

— *The Poems* (in 2 volumes), ed. John Pettigrew, supplemented and completed by Thomas J. Collins (Harmondsworth: Penguin, 1981).

Buckley, Jerome Hamilton, *The Victorian Temper: A Study in Literary Culture* (Cambridge: Cambridge University Press, 1981).

Budd, Malcolm, *Values of Art: Pictures, Poetry, and Music* (Harmondsworth: Penguin, 1995).

Bullen, A. H., *Lyrics from the Song-Books of the Elizabethan Age* (London: John C. Nimmo, 1887).

Burdett, Carolyn, ' "The Subjective Inside us can Turn into the Objective Outside": Vernon Lee's Psychological Aesthetics', *19* (2011), pp. 1–31.

Burnett, Timothy A. J., 'Swinburne at Work: the First Page of "Anactoria" ', in Rikky Rooksby and Nicholas Shrimpton (eds), *The Whole Music of Passion: New Essays on Swinburne* (Aldershot: Scolar Press, 1993), pp. 148–58.

Bush, Ronald, 'In Pursuit of Wile Possum: Reflections on Eliot, Modernism, and the Nineties', *Modernism/Modernity* 11.3 (2004), pp. 469–85.

Byron, Glennis, *Dramatic Monologue* (New York: Routledge, 2003).

Caine, T. H. Hall, 'The Poetry of Dante Gabriel Rossetti', *New Monthly Magazine* 116 (July 1879), pp. 800–12.

Cameron, Sharon, *Lyric Time: Dickinson and the Limits of Genre* (Baltimore: Johns Hopkins University Press, 1979).

Carr, Helen, *The Verse Revolutionaries: Ezra Pound, H.D. and The Imagists* (London: Jonathan Cape, 2009).

Chace, Wiliam M., *The Political Identities of Ezra Pound and T. S. Eliot* (Stanford: Stanford University Press, 1973).

Chapman, Alison, 'Defining the Feminine Subject: D. G. Rossetti's Manuscript Revisions to Christina Rossetti's Poetry', *Victorian Poetry* 35.2 (1997), pp. 139–56.

Chaytor, H. J., *The Troubadours of Dante* (Oxford: Clarendon Press, 1902).

Chew, Samuel C., Jr, 'Lyric Poetry', *Modern Language Notes* XXIX.6 (1914), pp. 173–8.

Childs, Peter, *Modernism* (London: Routledge, 2000).

Christ, Carol T., *The Finer Optic: The Aesthetics of Particularity in Victorian Poetry* (New Haven, CT: Yale University Press, 1975).

—*Victorian and Modern Poetics* (Chicago: University of Chicago Press, 1984).

Classen, Constance, *The Deepest Sense: A Cultural History of Touch* (Urbana: University of Illinois Press, 2012).

Coleridge, Samual Taylor, *Biographia Literaria*, 2 vols, ed. John Shawcross (Oxford: Clarendon Press, 1907).

Comentale, Edward P. and Andzej Gasiorek (eds), *T. E. Hulme and the Question of Modernism* (Aldershot: Ashgate, 2006).

Connor, Steven, *The Book of Skin* (Ithaca, NY: Cornell University Press, 2004).

— 'A Few Don'ts (And Dos) by a Cultural Phenomenologist', http://www.bbk.ac.uk/english/skc/cp/welcome.htm: 'What is it that it is?' (last accessed 17 March 2012).

— 'How to Get Out of Your Head: Notes Toward a Philosophy of Mixed Bodies' (talk given to the *London Consortium*, 26 January 2006), http://www.stevenconnor.com/mixedbodies.pdf, pp. 4–6 (last accessed 17 March 2012).

Costello, Bonnie, 'John Ashbery and the Idea of the Reader', *Contemporary Literature* 23 (1982), pp. 493–514.

Courthope, W. J., 'Life in Poetry: Poetical Decadence', *Nineteenth Century: A Monthly Review* 42.245 (July 1897), pp. 124–41.

Coventry, R. G. T., 'What Makes the Perfect Lyric?', *Academy* 1748 (November 1905), pp. 1149–51.

Covey, Neil, 'The Decline of Poetry and Hardy's Empty Hall', *Victorian Poetry* 31.1 (1993), pp. 61–78.

Coyle, Michael, *Ezra Pound, Popular Genres and the Discourse of Culture* (University Park: Pennsylvania State University Press, 1995).
— 'Hugh Selwyn Mauberley', in David Bradshaw and Kevin J. H. Dettmar (eds), *A Companion to Modernist Literature and Culture* (Oxford: Blackwell, 2006), pp. 431–9.
Craig, Cairns, *Yeats, Eliot, Pound and the Politics of Poetry* (Pittsburgh: University of Pittsburgh Press, 1982).
Craig, Edward, *The Mind of God and the Works of Man* (Oxford: Clarendon Press, 1987).
Crary, Jonathan, *Techniques of the Observer: On Vision and Modernity in the Nineteenth Century* (Cambridge, MA: MIT Press, 2001 [1990]).
Crowther, Paul, *The Kantian Sublime: From Morality to Art* (Oxford: Clarendon Press, 1989).
— 'Merleau-Ponty: Perception into Art', in *Critical Aesthetics and Postmodernism* (Oxford: Clarendon Press, 1993), pp. 40–55.
Culler, Jonathan, 'Changes in the Study of the Lyric', in Chaviva Hošek and Patricia Parker (eds), *Lyric Poetry: Beyond New Criticism* (Ithaca, NY: Cornell University Press, 1985), pp. 38–54.
— *The Pursuit of Signs* (London: Routledge, 1981).
— *Structuralist Poetics* (Ithaca, NY: Cornell University Press, 1975).
— 'Why Lyric?', *PMLA* 123.1 (2008), pp. 201–6.
Cunningham, Valentine, *The Victorians* (Oxford: Blackwell, 2000).
Curran, Stuart, *Poetic Form and British Romanticism* (Oxford: Oxford University Press, 1986).
Custance, Olive, *Opals* (London: John Lane, 1897).
— *Rainbows* (London: John Lane, 1902).
Das, Santanu, *Touch and Intimacy in First World War Literature* (Cambridge: Cambridge University Press, 2005).
Davidson, John, *In a Music-hall and Other Poems* (London: Ward and Downey, 1891).
Davie, Donald, *Studies in Ezra Pound* (Manchester: Carcanet, 1991).
Dee, Catherine, *Form and Fabric in Landscape Architecture: A Visual Introduction* (London: Taylor and Francis, 2001).
DeJean, Joan, 'Fictions of Sappho', *Critical Inquiry* 13.4 (1987), pp. 787–805.
Denisoff, Dennis, *Aestheticism and Sexual Parody* (Cambridge: Cambridge University Press, 2001).
DeShazer, Mary, *Inspiring Women: Reimagining the Muse* (Oxford: Pergamon Press, 1986).
Dolin, Tim, 'The *Early Life* and *Later Years of Thomas Hardy*: An Argument for a New Edition', *The Review of English Studies* NS 58 (2007), pp. 698–714.
Doolitle, Hilda [H.D.], *Collected Poems, 1912–1944*, ed. Louis L. Martz (New York: New Directions, 1986).
Douglas, Alfred, *The City of the Soul* (London: Grant Richards, 1899).
Dowling, Linda, *Language and Decadence in the Victorian Fin de Siècle* (Princeton: Princeton University Press, 1986).

Dowson, Ernest, *Collected Poems*, ed. R. K. R. Thornton with Caroline Dowson (Birmingham: Birmingham University Press, 2003).

Duff, David, *Romanticism and the Uses of Genre* (Oxford: Oxford University Press, 2009).

— 'The Retuning of the Sky: Romanticism and Lyric', in Marion Thain (ed.), *The Lyric Poem: Formations and Transformations* (Cambridge: Cambridge University Press, 2013), pp. 135–55.

Duffey, Bernard, 'The Experimental Lyric in Modern Poetry: Eliot, Pound, Williams', *Journal of Modern Literature* 3.5 (1974), pp. 1085–103.

Dufrenne, Mikel, 'The Phenomenological Approach to Poetry', *Philosophy Today* 20.1 (1976), pp. 13–19.

Eagleton, Terry, *How to Read a Poem* (Oxford: Blackwell, 2007).

Eliot, T. S., 'Isolated Superiority' (Review of *Personae: The Collected Poems of Ezra Pound*), *The Dial* 84.1 (1928), pp. 4–7.

— 'Reflections on *Vers libre*', in Frank Kermode (ed.), *Selected Prose of T. S. Eliot* (London: Faber and Faber, 1975), pp. 31–6.

— 'Swinburne', in *The Sacred Wood* (London: Methuen, 1920), pp. 144–50.

— *The Three Voices of Poetry* (London: Published for the National Book League by the Cambridge University Press, 1953).

— 'Tradition and the Individual Talent', in Frank Kermode (ed.), *Selected Prose of T. S. Eliot* (London: Faber and Faber, 1975), pp. 37–44.

Ellis, Havelock, *Man and Woman: A Study of Human Secondary Sexual Characteristics*, 7th rev. edn (Boston: Houghton Mifflin, 1929 [1894]).

Ellmann, Richard, *Oscar Wilde* (New York: Knopf, 1988).

Erkkila, Betsy (ed.), *Ezra Pound: The Contemporary Reviews* (Cambridge: Cambridge University Press, 2011).

Farnell, Ida, *The Lives of the Troubadours* (London: D. Nutt, 1896).

Faulk, Barry, 'Camp Expertise: Arthur Symons, Music-Hall, and the Defense of Theory', *Victorian Literature and Culture* 28.1 (2000), pp. 171–93.

Fehl, Philipp, 'The Hidden Genre: A Study of the Concert Champêtre in the Louvre', *The Journal of Aesthetics and Art Criticism* 16.2 (1957), pp. 153–68.

Fehr, Bernard, 'Walter Pater und Hegel', *Englische Studien* 50 (1916–17), pp. 300–8.

Feldman, Jessica R., *Victorian Modernism* (Cambridge: Cambridge University Press, 2002).

Ferkiss, Victor C., 'Ezra Pound and American Fascism', *The Journal of Politics* 17.2 (1955), pp. 173–97.

Field, Michael, *Underneath the Bough* (London: George Bell and Sons, 1893).

— *Wild Honey from Various Thyme* (London: T. Fisher Unwin, 1908).

FitzGerald, Edward, *Rubáiyát of Omar Khayyám*, ed. Christopher Decker (Charlottesville: University of Virginia Press, 1997).

Flint, Kate, ' "... As A Rule, I Does Not Mean I": Personal Identity and the Victorian Woman Poet', in Roy Porter (ed.), *Rewriting the Self: Histories from the Renaissance to the Present* (London: Routledge, 1997), pp. 156–66.

Fontana, Ernest, 'Dante Gabriel and the Interrogative Lyric', *Philological Quarterly* 80.3 (2001), pp. 253–71.

Fowler, Alastair, *Kinds of Literature: An Introduction to the Theory of Genres and Modes* (Oxford: Clarendon Press, 1982).

Frankel, Nicholas, *Oscar Wilde's Decorated Books* (Ann Arbor: University of Michigan Press, 2000).

— ' "A Wreath for the Brows of Time": The Books of the Rhymers' Club as Material Texts', in Joseph Bristow (ed.), *The Fin-de-Siècle Poem: English Literary Culture and the 1890s* (Athens: Ohio University Press, 2005), pp. 131–57.

Freedman, Ariela, *Death, Men and Modernism: Trauma and Narrative in British Fiction from Hardy to Woolf* (London: Routledge: 2003).

Freedman Jonathan, *Professions of Taste* (Stanford: Stanford University Press, 1990).

Frow, John, *Genre* (London: Routledge, 2006).

Frye, Northrop, 'Approaching the Lyric', in Chaviva Hošek and Patricia Parker (eds), *Lyric Poetry: Beyond New Criticism* (Ithaca, NY: Cornell University Press, 1985), pp. 31–7.

Fussell, Paul, Jr, *Poetic Meter and Poetic Form*, rev. edn (New York: McGraw-Hill, 1979).

Gadamer, Hans-Georg, 'On the Contribution of Poetry to the Search for Truth', trans. Nicholas Walker, in *The Relevance of the Beautiful and Other Essays*, ed. Robert Bernasoni (Cambridge: Cambridge University Press, 1986), pp. 105–15.

Gagnier, Regenia, *Idylls of the Marketplace* (Stanford: Stanford University Press, 1986).

Garber, Frederick, 'Address and its Dialects in American Romantic Poetry', in Angela Esterhammer (ed.), *Romantic Poetry* (Amsterdam: John Benjamins, 2002), pp. 373–400.

Garrington, Abbie, *Haptic Modernism* (Edinburgh: Edinburgh University Press, 2013).

— 'Touching Texts: The Haptic Sense in Modernist Literature', *Literature Compass* 7/9 (2010), pp. 810–23.

Gaunt, Simon, 'Poetry of Exclusion: A Feminist Reading of Some Troubadour Lyrics', *The Modern Language Review* 85.2 (1990), pp. 310–29.

Gaunt, Simon, and Sarah Kay (eds), *The Troubadours* (Cambridge: Cambridge University Press, 1999).

Gill, Stephen, *Wordsworth and the Victorians* (Oxford: Clarendon Press, 1998).

Goldfarb, Lisa, *The Figure Concealed: Wallace Stevens, Music and Valéryan Echoes* (Brighton: Sussex Academic Press, 2010).

Golding, Louis, 'Mr Hardy and the New Poetry', *The Saturday Review* (24 June 1922), pp. 649–50.

Gordon, Jan B., 'The Danse Macabre of Symons' "London Nights" ', *Victorian Poetry* 9.4 (1971), pp. 429–43.

Gosse, Edmund, 'Is Verse in Danger?', *Forum* 10 (1890–91), pp. 517–26.

— 'Mr Hardy's Lyrical Poems', *Edinburgh Review* 227.464 (April 1918), pp. 272–93.

— 'A Plea for Certain Exotic Forms of Verse', *Cornhill* XXXVI (1887), pp. 53–71.

Gowing, Lawrence, *Les Peintures du Louvre* (Paris: Éditions de la Martinière, 1994).

Gray, Elizabeth, *Christian and Lyric Tradition in Victorian Women's Poetry* (London: Routledge, 2009).

Gray, John M., Review of Michael Field's *Long Ago*, *Academy* (8 June 1889), in Marion Thain and Ana Parejo Vadillo (eds), *Michael Field: The Poet: Published and Manuscript Materials* (Peterborough, Ont.: Broadview Press, 2009).

Gregory, Melissa Valiska, 'Robert Browning and the Lure of the Violent Lyric Voice: Domestic Violence and the Dramatic Monologue', *Victorian Poetry* 38.1 (2000), pp. 191–510.

Grew, Eva Mary, 'Thomas Hardy as Musician', *Music and Letters* 21 (1940), pp. 120–42.

Grieve, Thomas F., *Ezra Pound's Early Poetry and Poetics* (Columbia: University of Missouri Press, 1997).

Grosskurth, P. M., 'Swinburne and Symonds: An Uneasy Literary Relationship', *The Review of English Studies* NS 14.55 (1963), pp. 257–68.

Guy, Josephine, and Ian Small, *The Textual Condition of Nineteenth-Century Literature* (London: Routledge, 2012).

Hallberg, Robert Von, *Lyric Powers* (Chicago: University of Chicago Press, 2008).

Hallet, J. P., 'Sappho and her Social Context: Sense and Sensuality', *Signs* 4 (1979), pp. 447–64.

Halpern, Rob, 'Baudelaire's "Dark Zone": The *Poème en Prose* as Social Hieroglyph; or The Beginning and the End of Commodity Aesthetics', *Modernist Cultures* 4 (2009), pp. 1–23.

Hardy, Florence Emily, *The Life of Thomas Hardy: 1840–1928* (London: Macmillan, 1965).

Hardy, Thomas, 'Apology' (Preface to *Late Lyrics and Earlier*), in Thomas J. Collins and Vivienne J. Rundle (eds), *Broadview Anthology of Victorian Poetry and Poetic Theory* (Peterborough, Ont.: Broadview Press, 1999), pp. 1441–5.

— *The Collected Letters*, Vols 1 to 4 (1840–1913), ed. Richard Little Purdy and Michael Millgate (Oxford: Clarendon Press, 1978–84).

— *The Complete Poems*, ed. James Gibson (London: Palgrave, 2001).

— *Wessex Tales* (London: Macmillan, 1919).

Harper, George Mills, and Karl Beckson, 'Victor Plarr on "The Rhymers' Club": An Unpublished Lecture', *English Literature in Transition* 45.4 (2002), pp. 379–401.

Harrington, Emily, *Second Person Singular: Late Victorian Women Poets and the Bonds of Verse* (Charlottesville: Virginia University Press, 2014).

Hart, Kevin, 'The Experience of Poetry', public lecture at the Centre for Comparative Literature and Cultural Studies, Monash University, May 1996, *Boxkite* 2 (1998), pp. 285–304.

Hegel, G. W. F., *Aesthetics: Lectures on Fine Art*, Vol. 2, trans. T. M. Knox (Oxford: Clarendon Press, 1975).

Heidegger, Martin, 'The Dasein-With of Others and Everyday Being-With', in Robert C. Solomon (ed.), *Phenomenology and Existentialism* (Lanham, MD: Rowman and Littlefield, 2001), pp. 437–8.

Helsinger, Elizabeth K., 'Listening: Dante Gabriel Rossetti and the Persistence of Song', *Victorian Studies* 51.3 (2009), pp. 409–21.

— *Poetry and the Pre-Raphaelite Arts* (New Haven, CT: Yale University Press, 2008).

— *Poetry and the Thought of Song in Nineteenth-Century Britain* (Charlottesville: Virginia University Press, 2015).

Henriksen, John, 'Poems as Song: The Role of the Lyric Audience', *Alif* 21 (2001), pp. 77–100.

Hertz, Neil, *The End of the Line: Essays on Psychoanalysis and the Sublime* (New York: Columbia University Press, 1985).

Hewlett, Henry G., 'Modern Ballads', *Contemporary Review* 26 (1875), pp. 958–80.

Hollander, John, *The Gazer's Spirit: Poems Speaking to Silent Works of Art* (Chicago: University of Chicago Press, 1995).

— 'The Poetics of *ekphrasis*', *Word and Image* 4.1 (1988), pp. 209–19.

— *Vision and Resonance: Two Senses of Poetic Form* (New York: Oxford University Press, 1975).

Holmes, John, *Dante Gabriel Rossett and the Late Victorian Sonnet Sequence* (Aldershot: Ashgate, 2005).

Homans, Margaret, *Bearing the Word: Language and Female Experience in Nineteenth-Century Women's Writing* (Chicago: University of Chicago Press, 1986).

Hopkins, Robert, 'Painting, Sculpture, Sight and Touch', *The British Journal of Aesthetics* 44 (2004), pp. 149–66.

Horne, Herbert P., 'Thoughts Towards a Criticism of the Works of Dante Gabriel Rossetti', *Century Guild Hobby Horse* 1.7 (1887), pp. 92–102.

Hošek, Chaviva, and Patricia Parker (eds), *Lyric Poetry: Beyond New Criticism* (Ithaca, NY: Cornell University Press, 1985).

Howarth, Peter, *British Poetry in the Age of Modernism* (Cambridge: Cambridge University Press, 2009).

Howe, Elisabeth A., *The Dramatic Monologue* (New York: Twayne, 1996).

Hueffer, Ford Madox, 'Thus to Revisit. . . (iii)', *English Review* (September 1920), pp. 209–17.

Hueffer, Francis, *The Troubadours: A History of Provençal Life and Literature in the Middle Ages* (London: Chatto and Windus, 1878).

Hughes, Glenn, *Imagism and the Imagists: A Study in Modern Poetry* (London: Bowes and Bowes, 1960).

Hughes, Linda K., 'Ironizing Prosody in John Davidson's "A Ballad in Blank Verse"', *Victorian Poetry* 49:2 (2011), pp. 161–80.

— (ed.), *New Woman Poets: An Anthology* (London: The Eighteen Nineties Society, 2001).

— 'A Woman on the Wilde Side: Masks, Perversity, and Print Culture's Role in Poems by "Graham R. Tomson"/Rosamund Marriott Watson', in Joseph Bristow (ed.), *The Fin-de-Siècle Poem: English Literary Culture and the 1890s* (Athens: Ohio University Press, 2005), pp. 101–30.

Hulme, T. E., 'Cinders', in Patrick McGuinness (ed.), *Selected Writings* (Manchester: Fyfield Books, 1998), pp. 18–36.

— 'A Lecture on Modern Poetry' (1908), in Patrick McGuinness (ed.), *Selected Writings* (Manchester: Fyfield Books, 1998), pp. 59–67.

Husserl, Edmund, *Zur Phänomenologie der Intersubjecktivität*, in *Husserliana* XIV (Dordrecht: Kluwer, 1973).

Hyder, Clyde K., 'Swinburne and the Popular Ballad', *PMLA* 49.1 (1934), pp. 295–309.

Image, Selwyn, *Poems and Carols* (London: Elkin Mathews, 1894).

Jackson, Thomas H., *The Early Poetry of Ezra Pound* (Cambridge, MA: Harvard University Press, 1968).

Jackson, Virginia, *Dickinson's Misery: A Theory of Lyric Reading* (Princeton: Princeton University Press, 2005).

— 'Lyric', in *The New Princeton Encyclopaedia of Poetry and Poetics*, ed. Roland Greene and Stephen Cushman, 4th edn (Princeton: Princeton University Press, 2012), pp. 826–34.

— 'Who Reads Poetry?', *PMLA* 123.1 (2008), pp. 181–7.

Jackson, Virginia, and Yopie Prins, 'Lyrical Studies', *Victorian Literature and Culture* 27.2 (1999), pp. 521–30.

— (ed.), *The Lyric Theory Reader: A Critical Anthology* (Baltimore: Johns Hopkins University Press, 2014).

Jarvis, Simon, 'Musical Thinking: Hegel and the Phenomenology of Prosody', *Paragraph* 28.2 (2005), pp. 57–71.

Jeffreys, Mark, 'Ideologies of Lyric: A Problem of Genre in Contemporary Anglophone Poetics', *PMLA* 110.2 (1995), pp. 196–205.

Johnson, James William, 'Lyric', in *The New Princeton Encyclopedia of Poetry and Poetics*, ed. T. V. F. Brogan, A. Preminger et al. (Princeton: Princeton University Press, 1993), pp. 713–27.

Johnson, Lionel, *Poems* (London: Elkin Mathews, 1895).

Johnson, W. R., *The Idea of Lyric: Lyric Modes in Ancient and Modern Poetry* (Berkeley: University of California Press, 1982).

Kaufman, Robert, 'Lyric Commodity Critique, Benjamin Adorno Marx, Baudelaire Baudelaire Baudelaire', *PMLA* 123.1 (2008), pp. 207–15.

Keats, John, *The Complete Poems*, ed. John Barnard (Harmondsworth: Penguin, 1988).

Kenner, Hugh, *The Poetry of Ezra Pound* (Lincoln: University of Nebraska Press, 1985).

— *The Pound Era* (Berkeley: University of California Press, 1971).

Kermode, Frank, *Romantic Image* (London: Routledge, 2002 [1957]).

Kern, Stephen, *The Culture of Time and Space, 1880–1918* (Cambridge, MA: Harvard University Press, 1983).

Keynes, Geoffrey (ed.), *The Letters of Rupert Brooke* (London: Faber and Faber, 1968).

Koestenbaum, Wayne, *Double Talk: The Erotics of Male Collaboration* (London: Routledge, 1989).

Kooistra, Lorraine Janzen, *The Artist as Critic; Bitextuality in Fin-de-Siècle Illustrated Books* (Aldershot: Scolar Press, 1995).

Kreilkamp, Ivan, *Voice and the Victorian Storyteller* (Cambridge: Cambridge University Press, 2005).

Laity, Cassandra, 'Editor's Introduction: Beyond Baudelaire, Decadent Aestheticism and Modernity', *Modernism/modernity* 15.3 (2008), pp. 427–30.

— 'T. S. Eliot and A. C. Swinburne: Decadent Bodies, Modern Visualities, and Changing Modes of Perception', *Modernism/modernity* 11.3 (2004), pp. 425–48.

Langer, Susanne K., *Feeling and Form: A Theory of Art* (New York: Charles Scribner's Sons, 1953).

Lanzoni, Susan, 'Practicing Psychology in the Art Gallery: Vernon Lee's Aesthetics of Empathy', *Journal of the History of the Behavioral Sciences* 45.4 (2009), pp. 330–54.

LaPorte, Charles, 'Post-Romantic Ideologies and Victorian Poetic Practice, or, the Future of Criticism at the Present Time', *Victorian Poetry* 41.4 (2003), pp. 519–25.

Lawrence, D. H., *Complete Poems*, ed. Vivian de Sola Pinto and F. Warren Roberts (Harmondsworth: Penguin, 1993).

— 'Poetry of the Present', in Vivian de Sola Pinto and F. Warren Roberts (eds), *Complete Poems* (Harmondsworth: Penguin, 1993), pp. 181–6.

Lee, Vernon, *The Handling of Words, and Other Studies in Literary Psychology* (London: John Lane, The Bodley Head, 1923).

— 'Vital Tempo', letter to the Editor, *The Times* (14 November 1924), p. 8.

Lee, Vernon, and C. Anstruther-Thomson, *Beauty and Ugliness and Other Studies in Psychological Aesthetics* (London: John Lane, 1912).

Leighton, Angela, 'In Time, and Out: Women's Poetry and Literary History', *Modern Language Quarterly* 65 (2004), pp. 131–48.

— *On Form* (Oxford: Oxford University Press, 2007).

— *Victorian Women Poets: Writing Against the Heart* (Charlottesville: University of Virginia Press, 1992).

Lenoski, Daniel, 'The Symbolism of Rhythm in W. B. Yeats', *Irish University Review* 7.2 (1977), pp. 201–12.

Lessing, G. E., *Laocoön* (1766), trans. Edward Allen McCormick (Indianapolis: The Library of Liberal Arts, 1962).

Leverson, Ada, 'Reminiscences', in Violet Wyndham, *The Sphinx and Her Circle* (London: André Deutsch, 1963), pp. 103–23.

Levin, Yisrael (ed.), *A. C. Swinburne and the Singing Word: New Perspectives on the Mature Work* (Aldershot: Ashgate, 2010).

Levinson, Marjorie, 'Object-loss and Object-bondage: Economies of Representation in Hardy's Poetry', *ELH* 73 (2006), pp. 549–80.

Lewis, C. Day, *The Lyric Impulse* (London: Chatto and Windus, 1965).

Lindley, David, *Lyric* (London: Methuen, 1985).

Lipking, Lawrence, 'A Trout in the Milk', in Marshall Brown (ed.), *The Uses of Literary History* (Durham, NC: Duke University Press, 1995), pp. 1–12.

Livesey, Ruth, *Socialism, Sex and the Culture of Aestheticism in Britain, 1880–1914* (Oxford: Oxford University Press, 2007).

McDougal, Stuart Y., *Ezra Pound and the Troubadour Tradition* (Princeton: Princeton University Press, 1972).

McFarland, Ronald E., 'Victorian Villanelle', *Victorian Poetry* 20.2 (1982), pp. 125–38.

McGann, Jerome, *Dante Gabriel Rossetti and the Game that Must be Lost* (New Haven, CT: Yale University Press, 2000).

— (ed.), *The Rossetti Archive*, http://www.rossettiarchive.org.

— *Swinburne: An Experiment in Criticism* (Chicago: University of Chicago Press, 1972).

— *The Textual Condition* (Princeton: Princeton University Press, 1991).

— 'Wagner, Baudelaire, Swinburne: Poetry in the Condition of Music', *Victorian Poetry* 47.4 (2009), pp. 619–32.

McLane, Maureen, *Balladeering, Minstrelsy, and the Making of British Romantic Poetry* (Cambridge: Cambridge University Press, 2008).

McSweeney, Kerry, *What's the Import? Nineteenth-Century Poems and Contemporary Critical Practice* (Montreal and Kingston: McGill-Queen's University Press, 2007).

Maitland, Thomas, 'The Fleshly School of Poetry: Mr D. G. Rossetti', *Contemporary Review* 18 (1871), pp. 334–50.

Mallarmé, Stéphane, 'Crisis in Poetry', in Bradford Cook (trans.), *Selected Prose, Poems, Essays, and Letters* (Baltimore: Johns Hopkins University Press, 1956), pp. 34–43.

Malpas, Simon, 'Touching Art: Aesthetics, Fragmentation and Community', in John J. Joughin and Simon Malpas (eds), *The New Aestheticism* (Manchester: Manchester University Press, 2003), pp. 83–95.

Man, Paul de, 'Lyric and Modernity', in *Blindness and Insight: Essays in the Rhetoric of Contemporary Criticism*, 2nd edn (London: Methuen, 1983), pp. 166–86.

Martineau, Jane, *Andrea Mantegna* (Royal Academy of Arts, London and The Metropolitan Museum of Art, New York, in association with the publisher: Milan: Electa, 1992).

Mason, Emma, 'Christina Rossetti and the Doctrine of Reserve', *Journal of Victorian Culture* 7.2 (2002), pp. 196–219.

Matthews, Eric, *The Philosophy of Merleau-Ponty* (Chesham: Acumen, 2002).

Matz, Jesse, *Literary Impressionism and Modernist Aesthetics* (Cambridge: Cambridge University Press, 2001).

Maxwell, Catherine, ' "Devious Symbols": Dante Gabriel Rossetti's Purgatorio', *Victorian Poetry* 31.1 (1993), pp. 19–40.

— *The Female Sublime From Milton to Swinburne: Bearing Blindness* (Manchester: Manchester University Press, 2001).

— *Second Sight: The Visionary Imagination in Late Victorian Literature* (Manchester: Manchester University Press, 2008).

— *Swinburne* (Plymouth: Northcote House, 2006).

Meisel, Perry, *The Absent Father: Virginia Woolf and Walter Pater* (New Haven, CT: Yale University Press, 1980).

Merleau-Ponty, Maurice, 'The Body, Motility and Spatiality', in Robert C. Solomon (ed.), *Phenomenology and Existentialism* (Lanham, MD: Rowman and Littlefield, 1972), pp. 353–86.

— 'Eye and Mind', trans. Carleton Dallery, in *Phenomenology, Language and Sociology: Selected Essays of Maurice Merleau-Ponty*, ed. John O'Neill (London: Heinemann, 1974), pp. 280–311.

— 'The Intertwining – The Chiasm', in Clive Cazeaux (ed.), *The Continental Aesthetics Reader* (London: Routledge, 2000), pp. 164–80.

— 'Metaphysics and the Novel', in John O'Neill (ed.), *Phenomenology, Language and Sociology: Selected Essays of Maurice Merleau-Ponty* (London: Heinemann, 1974), pp. 136–50.

— 'Other People and the Human World', trans. Colin Smith, in *Phenomenology of Perception* (London: Routledge and Kegan Paul, 1962), pp. 346–65.

— *Phenomenology of Perception*, trans. Colin Smith (London: Routledge and Kegan Paul, 1962).

— *The Prose of the World*, trans. J. O'Neill, ed. Claude Lefort (Evanston: Northwestern University Press, 1973).

Mermin, Dorothy, 'The Damsel, the Knight, and the Victorian Woman Poet', *Critical Inquiry* 13 (1986), pp. 64–80.

Meynell, Alice, 'Christina Rossetti', *The New Review* 12.69 (February 1895), pp. 201–6.

— 'Dante Gabriel Rossetti and Contemporary Poets', *The Academy* 520 (22 April 1882), p. 286.

— 'The Lady of the Lyrics', in F.P., V.M., O.S., and F.M. (eds), *Prose and Poetry* (London: Jonathan Cape, 1947), pp. 49–51.

— *The Last Poems* (London: Burns, Oates and Washbourne, 1923).

— *Poems* (London: Hollis and Carter, 1947).

— *Preludes* (London: H. S. King and Co., 1875).

— 'The Rhythm of Life', in F.P., V.M., O.S., and F.M. (eds), *Prose and Poetry* (London: Jonathan Cape, 1947), pp. 216–19.

— *The Second Person Singular and Other Essays* (London: Oxford University Press, 1922).

Mill, John Stuart, *Early Essays by John Stuart Mill, J. W. M. Gibbs, Edward Bulwer Lytton*, compiled by J. W. M. Gills (London: G. Bell and Sons, 1897).

— (as 'Antiquus'), 'The Two Kinds of Poetry', *Monthly Repository* 7.80 (August 1833), pp. 714–24.

— (as 'Antiquus'), 'What is Poetry', *Monthly Repository* 7.73 (January 1833), pp. 60–70.

Miller, J. Hillis, *Illustration* (Cambridge, MA: Harvard University Press, 1992).

— *Thomas Hardy: Distance and Desire* (Cambridge, MA: The Belknap Press of Harvard University Press, 1970).

— 'Time in Literature', *Daedalus* 132.2 (2003), pp. 86–97.

Miller, Paul Allen, *Lyric Texts and Lyric Consciousness: The Birth of a Genre from Archaic Greece to Augustan Rome* (London: Routledge, 1994).

Millgate, Michael (ed.), *The Life and Work of Thomas Hardy* (London: Macmillan, 1984).

— *Thomas Hardy: A Biography* (Oxford: Oxford University Press, 1982).

Monkhouse, William Cosmo, Review of *Ballades and Rondeaus, Chants Royal, Sestinas, Villanelles, etc.* by Gleeson White, *Academy* 806 (October 1887), pp. 246–7.

Montefiore, Jan, *Feminism and Poetry: Language, Experience, Identity in Women's Writing* (London: Pandora, 1994).

Moody, A. David, *Ezra Pound: Poet: A Portrait of the Man and His Work. 1: The Young Genius, 1885–1920* (Oxford: Oxford University Press, 2007).

Morgan, Benjamin, 'Critical Empathy: Vernon Lee's Aesthetics and the Origins of Close Reading', *Victorian Studies* 55.1 (2012), pp. 31–56.

Morgan, Monique R., 'Lyric Narrative Hybrids in Victorian Poetry', *Literature Compass* 4 (2007), pp. 917–34.

— *Narrative Means, Lyric Ends: Temporality in the Nineteenth-Century British Long Poem* (Columbus, OH: Ohio State University Press, 2009).

Morgan, Thaïs E., 'Influence, Intertextuality and Tradition in Swinburne and Eliot', in Rikky Rooksby and Nicholas Shrimpton (eds), *The Whole Music of Passion: New Essays on Swinburne* (Aldershot: Scolar Press, 1993), pp. 136–47.

Morris, Bruce, 'Mallarmé's Letters to Arthur Symons: Origins of the Symbolist Movement', *English Literature in Transition (1880–1920)* 28.4 (1985), pp. 346–53.

Nadel, Ira B., *Ezra Pound: A Literary Life* (Basingstoke: Palgrave Macmillan, 2004).

Nathan, Leonard, 'The Ballad of Reading Gaol: At the Limits of the Lyric', in Regenia Gagnier (ed.), *Critical Essays on Oscar Wilde* (New York: G. K. Hall, 1991), pp. 213–22.

Newbolt, Henry, 'The Future of English Verse', *International Quarterly* 9 (March/June 1904), pp. 366–81.

Nicholls, Peter, *Modernisms: A Literary Guide*, 2nd edn (London: Palgrave Macmillan, 2009).

Nietzsche, Friedrich, *On the Uses and Disadvantages of History for Life*, trans. R. J. Hollingdale, in *Untimely Meditations*, with an introduction by J. P. Stern (Cambridge: Cambridge University Press, 1983), pp. 58–123.

Noyes, Alfred, 'The Poetry of Thomas Hardy', *North American Review* 194.1 (1911), pp. 96–105.

O'Neal, Michael J., 'English Decadence and the Concept of Visual Perspective', *British Journal of Aesthetics* 23 (1983), pp. 240–51.

Ong, Walter J., 'The Poem as a Closed Field', in *Interfaces of the World: Studies in the Evolution of Consciousness and Culture* (Ithaca, NY: Cornell University Press, 1977), pp. 222–3.

Ormond, Leonée, 'Framing the Painting: The Victorian "Picture Sonnet"', *Movable Type* 2 (2006), n.p.

Ostermark-Johansen, Lene, 'Caught between Gautier and Baudelaire: Walter Pater and the Death of Sculpture', *Yearbook of English Studies* 40.1–2 (2010), pp. 180–95.

Paden, William D., Jr, 'Pound's Use of Troubadour Manuscripts', *Comparative Literature* 32.4 (1980), pp. 402–12.

Page, Norman, 'Art and Aesthetics', in Dale Kramer (ed.), *The Cambridge Companion to Thomas Hardy* (Cambridge: Cambridge University Press, 1999), pp. 38–53.

Paglia, Camille, *Sexual Personae: Art and Decadence from Nefertiti to Emily Dickinson* (New Haven, CT: Yale University Press, 2001).

Palgrave, Francis Turner (ed.), *The Golden Treasury of the Best Songs and Lyrical Poems in the English Language* (Oxford: Oxford University Press, 1964 [1861]).

Pater, Walter, *Walter Pater: Three Major Texts (The Renaissance; Appreciations; and Imaginary Portraits)*, ed. William E. Buckler (New York: New York University Press, 1986).

Paterson, Linda M., *The World of the Troubadours* (Cambridge: Cambridge University Press, 1993).

Patmore, Coventry, *Essay on English Metrical Law: A Critical Edition with a Commentary*, ed. Sister Mary Roth (Washington, DC: Catholic University of America Press, 1961 [1878]).

Paulin, Tom, *Thomas Hardy: The Poetry of Perception* (Basingstoke: Macmillan, 1975).

Perloff, Marjorie, *The Dance of the Intellect: Studies in the Poetry of the Pound Tradition* (New York: Cambridge University Press, 1985).

— 'Presidential Address 2006: It Must Change', *PMLA* 122.3 (2007), pp. 652–62.

Phelan, James, *Living to Tell About It: A Rhetoric and Ethics of Character Narration* (Ithaca, NY: Cornell University Press, 2005).

Phillips, Adam, 'Five Short Talks on Excess', in *On Balance* (Harmondsworth: Penguin, 2010).

Pite, Ralph, *Thomas Hardy: The Guarded Life* (London: Picador, 2006).

Pound, Ezra, and Margaret Cravens, *A Tragic Friendship, 1910–1912*, ed. Omar Pound and Robert Spoo (Durham, NC: Duke University Press, 1988).

Pound, Ezra, *Collected Early Poems*, ed. Michael John King and Louis L. Martz (London: Faber and Faber, 1976).

— *Guide to Kulchur* (New York: New Directions, 1970).

— *Literary Essays*, ed. T. S. Eliot (New York: New Directions, 1968 [1918]).

— *Personae: The Shorter Poems*, prepared by Lea Baechler and A. Walton Litz, rev. edn (London: Faber and Faber, 2001).

— (ed.), *The Poetical Works of Lionel Johnson* (London: Elkin Matthews, 1915).

— *The Selected Letters of Ezra Pound 1907–1941*, ed. D. D. Paige (New York: New Directions, 1971).

— *Selected Prose 1909–1965*, ed. William Cookson (New York: New Directions, 1973).

— *The Spirit of Romance* (London: Peter Owen, 1970).

— 'Two Early Letters of Ezra Pound', ed. Tanselle, *American Literature* XXXIV.1 (1962), pp. 114–19.

— 'Vorticism', *Fortnightly Review* 96.573 (September 1914), pp. 461–71.

Preda, Roxana, 'D. G. Rossetti and Ezra Pound as Translators of Cavalcanti: Poetic Choices and the Representation of Woman', *Translation and Literature* 8.2 (1999), pp. 217–34.

Prendergast, Christopher, *Paris and the Nineteenth Century* (Oxford: Blackwell, 1992).

Price, Leah, *How to Do Things with Books in Victorian Britain* (Princeton: Princeton University Press, 2012.)

Prins, Yopie, 'Historical Poetics, Dysprosody, and *The Science of English Verse*', *PMLA* 123.1 (2008), pp. 229–34.

— 'A Metaphorical Field: Katherine Bradley and Edith Cooper', *Victorian Poetry* 33.1 (1995), pp. 129–48.

— 'Patmore's Law, Meynell's Rhythm', in Joseph Bristow (ed.), *The Fin-de-Siècle Poem: English Literary Culture and the 1890s* (Athens: Ohio University Press, 2005), pp. 261–84.

— *Victorian Sappho* (Princeton: Princeton University Press, 1999).

Psomiades, Kathy Alexis, *Beauty's Body: Femininity and Representation in British Aestheticism* (Stanford: Stanford University Press, 1997).

Rader, R. W., 'The Dramatic Monologue and Related Lyric Forms', *Critical Inquiry* 3 (1976–77), pp. 131–51.

Radford, Dollie, *A Light Load* (London: Elkin Matthews, 1891).

Reeves, James (ed.), *Georgian Poetry* (Harmondsworth: Penguin, 1962).

Remoortel, Marianne Van, '(Re)gendering Petrarch: Elizabeth Barrett Browning's "Sonnets from the Portuguese"', *Tulsa Studies in Women's Literature* 25.2 (2006), pp. 247–66.

Reynolds, Margaret (ed.), *The Sappho Companion* (London: Chatto and Windus, 2000).

Rhymers' Club, *The Book of the Rhymers' Club* (London: Elkin Mathews, 1892).

— *The Second Book of the Rhymers' Club* (London: Elkin Mathews and John Lane, 1894).

Richardson, James, *Thomas Hardy: The Poetry of Necessity* (Chicago: University of Chicago Press, 1977).

Robbins, Ruth, *Pater to Forster, 1873–1924* (Basingstoke: Palgrave, 2003).

Robertson, Eric S., *English Poetesses: A Series of Critical Biographies, with Illustrative Extracts* (London: Cassell, 1883).

Robinson, A. Mary F., *The Collected Poems* (London: T. Fisher Unwin, 1901).

Robinson, James K., 'A Neglected Phase of the Aesthetic Movement: English Parnassianism', *PMLA* 68.4 (1953), pp. 733–54.

Robson, Catherine, *Heart Beats: Everyday Life and the Memorized Poem* (Princeton: Princeton University Press, 2012).

Rodaway, Paul, *Sensuous Geographies: Body, Sense and Place* (London: Routledge, 1994).

Roe, Dinah, ' "Good Satan": The Unlikely Poetic Affinity of Swinburne and Christina Rossetti', in Catherine Maxwell and Stefano Evangelista (eds), *Algernon Charles Swinburne: Unofficial Laureate* (Manchester: Manchester University Press, 2013), pp. 157–73.

Rogers, William Elford, *The Three Genres and the Interpretation of Lyric* (Princeton: Princeton University Press, 1983).

Rooksby, Rikky, 'Swinburne in Miniature: *A Century of Roundels*', *Victorian Poetry* 23.3 (1985), pp. 249–56.

— 'Swinburne Without Tears: A Guide to the Later Poetry', *Victorian Poetry* 26.4 (1988), pp. 413–30.

Rosenberg, John D., *Elegy for an Age: The Presence of the Past in Victorian Literature* (London: Anthem Press, 2005).

Rosenthal, M. L., and Sally M. Gall, *The Modern Poetic Sequence: The Genius of Modern Poetry* (Oxford: Oxford University Press, 1983).

Rosmarin, Adena. *The Power of Genre* (Minneapolis: University of Minnesota Press, 1985).

Rossetti, D. G., *Ballads and Sonnets* (London: Ellis and White, 1881).

— *The Correspondence of Dante Gabriel Rossetti 1: Charlotte Street to Cheyne Walk, 1835–1854, II*, ed. William E. Fredeman (Woodbridge: D. S. Brewer, 2002).

— *The Correspondence 4: The Chelsea Years, 1863–1872, II. 1868–1870*, ed. William E. Fredeman (Woodbridge: D. S. Brewer, 2004).

— *Poems* (London: F. S. Ellis, 1870).

— *Poems* (London: Elkin Matthews and John Lane, 1892; first published 1881 as a new edition, with revised contents, of the 1870 *Poems*).

— *Poems, Ballads, and Sonnets*, ed. Paull Franklin Baum (New York: Doubleday Doran, 1937).

— 'Sonnets for Pictures', *The Germ* 4 (30 April 1850), pp. 180–2, http://www.rossettiarchive.org.

Rossetti, William Michael (ed.), *The Works of Dante Gabriel Rossetti* (London: F. S. Ellis, 1911).

Roth, Christine, 'Ernest Dowson and the Duality of Late-Victorian Girlhood: "Her Double Perversity" ', *English Literature in Transition (1880–1920)* 45 (2002), pp. 158–75.

Rowlinson, Matthew, 'Lyric', in Richard Cronin, Alison Chapman and Antony H. Harrison (eds), *A Companion to Victorian Poetry* (Oxford: Blackwell, 2002), pp. 59–79.

— 'The Thing in the Poem: Maud's Hymen', *differences: A Journal of Feminist Cultural Studies* 12.3 (2001), pp. 128–65.

Ruthven, K. K., *A Guide to Ezra Pound's Personae: 1926* (Berkeley: University of California Press, 1969).

Sailer, Susan Shaw, 'Time against Time: Myth in the Poetry of Yeats and Heaney', *The Canadian Journal of Irish Studies* 17.2 (1991), pp. 54–63.

Scarry, Elaine, 'Counting at Dusk (Why Poetry Matters When the Century Ends)', in Elaine Scarry (ed.), *Fins de Siècle: English Poetry in 1590, 1690, 1790, 1890, 1990* (Baltimore: Johns Hopkins University Press, 1995).

— *Resisting Representation* (Oxford: Oxford University Press, 1994).

Schaffer, Talia, *The Forgotten Female Aesthetes: Literary Culture in Late-Victorian England* (Charlottesville: University Press of Virginia, 2000).

Schaffer, Talia, and Kathy Alexis Psomiades, 'Introduction', in Talia Schaffer and Kathy Alexis Psomiades (eds), *Women and British Aestheticism* (Charlottesville: University Press of Virginia, 1999), pp. 1–22.

Schlegel, Friedrich, *Dialogue on Poetry and Literary Aphorisms*, trans. Ernst Behler and Roman Struc (University Park: Pennsylvania State University Press, 1989).

Schleifer, Ronald, *Modernism and Time: The Logic of Abundance in Literature, Science, and Culture, 1880–1930* (Cambridge: Cambridge University Press, 2000).

Sedgwick, W. B., 'The Lyric Impulse', *Music and Letters* 5.2 (1924), pp. 97–102.

Seeley, Tracy, ' "The Sun Shines on a World Re-Arisen to Pleasure": The Fin-de-Siècle Metaphysical Revival', *Literature Compass* 3.2 (2006), pp. 195–217.

Shairp, J. C., 'Aesthetic Poetry: Dante Gabriel Rossetti', *Contemporary Review* 42 (July 1882), pp. 17–32.

Sharp, William (ed.), *Romantic Ballads and Poems of Phantasy* (London: Walter Scott, 1888).

Shaw, W. David, *The Lucid Veil: Poetic Truth in the Victorian Age* (London: The Athlone Press, 1987).

— *Victorians and Mystery: Crises of Representation* (Ithaca, NY: Cornell University Press, 1990).

Shelley, P. B., 'A Defence of Poetry' (in a volume with Peacock's 'Four Ages of Poetry' and Browning's 'Essay on Shelley'), ed. H. F. B. Brett-Smith (Oxford: Basil Blackwell, 1937), pp. 21–59.

Sherman, Elna, 'Music in Thomas Hardy's Life and Work', *The Musical Quarterly* XXVI.4 (1940), pp. 419–45.

— 'Thomas Hardy: Lyricist, Symphonist', *Music and Letters* 21 (1940), pp. 143–71.

Sherry, Vincent, *Modernism and the Reinvention of Decadence* (Cambridge: Cambridge University Press, 2015).

Shrimpton, Nicholas, 'Swinburne and the Dramatic Monologue', in Rikky Rooksby and Nicholas Shrimpton (eds), *The Whole Music of Passion: New Essays on Swinburne* (Aldershot: Scolar Press, 1993), pp. 22–40.

— 'The Old Aestheticism and the New', *Literature Compass* 2 (2005), n.p.

Shuter, William, 'History as Palingenesis in Pater and Hegel', *PMLA* 86.3 (1971), pp. 411–21.

Sidnell, Michael J., *Yeats's Poetry and Poetics* (Basingstoke: Macmillan, 1996).

Sieburth, Richard, 'Poetry and Obscenity: Baudelaire and Swinburne', *Comparative Literature* 36.4 (1984), pp. 343–53.

Siegel, Jonah, *Desire and Excess: The Nineteenth-Century Culture of Art* (Princeton: Princeton University Press, 2000).

Silverman, Hugh, 'Dufrenne's Phenomenology of Poetry', *Philosophy Today* 20.1 (1976), pp. 20–4.

Slinn, E. Warwick, 'Dramatic Monologue', in Richard Cronin, Alison Chapman and Antony H. Harrison (eds), *A Companion to Victorian Poetry* (Oxford: Blackwell, 2002).

— *The Discourse of Self in Victorian Poetry* (Charlottesville: University of Virginia Press, 1991).

— *Victorian Poetry as Cultural Critique: The Politics of Performative Language* (Charlottesville: University of Virginia Press, 2003).

Smith, A. D., *Husserl and the Cartesian Meditations* (London: Routledge, 2003).

Smith, Paul, ' "Le Peinture de la vie modern" and "La Peinture de la vie ancienne" ', in Richard Hobbs (ed.), *Impressions of French Modernity: Art and Literature in France, 1850–1900* (Manchester: Manchester University Press, 1998), pp. 76–96.

Smith, Roger, *Free Will and the Human Sciences in Britain, 1870–1910* (London: Pickering and Chatto, 2013).

Snodgrass, Chris, 'Decadent Mythmaking: Arthur Symons on Aubrey Beardsley and Salome', *Victorian Poetry* 28.3/4 (1990), pp. 61–109.

Soloman, Robert C. (ed.), *Phenomenology and Existentialism* (Lanham, MD: Rowman and Littlefield, 1972).

Sontag, Susan, 'Notes on "Camp" ' (1964), in Fabio Cleto (ed.), *Camp: Queer Aesthetics and the Performing Subject* (Edinburgh: Edinburgh University Press, 1999), pp. 53–65.

Spencer, Herbert, *The Principles of Psychology* (London: Longman, Brown, Green, and Longmans, 1855).

Stark, Robert, 'Pound Among the Nightingales: From the Troubadours to a Cantabile Modernism', *Journal of Modern Literature* 32.2 (2009), pp. 1–19.

Stein, Richard, *The Ritual of Interpretation: Literature and Art in Ruskin, Rossetti, and Pater* (Cambridge, MA: Harvard University Press, 1975).

Stephens, Sonya, *Baudelaire's Prose Poems: The Practice and Politics of Irony* (Oxford: Oxford University Press, 1999).

Stewart, Susan, *Poetry and the Fate of the Senses* (Chicago: University of Chicago Press, 2002).

— 'Preface to a Lyric History', in Marshall Brown (ed.), *The Uses of Literary History* (Durham, NC: Duke University Press, 1995), pp. 199–218.

Swinburne, A. C., *Collected Poetical Works*, 6 vols (London: Chatto and Windus, 1904).

— *Essays and Studies* (London: Chatto and Windus, 1875).

— 'Notes on Poems and Reviews' (London: John Camden Hotten, 1866).

— *Poems and Ballads & Atalanta in Calydon*, ed. Kenneth Haynes (Harmondsworth: Penguin, 2000).

— 'The Poems of Dante Gabriel Rossetti', *Fortnightly Review* 7.41 (1870), pp. 551–79. Subsequently published in *Essays and Studies*, pp. 60–109.

Symonds, John Addington, 'A Comparison of Elizabethan with Victorian Poetry', *Fortnightly Review* 45.265 (January 1889), pp. 55–79.

— (ed. and trans.), *The Sonnets of Michael Angelo Buonarroti and Tommaso Campanella* (London: Smith, Elder & Co., 1878).

Symons, Arthur, *The Collected Works* (London: Martin Secker, 1924).

— 'The Decadent Movement in Literature', *Harper's New Monthly Magazine* 87 (June/November 1893), pp. 858–68.

— *Images of Good and Evil* (London: William Heinemann, 1899).

— *London Nights*, 2nd rev. edn (London: Leonard Smithers, 1897).

— 'Modernity in Verse' (1892), in *Studies in Two Literatures* (London: Martin Secker, 1924 [1897]), pp. 44–59.

— *Silhouettes*, 2nd rev. edn (London: Leonard Smithers, 1896).

— 'The World as Ballet' (1898), in *Studies in Seven Arts* (London: Martin Secker, 1924), pp. 244–6.

Tennyson, Alfred, Lord, *The Poems of Tennyson*, ed. Christopher Ricks (London: Longman, 1969).

Terada, Rei, 'After the Critique of Lyric', *PMLA* 123.1 (2008), pp. 195–200.

Thacker, Andrew, 'A Language of Concrete Things: Hulme, Imagism and Modernist Theories of Language', in Edward Comentale and Andrzej Gasiorek (eds), *T. E. Hulme and the Question of Modernism* (Aldershot: Ashgate, 2006).

Thain, Marion, (ed.), *The Lyric Poem: Formations and Transformations* (Cambridge: Cambridge University Press, 2013).

— *Michael Field: Poetry, Aestheticism and the Fin de Siècle* (Cambridge: Cambridge University Press, 2007).

— 'Victorian Lyric Pathology and Phenomenology', in Thain (ed.), *The Lyric Poem: Formations and Transformations*, pp. 156–76.

Thomas, Calvin, 'Have We Still Need of Poetry', *Forum* 25 (1898), pp. 510–11.

Thompson, Francis, 'Mrs Meynell's Poems' (1893), in Terence L. Connolly (ed.), *Literary Criticisms by Francis Thompson* (New York: E. P. Dutton, 1948), pp. 187–91.

Thornton, R. K. R., *The Decadent Dilemma* (London: Edward Arnold, 1983).

Tiedemann, Rolf, 'Dialectics at a Standstill: Approaches to the Passagen-Werk', trans. Gary Smith and André Lefevere, in Walter Benjamin, *The Arcades Project*, trans. Howard Eiland and Kevin McLaughlin, prepared on the basis of the German volume ed. Rolf Tiedemann (Cambridge, MA: The Belknap Press of Harvard University Press, 1999), pp. 929–45.

Tomson, Graham R., 'Mrs Meynell's Poems and Essays', *Academy* 1081 (21 January 1893), pp. 53–4.

Tucker, Herbert F., 'Dramatic Monologue and the Overhearing of Lyric', in Chaviva Hošek and Patricia Parker (eds), *Lyric Poetry: Beyond New Criticism* (Ithaca, NY: Cornell University Press, 1985), pp. 226–43.

— 'The Fix of Form: An Open Letter', *Victorian Literature and Culture* 27.2 (1999), pp. 153–5.

— 'What Goes Around: Swinburne's *A Century of Roundels*', in Catherine Maxwell and Stefano Evangelista (eds), *Algernon Charles Swinburne: Unofficial Laureate* (Manchester: Manchester University Press, 2013), pp. 125–37.

Tucker, John J., 'Pound, Vorticism and the New Esthetic', *Mosaic* 16.4 (1983), pp. 83–96.

Vadillo, Ana Parejo, 'Immaterial Poetics: A. Mary F. Robinson and the Fin-de-Siècle Poem', in Joseph Bristow (ed.), *The Fin-de-Siècle Poem: English Literary Culture and the 1890s* (Athens: Ohio University Press, 2005), pp. 231–60.

— *Women Poets and Urban Aestheticism* (Basingstoke: Palgrave Macmillan, 2005).

Vendler, Helen, *The Art of Shakespeare's Sonnets* (Cambridge, MA: The Belknap Press of Harvard University Press, 1997).

— (ed.), *Poems – Poets – Poetry: An Introduction and Anthology* (New York: Bedford/St. Martin's, 2002 [1996]).

Wagner-Lawlor, Jennifer, 'Metaphorical "Indiscretion" and Literary Survival in Swinburne's "Anactoria"', *Studies in English Literature, 1500–1900* 36.4 (1996), pp. 917–34.

Ward, Anthony, *Walter Pater: The Idea in Nature* (London: MacGibbon and Kee, 1966).

Waters, William, *Poetry's Touch: On Lyric Address* (Ithaca, NY: Cornell University Press, 2003).

Weiner, Stephanie Kuduk, 'Sight and Sound in the Poetic World of Ernest Dowson', *Nineteenth-Century Literature* 60.4 (2006), pp. 481–509.

Weir, David, *Decadence and the Making of Modernism* (Amherst, MA: University of Massachusetts Press, 1995).

Wellek, René, 'Genre Theory, the Lyric, and *Erlebnis*', in *Discriminations: Further Concepts of Criticism* (New Haven, CT: Yale University Press, 1970), pp. 225–52.

Wharton, Henry Thornton. *Sappho: Memoir, Texts, Selected Renderings, and a Literal Translation* (London: David Stott, 1885).

White, Gleeson, (ed.), *Ballades and Rondeaus, Chants Royal, Sestinas, Villanelles, &c* (London and Felling-on-Tyne: Walter Scott, 1887).

Wilde, Oscar, *The Artist as Critic: The Critical Writings of Oscar Wilde*, ed. Richard Ellmann (Chicago: University of Chicago Press, 1969).

— 'The Critic as Artist', in Richard Ellmann (ed.), *The Artist as Critic: Critical Writings of Oscar Wilde* (New York: Random House, 1968), pp. 371–408.

— 'Mr Swinburne's Last Volume' (1889), in Richard Ellmann (ed.), *The Artist as Critic: Critical Writings of Oscar Wilde* (New York: Random House, 1968), pp. 146–9.

— *Poems* (London: Elkin Matthews and John Lane, 1892).

Wilhelm, James J., 'Guido Cavalcanti as a Mask for Ezra Pound', *PMLA* 89.2 (1974), pp. 332–40.

Winn, James Anderson, *Unsuspected Eloquence: a History of the Relations between Poetry and Music* (New Haven, CT: Yale University Press, 1981).

Witemeyer, Hugh, *The Poetry of Ezra Pound: Forms and Renewals, 1908–1920* (Berkeley: University of California Press, 1969).

Wittgenstein, Ludwig, *Zettel*, trans. G. E. M. Anscombe, ed. G. E. M. Anscombe and G. H. von Wright (Oxford: Blackwell, 1967).

Wordsworth, William, 'Preface' to *Lyrical Ballads*, ed. R. L. Brett and A. R. Jones (London: Routledge, 1991). This book includes the text of the 1798 edition with the additional 1800 poems and the prefaces.

Wyndham, Violet, *The Sphinx and Her Circle* (London: André Deutsch, 1963).

Yeats, W. B. *Collected Poems* (London: Macmillan, 1982).

— 'Nationality and Literature', in John P. Frayne (ed.), *Uncollected Prose 1: First Reviews and Articles, 1886–1896* (London: Macmillan, 1970), pp. 266–75.

— 'Symbolism of Poetry', in Thomas G. West (ed.), *Symbolism, An Anthology* (London: Taylor and Francis, 1980), pp. 14–23.

— 'What is Popular Poetry', *Cornhill* 12 (1902), pp. 344–9.

Zonana, Joyce, 'Swinburne's Sappho: The Muse as Sister-Goddess', *Victorian Poetry* 28.1 (1990), pp. 39–50.

Zuckerkandl, Victor, *Sound and Symbol: Music and the External World*, trans. Willard R. Trask (New York: Pantheon, 1956).

Index